Drought-Tolerant Plants

Drought-Tolerant Plants
Waterwise Gardening
for Every Climate

JANE TAYLOR

Foreword by W. George Waters

A **Horticulture** Book

PRENTICE HALL

New York ● London ● Toronto ● Sydney ● Tokyo ● Singapore

Prentice Hall General Reference
15 Columbus Circle
New York, New York 10023

First published in the UK as *Plants for Dry Gardens*
by Frances Lincoln Limited

PRENTICE HALL and colophon are registered trademarks
of Simon & Schuster, Inc.

A **Horticulture** Book
An Affiliate of *Horticulture*,
The Magazine of American Gardening

Library of Congress Cataloging-in-Publication Data
Taylor, Jane, 1944–
    Drought-tolerant plants / Jane Taylor.
        p.   cm.
    Includes bibliographical references and index.
    ISBN 0-671-86500-5
    1. Drought-tolerant plants. 2. Landscape gardening—Water
conservation. I. Title.
SB439.8.T38   1993
635.9'5—dc20   92-40097
                                               CIP

Printed in Hong Kong

10 9 8 7 6 5 4 3 2 1

First Prentice Hall Edition

Half-title page: *Argemone platyceras*

Frontispiece: *Phalaris arundinacea picta* and *Rosa* 'Iceberg'
above *Lavandula* 'Hidcote'

Title page: *Eryngium maritimum*

Opposite: A path descends through a terrace covered
with a host of drought-tolerant plants including white
Cerastium tomentosum, *Acanthus mollis*, senecio, box,
ceanothus and pink erysimum, with osteospermum
spilling over the wall

Contents

Forming the framework of the garden

Dramatic silhouettes giving a tropical feel to the garden

Elegantly shaped evergreens in a range of colors and forms

Colorful and scented plants providing backdrops, shade, and cover for vertical surfaces

Dry Garden Maintenance 176

STARTING WITH THE SOIL

Recognizing problems; improving and enriching

PLANTING

Ensuring a good start; mulching and minimizing water loss

WINDBREAKS

Protection from the drying effects of wind

LAWNS AND LAWN SUBSTITUTES

Hard surfaces and drought-proof ground cover

IRRIGATION TECHNIQUES

Saving water and using it efficiently

Foreword

Here in the United States each of us uses two hundred gallons of water a day. Our profligacy with water is encouraged by the spigot, a turn of which makes the water flow. Habitually wasteful use of it makes it difficult for us to think of water as anything but cheap and inexhaustible, whereas it is precious and the supply erratic.

Now and again we are reminded of the value of water by shortages; rains fail, reservoirs dry up, and drought descends. In times of drought we resolve to use less water, but when the rains return the resolutions are forgotten. Meanwhile, however, gardeners learn that some plants are less thirsty than others. Gradually word gets around that gardens of unthirsty plants are easy to make and maintain.

Almost half the water supplied to homes is used in gardens, and so the plants we choose for our gardens can make a big difference in water use. Many popular plants such as hybrid tea roses need large amounts of water throughout the summer to flower well. It would be good for our water supply if gardeners could learn to love less thirsty plants and use fewer roses, but that seems too much to ask. But it may be possible for us to learn to group our plants according to their need for water – putting plants that need frequent irrigation close to the lawn, which must also be watered regularly, and furnishing as much of the remainder of the garden as possible with less thirsty plants. This is not simply sound water use, it is good for the plants.

For many of us the difficulty is knowing which are the unthirsty plants. Some books have lists of plants for special purposes; for wet, dry, sunny, and shady places for example, but they give just a dozen or so suggestions, and seldom are the lists rigorously assembled; they may group those that survive for a week or two between rains along with desert dwellers accustomed to months without moisture. We in the dry Southwest need more; we need to know which plants flourish, not merely survive, where water is scarce and temperatures high.

Jane Taylor fills our need for a careful compilation of plants that are genuinely drought tolerant. She brings to-the-task experience of gardening not only in her native England, but in some of the driest parts of the world, including California and Pakistan. In her *Drought-Tolerant Plants* she provides the reference we need to make gardens that remain easy on the eye while drawing off far fewer gallons of our precious water.

George Waters
Editor, *Pacific Horticulture*
Berkeley, California

Origanum 'Kent Beauty'

The Drought-Tolerant Garden

Drought is a relative term. For people in stricken areas of Africa or Asia, it may be a matter of life and death, as crops shrivel under the relentless, rainless skies. For those of us who live in the developed world, it may represent the comparatively mild annoyance of having to shower into a bucket, direct the washing machine outlet into a rain barrel, and drive a car covered in dust (which, if we live in Europe, might have blown over from the Sahara). One definition is that drought occurs when there has been inadequate precipitation for long enough to cause moisture deficits in the soil that disrupt normal biological and human activities. Out of that rather ponderous sentence emerges a picture familiar to an increasing number of gardeners throughout the world: dry, cracked soil, wilting plants, and the chore of lugging water – if the water is there to be had.

There is little agreement yet between scientists and environmentalists about climatic changes: are we experiencing a blip, or the start of serious global warming? And what will be the long-term effects of our environmental behavior? The practical and immediate effects for gardeners, however, are not in doubt: more or less severe droughts, intermittent, recurrent or persistent, are forcing many of us, in many parts of the world, to think again about the plants we take for granted.

For years, people making gardens in desert areas would use water prodigally to create lush green oases. Not any more: xeriscaping is the rage, using plants adapted to desert conditions to create landscapes that call for the minimum of water. In less extreme climates, dwellers in areas blessed with a Mediterranean climate are experienced at coping with summer droughts by using plants with minimal water needs. But lately, gardeners in continental or even maritime climates have had to learn to cope with droughts made more challenging by reduced water reserves caused by increased demand for water and cumulative precipitation shortfalls in successive wet seasons: reservoirs are low, the soil moisture deficit is increasing, and the water companies charge ever more for the use of ever less water.

Dry and droughty climates

Gardeners used to maritime and island climates are perhaps most affronted by drought. For those accustomed to the ease of gardening through cool summers and relatively mild winters, with rain in every month, and to the luxury of using a hose or sprinkler freely during the brief dry spells of summer, it is hard to cope with the new reality of watering bans, water-saving measures, brown lawns in place of the famous velvet sward, and annuals that rush into flower almost before you have had time to plant them out. For instance, a typical British garden with its flowery borders and green lawns needs the equivalent of 1in/2.5cm of rain every ten days to

look its best. By choosing from the plants in the chapters that follow, and using the techniques in the final chapter, canny gardeners will quickly learn to give their gardens the best chance of looking respectable, even through prolonged dry spells.

Some of the plants described in the following chapters are suitable for very arid, desert climates, but I do not attempt to cover the highly specialized techniques of greening deserts; deserts occur where there is an imbalance between rainfall and soil moisture, evaporation exceeding the amount of rain falling on the ground so that there is a permanent soil moisture deficit. A little less challenging for the gardener are the climates classed as semi-desert, which range from warm (often with hot summers) to cool, are sometimes very cold in winter, and are characterized by low seasonal rainfall. The rainfall may be scarcely more than in true desert areas, but the rain falls at a time when it can accumulate in the soil rather than being lost through evaporation and run-off. The native flora is often of the type known as steppe (in central Asia), savanna (in South America), or arid grassland, because the soil is, for a short time each year, sufficiently moist to support a complete cover of grass, usually an annual grass. These climates are found in parts of the western United States and the Cape District of South Africa, in much of Central Asia, in large areas of Australia, and in Argentina.

Less extreme seasonal soil moisture deficits occur in a Mediterranean climate, which is characterized by warm dry summers and mild wettish winters. In addition to the Mediterranean region itself, other regions lying

In this soft-toned group are plants that will withstand spells of summer drought. There is *Allium karataviense* with its broad leaves and globe flowerheads, the dwarf *Geranium cinereum* 'Ballerina,' and border pinks: *Dianthus* 'Musgrave's Pink,' with white flowers, and pink *D. turkestanicus* 'Patricia Bell.'

In this Riviera garden, gnarled olive trees underplanted with irises cast their friendly shade across the formal walks. Other flowering plants that will thrive in the shade of olives include osteospermums, garden pinks, agapanthus, and echiums.

on the western side of continents, such as California and the southwestern Cape District in South Africa, parts of Chile, and some of south and western Australia, enjoy this type of climate. It has its own typical vegetation, known as maquis in southern France, where rosemary, lavender, and other aromatic evergreen shrubs grow on the rocky hills, with myrtle, kermes oak, lentisk, and strawberry trees, and where the olive and the vine of classical times still thrive. In the driest areas, the vegetation is called garrigue; it is sparser than the dense maquis cover, and its typical plants are cistus, sage, Jerusalem sage, and bulbs. California has its own equivalent of maquis in the chaparral, also a scrub vegetation with its own unmistakable aroma, composed of California lilac, manzanita, sumac, and native oaks, with *Fremontodendron* and tree poppy on the hottest, stoniest slopes. In both the Mediterranean and California, plants from the Australian bush, notably eucalyptus, have become part of the landscape.

The so-called continental climate of warm to hot summers and cold winters, combined with a higher average rainfall than that of the arid grasslands, is typical of much of Asia Minor and eastern North America. It was the evolutionary cradle of many of our favorite border plants – oriental poppy, iris, New England aster, phlox, and bergamot – and of the trees and shrubs we value for flowers and fall color, such as maple, oak, and dogwood. These are not on the whole what we think of as drought-tolerant, yet among them are plants adapted to periods without rain, and valuable in colder zones where Mediterranean or Californian plants would not survive. The books of Gertrude Jekyll, or more recently of Beth Chatto, whose garden in East Anglia in England is open to visitors, show what can be done on dry, hungry soils with the right choice of plants and a willingness to improve the soil.

How plants cope with drought

Over the millennia of their existence on this planet, plants have evolved a range of strategies for surviving hostile conditions such as drought. Some have developed natural defenses, enabling us to recognize a species that is likely to have a natural tolerance of droughty spells and of the elements of the climate that exacerbate soil moisture deficits, such as wind and hot sun. These adaptations are not only practical, helping to guarantee the plant's survival, but by kind providence often give the plant its esthetic garden value as well.

Perhaps of none is this more true than of the plants gardeners call the "silvers and grays." These have developed a coating of fine hairs on the leaf surface, giving the familiar silken, satiny, felted, cobweb, or wooly texture belonging to plants such as *Artemisia schmidtiana*, *Leucophyta brownii*, *Convolvulus cneorum*, *Brachyglottis* 'Sunshine,' or *Stachys byzantina*. The coating reflects light, reducing the temperature within the leaf tissues and hence cutting back on moisture loss through transpiration, and it gives extra protection against the desiccating effects of wind. Sometimes it is combined with another adaptation providing similar defenses; a thick pellicle protecting the tender inner tissues. Thus the mature leaves of *Brachyglottis* 'Sunshine' are leathery on the upper surface and felted beneath. Silver-leaved plants are not, as a general rule, hardy except in the warmer zones, though the directory includes some exceptions: the white poplar, *Populus alba*, for z4, and silver-leaved shrubby potentillas, for z3, among them.

Other plants protect themselves with a waxy outer coating on the leaf, giving the familiar bluish cast of glaucous foliage belonging to plants like rue, eucalyptus, and the California *Mahonia fremontii*, which are also adapted to dry, hot, sunny places.

Other things being equal, the larger the leaf surface, the greater the moisture loss through transpiration. Some plants, instead of evolving a protective leaf coating, reduce moisture loss by dispensing with leaves altogether, or almost. Many brooms have only vestigial leaves, and their green stems have taken over the function of photosynthesis. The Mexican palo verde (*Parkinsonia aculeata*), a desert plant, adapts itself to continuing drought in a variety of ways, including leaf loss; first it sheds its tiny leaflets, then the midribs, and finally even twigs if the drought becomes very severe. In this plant, too, the bark is green with chlorophyll and can continue the process of photosynthesis even after every leaf has fallen.

Some plants have not lost their leaves, but resort to other devices to protect themselves from the sun – folding their leaves or turning them at right angles to the sun's rays: this is the trick of several of the manzanitas,

Grays and silvers, and a scattering of bright flowers, set off the rich mahogany bark of the manzanita, *Arctostaphylos manzanita*, a typical component of the California chaparral.

among them *Arctostaphylos patula* and *A. manzanita*. The California buckeye, *Aesculus californica*, is winter-deciduous in areas with maritime or island climates, but in its native habitat sheds its leaves in summer to cope with the seasonal drought and heat. Narrow or spiky, hard-textured sword leaves such as those of *Yucca glauca* also lose little moisture through transpiration, while the fine needles of conifers from high altitudes or latitudes enable them to survive the cold-induced drought of winter; yet, being evergreen, they are ready to take advantage of the short growing season without having to unfurl a new set of leaves each spring before they can begin to photosynthesize again.

Some plants have adapted to dry conditions by developing massive, spreading root systems, or deep taproots, able to gather moisture where other plants cannot reach: eucalyptus, desert hackberry (*Celtis pallida*), and mesquite (*Prosopis* species) among them. The Mexican palo verde, already mentioned for its leaf-shedding tactics, has both a deep, moisture-seeking taproot and a shallow, fibrous root system extending outward near the surface to absorb every trace of rainfall, and its open silhouette is adapted to collect every drop of dew and guide it to the roots. Other desert plants are thought to survive by making their surroundings hostile to competition: the creosote bush, *Larrea tridentata*, seems to produce a toxic substance, while some tamarisks probably achieve the same end by shedding their salt-rich leaves.

Another group of plants, the succulents, challenge drought by storing water when it is available in their fleshy leaves, stems, or caudex. An extreme example of water storage is the Queensland bottle tree, *Brachychiton rupestris*, its trunk not only bottle-shaped, but also, like any self-respecting bottle, full of liquid. The thick leaves of agaves, echeverias, and Cape vygies are all efficient reservoirs of moisture, and cacti are also water-holders, with a tough, waxy skin, reducing moisture loss through transpiration. The corrugated ribs of some cacti and succulent euphorbias are designed to guide moisture, when it is available, down toward the roots. The fleshy roots of the cat's claw vine (*Macfadyena unguis-cati*), asparagus fern, and *Antigonon leptopus* or queen's wreath also act as water-storage organs.

The leaves of the desert-dwelling shrub *Leucophyllum frutescens* borrow some of the tricks of the succulents, for they are spongy-plump and green during rains, but after using the stored moisture become small, silver and reflective. Some desert plants not only store water, but can also go into drought-induced dormancy by shutting down their stomata or leaf pores, either during the hottest days or even, in extreme adaptations, for long periods when they store carbon dioxide as well as water and continue to metabolize internally until rain again falls. The giant saguaro cactus behaves in this way, and is, typically of such plants, slow-growing but long-lived.

Going to ground is a more familiar form of dormancy in areas where drought is regularly seasonal. The huge number of bulbous plants that grow in the Mediterranean regions, in South Africa, and above all in Central Asia testify to the success of this strategy. The plants emerge and flower in a short and brilliant season after the rains, their leaves returning nourishment to the bulb, corm, or tuber below ground, to be stored until the next burst of activity a year later. Even some non-bulbous plants have a short growing season and take early dormancy, such as oriental poppies, which die down almost immediately after flowering in early summer. For other plants, seeds that are capable of remaining dormant for long periods guarantee their survival until the right conditions of temperature and humidity stimulate germination and growth.

Drought-tolerant plants in the garden

The chaparral and maquis can be the model for dry-garden plantings where plants such as California lilac (*Ceanothus* spp.), sun roses (*Cistus* spp.), and rosemary survive. A close-knit grouping of silver-leaved and waxy-glaucous plants, contrasting with shades of green such as the dark glittering foliage of kermes oak (*Quercus coccifera*) or myrtle from the Mediterranean, is enlivened in due season by the flowers of cistus or oleander (*Nerium oleander*), tree poppy (*Romneya* spp.), or all the blues, from mist to ultramarine, of ceanothus. Overhead may be the wide, dark canopy of umbrella pine or the startling pink pea flowers of the Judas tree (*Cercis siliquastrum*); beneath, a *primavera* of spring bulbs in all their bright colors.

Few gardeners in California or the Mediterranean regions restrict themselves to native plants, however. If you want to emulate a Riviera garden, or one from the still warmer Costa del Sol, you can hardly ignore the mimosa (*Acacia* spp.), the pepper tree (*Schinus molle*), the proteaceous *Hakea laurina*, aloes and agaves, or the Atlantic island echiums. In California and the Mediterranean alike, eucalyptus, bougainvillea, and a variety of palms add their distinctive notes to the garden landscape. Even in the maritime and island climates of western Europe, it is often possible to create a garden with some of the feel of the Riviera or of California, with the added advantage of a lawn of fine grass that, though it may turn brown

The colors of the orange California poppy, *Eschscholzia californica*, and crimson linaria contrast well in this casual group of self-sown summer annuals adapted to dry soils.

during summer drought, will recover quickly when the rain comes, and is a good deal pleasanter to walk on than coarse bahia grass.

None of this makes much sense to the gardener in regions where cold winters prevail. In our Swiss garden, which is roughly equivalent to Zone 6–7, we can get away with the tougher Mediterraneans such as rosemary and lavender because of our very sharply draining sandy soil, sunny summers which ripen the wood, and shelter from the cutting north wind. In most regions of continental climate, the range of evergreens is more restricted, and the garden in winter may look almost derelict, with little more than the silhouettes of the trees and the dark, looming presence of the hardiest conifers for relief. In compensation, though, the fall colors of deciduous trees and shrubs are more vivid, and the garden can be bright and flowery even in droughty summers with the right choice of border plants, and flowering shrubs such as the indestructible potentillas.

If you live in a near-desert area, you may feel an irresistible urge for your own green oasis. To square this with water conservation, choose drought-tolerant plants for your screens, ground-cover, shade trees – and confine the lush, green, water-demanding plantings to the smallest area possible near the house, where the plants can be supplied with efficient irrigation in the shape of submerged drip-lines. Elsewhere, a tapestry of drought-resisters such as dwarf coyote brush (*Baccharis pilularis*), saltbush (*Atriplex* spp.), and, for flower, Hottentot fig (*Carpobrotus edulis*), trailing lantana, and the annual California poppy (*Eschscholzia californica*) demands minimal water. Overhead shade comes from bougainvillea or

queen's wreath (*Antigonon leptopus*) grown on a trellis or pergola, or from trees – a selection of fast-growing trees for shade in arid climates is given in the introduction to the tree and shrub chapter.

Accentuating, rather than seeking to deny, the desert ambiance is the approach other gardeners prefer. For the atmosphere of the American West, for example, they use spiky yuccas and the flat juicy pads of prickly pear (*Opuntia* spp.), the fleshy rosettes of massive agaves and small echeverias, and feathery trees such as tamarisk or mesquite (*Prosopis* spp.) in schemes where contrasting textures and form are more important than color or greenery. These plants look right among stones, with raked sand or gravel paths, rather than amid green lawns. Provided the plants are chosen with regard to hardiness, "desert" plantings can be made in cooler climate zones, too. Here the purpose is not to emphasize the desert outside, but to create its simulacre within the garden as a deliberate piece of artificiality. The setting might be a hot, sunny courtyard or a rocky quarry: even an artificial desert needs the hint of a *raison d'être* if it is not to look absurd.

In the chapters that follow, all the plants described are assessed for hardiness, the zone numbers giving the lowest winter temperatures a plant will tolerate (see page 186). There could have been many more plants listed: the factors that make a plant resistant to or tolerant of drought are many, and they include not only the evolutionary forces that have molded the plant's character, which I have touched upon in this chapter, but also those that are to some extent within our control as gardeners. Some of these factors are considered in the last chapter.

One of the most attractive of prickly pears is *Opuntia macrocentra*, formerly known by the more descriptive name of *O. violacea* on account of the unusual color of its fleshy pads, contrasting here with the amber and gold of the silky flowers.

Trees & Shrubs

OPPOSITE ABOVE *Cistus* × *hybridus* (*C.* × *corbariensis*) is one of the hardiest members of this sun-loving, drought-resistant group of Mediterranean evergreens. In winter the foliage turns bronze and mahogany.

OPPOSITE BELOW The slender, open branches of *Genista aetnensis*, the Mount Etna broom, cast the lightest of shade all year and are transformed into a bright fountain of yellow in summer.

Woody plants form the framework, or to use another metaphor, the backbone of our gardens. Trees and the larger shrubs provide welcome shade from the hot sun, shelter from wind, a barrier to sound and a shield for our privacy. The smaller shrubs are equally versatile, performing a range of functions from weed-exclusion to hedging to erosion control. Even more important, many woody plants are also beautiful in leaf or flower or both, or have colorful or tasty fruits, while some have fragrant flowers or aromatic foliage. The bare silhouette of a deciduous tree forms a pattern of tracery against the winter sky, and in summer the leaves shimmer and tremble in the breeze. In colder climates we value evergreens for their stubborn endurance of winter, while in hot areas we welcome trees and shrubs that remain green throughout the dry season as all around becomes bleached to the color of old bones.

Even in the coldest climates (zones 1, 2 and 3 in the USDA classification; see page 186), there are woody plants that will stand dry spells: the quaking aspen (*Populus tremuloïdes*) and the gray sallow (*Salix cinerea*), the shrubby potentillas, the buffalo berries (*Shepherdia* spp.), the nine bark (*Physocarpus opulifolius*), and others. For those who garden in more temperate climates, the range is much wider, while in the blessed regions of zones 8, 9 and 10 the possibilities are enormous. Here, shelter from the sun's fierce rays at the height of summer is a priority. Winter-deciduous trees, especially if they form a high, broad canopy, are ideal for shading the house in summer; a house with a shaded roof may be as much as 10–20F/6–12C cooler, representing a significant gain in comfort and saving some of the energy costs of air conditioning. The tree should be sited to shade the house during the afternoon, when the sun is at its hottest. In winter the sun shines through the bare branches, warming the house – and again saving energy costs.

Some of the best fast-growing trees for desert areas include the western hackberry (*Celtis reticulata*), the velvet ash (*Fraxinus velutina*), the Fremont cottonwood (*Populus fremontii*), and the white mulberry (*Morus alba*). For shadow against the setting summer sun, evergreens such as *Eucalyptus microtheca*, the Aleppo pine (*Pinus halepensis*), the silk oak (*Grevillea robusta*), and the casuarinas also make good, quick-growing shade trees. Provided you site them properly, the winter sun, setting at a different angle, will still warm the house.

In less extreme climates, such as that of the Mediterranean, the best large deciduous trees include the London plane (*Platanus* × *hispanica*), the tree of heaven (*Ailanthus altissima*), the honey locust (*Gleditsia triacanthos*), and the honeyberry (*Celtis australis*). Moving down a size or two to something more suitable for a small plot, there are the olive (*Olea europaea*), which of course is evergreen, and deciduous trees including the silk tree

(*Albizia julibrissin*) and the more restrained acacias, the Judas tree (*Cercis* spp.), jacaranda and many others to choose from.

Shrubs form the major component of the natural vegetation in the Mediterranean region known as maquis or garrigue, a community of mainly evergreen, often aromatic shrubs adapted to dry, sunny slopes. Maquis is the shrubby growth which was once the understory of evergreen forest; a few pines and evergreen oaks may remain, amid the cistuses, rosemary, lavender, broom, strawberry trees and tree heaths. Garrigue, the vegetation of the hottest and driest slopes, is much sparser; sage, rue and Jerusalem sage grow among the rocks, with bulbous plants that briefly color the rubble in spring. The Californian chaparral is similar in nature to maquis, though its components are different: *Ceanothus*, *Arctostaphylos*, dwarf evergreen oaks, sumacs.

The maquis and the chaparral both inspire planting schemes where low, spreading evergreens, some with aromatic foliage, are punctuated by taller shrubs, a myrtle perhaps or a tree-sized ceanothus, to make a tapestry of foliage in shades of silver, gray and dark green. In colder climates, hardy deciduous shrubs and cold-resistant conifers can knit together in similar weed-excluding, many-colored carpets.

There is a wide choice of small, trailing shrubs that can drape a low wall or clothe a bank: several *Lotus* species in silver, rosemaries in gray-green, *Haplopappus coronopifolius* in dark green with cheery yellow daisies, the *Felicia* species still often called *Diplopappus*, their foliage smothered with tiny mauve daisies over a long season, and the prostrate *Cistus salvifolius* 'Prostratus' and *C.* × *dansereaui* 'Decumbens.'

The variety of foliage, from the silver, satiny fingers of *Lupinus chamissonis* to the almost metallic, aromatic blue-gray eucalypt leaves, from the thread-fine *Grevillea thelemanniana* to the bold green blades of *Eriobotrya japonica* or the massive paddles of bananas, is in itself a feast for the eyes. But many shrubs also bear flowers of striking beauty, either for their massed color, as in *Ceanothus*, or for their elegance of form, as in *Alyogyne* or, even more dramatically, *Brugmansia*. Then there is fragrance, from leaves and flowers alike. The brugmansias again, frangipani (*Plumeria rubra*), orange blossom, and the sweet osmanthus (*O. fragrans*) are just some of the shrubs and trees that evoke perfumed, tropical nights in warm climates, while in cooler regions the southern magnolia (*Magnolia grandiflora*), and in cold climates the Russian olive (*Elaeagnus angustifolia*), are among those that bring fragrance to our gardens.

Acacia LEGUMINOSAE

All acacias are tolerant of periods of drought, and some will stand prolonged drought or desert conditions. They grow more slowly where moisture supplies are limited. Native to many areas in the Old and New Worlds, they vary in their tolerance of frost, but none is suitable for very cold areas. They are increased by seed (pour boiling water over the seeds, and sow those that have swollen). Named varieties of *Acacia dealbata* are propagated by grafting.

Some acacias have compound leaves, often finely feathery; others have needle-like leaves. Still others dispense with true leaves, their function performed by modified stems or phyllodes that vary in shape. The familiar mimosa or silver wattle of southern France, *A. dealbata* (z8–11), is typical of the first kind, with its gray-green, white-dusted, feathery foliage and yellow bobbles of flower in early spring. It makes a tall tree or can be cut down to form a thicket of stems. Cultivars include 'Le Gaulois,' 'Mirandole,' and

'Toison d'Or.' The related *A. decurrens* (z9–11), the green wattle, is a medium-sized tree with pale yellow flower panicles in early spring. *A. mearnsii* (*A. mollissima*) (z9–11), the black wattle, resembles *A. decurrens* except that the leaves are softer, and the bigger flowers are paler primrose in color. Neither can compare with *A. baileyana* (z9–11), a small tree with beautiful foliage, the double pinnate, feathery leaves bright glaucous-blue in contrast to the bright yellow mimosa fluff very early in the year. The foliage of 'Purpurea' is flushed with purple. Both the type and 'Purpurea' can be raised from seed. Another very choice mimosa is *A. verniciflua* (z9–11), the varnish wattle, popular in the selection 'Clair de Lune,' one of the most delicate mimosas of the Riviera, with silver-gray foliage and fragrant fluffy blossom in early spring.

Named for the creator of the famous garden at La Mortola on the Riviera, *A. hanburyana* (z8–11) is possibly a cross between *A. dealbata* and *A. podalyriifolia*. It is a beautiful mimosa, bearing both blue-gray, feathered foliage and flat phyllodes; the fuzzy yellow flower bobbles form very long panicles. *A. podalyriifolia* (z9–11) itself, the Queensland silver wattle or pearl acacia, has striking foliage, the large triangular phyllodes bright silvery glaucous and downy in texture. The fragrant flowers, borne in long racemes, open in late winter. One of the prettiest for small spaces is *A. pravissima* (z9–11), Ovens wattle, which makes an elegant small tree with slim branchlets densely set with triangular, blue green phyllodes, smaller than those of the pearl acacia. The rounded flower heads form long compound racemes and open in spring. *A. cultriformis* (z9–11), which has triangular, silver-gray phyllodes each with a hooked point, and long sprays of yellow spring flowers.

Other wattles as well as *A. hanburyana* bear both compound leaves and willow-like phyllodes. *A. melanoxylon* (z9–11), the Australian blackwood, is one, bearing both feathery leaves and scimitar-shaped phyllodes; the

Acacia dealbata

blossom is pale yellow and rather sparse. Narrow, willow-like or sickle-shaped phyllodes characterize several other acacias, some of which are almost eucalypt-like except when in flower. *A. longifolia* (z9–11), the Sydney golden wattle, is both fast growing to medium size, and very tolerant of wind and of sandy soils. The foliage is willow-like, the flowers slim catkin-like spikes of bright yellow. *A. pycnantha* (z9–11), the golden wattle, has the look of a eucalyptus, with its glossy green, sickle-shaped phyllodes; the flowers are typical fluffy mimosa balls, in spring. *A.* Exeter Hybrid is a fine mimosa, very free with its slim, fluffy spikes of pale yellow flowers amid long, slender leaves. The blue-leaf wattle or golden wreath, *A. saligna* (*A. cyanophylla*) (z9–11), is very tolerant of salt or poor soils; its weeping branchlets are set with curving, blue-glaucous foliage and bear deep yellow flowers all along their length. Another that is tolerant of a wide range of soil types is *A. retinodes* (z9–11), the wirilda, often used as a stock for grafted mimosas in southern France, as it is lime-tolerant. It has its own value, too, as a small tree, with narrow leaves and soft yellow flowers borne almost constantly, earning it the name "mimose de quatre saisons."

Acacia melanoxylon

Wattles are not only tree-like. *A. redolens* 'Prostrata' (z9–11) is a low-growing, dense-habited shrub with aromatic, bright golden-green phyllodes and short spikes of yellow flowers. The river wattle, *A. subporosa* (z9–11), is a beautiful small- to medium-sized weeping tree with narrow phyllodes and yellow flowers; 'Emerald Cascade' has a low, spreading habit, with very narrow, bright green leaves. As its name, the shoestring acacia, implies, *A. stenophylla* (z9–11), also known as the Dalby myall or eumong, has pendulous, long, thread-like leaves. A small Australian tree, it casts a very light shade and has creamy white puffballs open from fall to spring. It is very tolerant of drought, heat, and poor soil.

The needle-leaved acacias are sometimes known as prickly Moses (Moses is probably a corruption of mimosa). *A. paradoxa* (*A. armata*) (z9–11) has dark green, needle-like leaves armed with sharp spines; it grows to become a medium-sized, densely bushy shrub and bears bright yellow bobbles along the branches in spring. The juniper wattle, *A. ulicifolia* (*A. juniperina*) (z9–11), has branching growth reaching small-tree dimensions. It has dark green, needle leaves and lemon-yellow flowers in bottlebrush spikes in spring. *A. riceana* (z9–11) is taller, with slender, weeping shoots and sharp, needle-like foliage. The pale yellow, arching flower spikes open in spring. It is somewhat less tolerant of dry soils than other acacias. *A. verticillata* (z9–11) is a prickly Moses forming a much-branched large shrub or small tree, with dark green, whorled needle leaves and cylindrical spikes of lemon-yellow flowers in spring.

The acacias of Africa and America are often ferociously thorny, and many are very tolerant of drought. *A. nilotica* ssp. *tomentosa* (*A. arabica*) (z9–11), the gum arabic tree, Egyptian mimosa or Egyptian thorn, also stands salt soils and wind. It is viciously armed with large thorns; the small flowers are yellow. Its natural habit is untidy, but it can be trimmed to shape. *A. abyssinica* (z9–11) is an attractive Ethiopian species resembling a small jacaranda, forming a small spreading tree with feathery green foliage composed of tiny leaflets. The creamy yellow puffball flowers open in mid-spring and are only slightly fragrant.

A. constricta (z9–11), the mescat or whitethorn acacia, is native to the deserts of the southwestern United States. Worth keeping if it is already growing in gardens in these areas, it is not one of the most garden-worthy acacias. The thorny, thickety growth to head height makes it useful for erosion control on banks, or for replanting disturbed desert areas, as it

Acacia farnesiana surrounded by a carpet of *Senecio haworthii* with California poppies.

needs scarcely any moisture and seeds itself freely. It can also be trained to tree form. The flowers are fragrant puffballs in mid-spring. The sweet acacia, *A. farnesiana* (z9–11), also called cassie, popinac or opopanax, is native to subtropical America, and tolerant of very low rainfall and salt soils; it makes a small tree or a multistemmed thicket. The very fragrant yellow flowers open in early spring; an essential oil is extracted from them and used in perfumery. *A. smallii* (z9) is similar, possibly slightly hardier, and tolerates lime. The Texas mimosa, *A. greggii* (z8–11), more descriptively called the catclaw acacia or devil's claw, forms a tangle of thorny branches, or, with training, a spreading, multistemmed small tree suitable for shading a courtyard or patio. The gray-green foliage sets off fuzzy, pale yellow catkin flowers in late spring or early summer, and again after summer rain.

Acca MYRTACEAE

Acca sellowiana (*Feijoa sellowiana*) (z8–11), the pineapple guava of South America, is tolerant of heat and poor soil; it will grow with little water but appreciates occasional deep irrigation. It forms a large shrub, with elliptical, dark gray-green, white-backed leaves, and flowers formed of fleshy, edible, pink and white petals surrounding a brush of crimson stamens. The green fruits that follow have a delicious flavor; gather them when they fall to the ground. The pineapple guava can be propagated by seed or half-ripe cuttings.

Acer ACERACEAE

Most maples need reasonably moist soils, but a few will tolerate drought. *Acer negundo* (z2–9), the box elder, is a fast-growing and undemanding medium-sized to large tree with pinnate leaves, often seen in its variegated forms: 'Variegatum' with white-margined leaves, or 'Elegans' with bright yellow-edged leaves. *A. negundo* var. *violaceum* has purple white-bloomed young shoots and showy pink flower sprays in spring. Named kinds are increased by budding on *A. negundo* stock. The trident maple, *A. buergerianum* (z5–8), has brilliant scarlet late fall color and tawny, peeling bark. Another grown chiefly for its brilliant colors is *A. tataricum* ssp. *ginnala* (z4–7), a shrubby tree with bright green, three-lobed leaves, reddish in spring, fragrant flowers and rose-red winged fruits. It can be grown from seed. The very slow-growing, ultimately quite large *A. nigrum* (z4–8), the black maple, forms a mushroom-shaped tree, yellow or rosy pink to apricot in the fall. The silver maple, *A. saccharinum* (z3–9) is a large tree tolerant of difficult conditions; cultivars with dissected leaves are the best choice for gardens. Its sterile hybrid with the red maple is *A.* × *freemanii* (z3–8), of which 'Marmo' is an excellent cultivar, resistant to extremes of both drought and wet. The Rocky Mountain maple, *A. glabrum* (z3–5), dislikes heat, but is tolerant of drought in cool climates; it forms a small multistemmed tree with red branchlets and glossy leaves turning pure yellow in the fall.

Adenocarpus LEGUMINOSAE

Natives of the Mediterranean area, these are leafy evergreen shrubs for a hot, dry site, easily raised from seed, with bright yellow to orange, gorse-like flowers. In *Adenocarpus anagyrifolius* (z9–11) these contrast with slightly glaucous foliage, and in *A. foliosus* (z8–11) with grayish foliage. *A. decorticans* (z9–11) is a rather leggy shrub with leafy branches.

Aesculus HIPPOCASTANACEAE

Aesculus californica (z7–9), the California buckeye, is a wide-spreading, shrubby tree, summer deciduous in dry areas, leafing up with fall rains. The fragrant white or blush flowers in long, dense, upright panicles are followed by very large fruits from which new plants can be raised.

Ailanthus SIMAROUBACEAE

Ailanthus altissima (z5–8), the tree of heaven, is very tolerant of harsh conditions, including pollution, and will grow in areas with as little as 10in/250mm of rain annually. Its bold pinnate foliage is handsome, and the cream flower sprays are followed on female trees by showy, tawny to crimson-brown seed heads. It can be raised from seed (and often self-sows), or from root cuttings to guarantee plants of a given sex. It is fast-growing and ultimately quite tall.

Albizia LEGUMINOSAE

Albizia distachya (*A. lophantha*; now *Paraserianthes distachya*) (z9–11) has finely feathered, mimosa-like foliage, composed of up to twenty pinnae, each set with as many as sixty silky leaflets. It bears soft primrose or sulfur-yellow, green-tinted bottlebrush flowers from late winter. The much more frost-resistant *A. julibrissin* (z7–9), the silk tree, does well in poor or gravel soil, and needs good drainage. The selection 'E.H. Wilson' is hardier still. *A. julibrissin* thrives in continental climates where it is well ripened by the summer sun. Sometimes slow to start, it forms a small tree suitable for shading a patio, though it has the habit of dropping a litter of pods. The flowers are a silky fuzz of pink, brightest in the cultivar 'Rosea.' Both species can be raised from seed.

Albizia julibrissin

Allocasuarina CASUARINACEAE

Allocasuarina verticillata (*Casuarina stricta*) (z9–11) is the beefwood or she oak, a small, fast-growing, upright, open-canopied, slender tree with jointed, thin branchlets resembling horsetail (*Equisetum*). It is a valuable timber tree, unsuited to windy, exposed areas.

Alyogyne MALVACEAE

These shrubby mallows with wide, hibiscus-like flowers are easily increased by softwood cuttings, so that though barely frost-tolerant, they can be grown as seasonal plants in cooler zones. Where not frosted they will grow to head height or more. *Alyogyne hakeifolia* (z10–11) has thread-like leaves and wide mauve saucer flowers over a long season; *A. huegelii* 'Santa Cruz' and 'Purple Delight' (z10–11) are selected forms of the satin hibiscus, with large violet-mauve flowers all summer long.

Amorpha LEGUMINOSAE

The false indigos are soft-wooded shrubs with acacia-like foliage, raised from seed or half-ripe cuttings. *Amorpha brachycarpa* (*A. canescens*) (z3–9), also known as the lead plant, is a small shrub with silver-gray leaves and long paniculate sprays of violet pea flowers enlivened by orange anthers in late summer; *A. fruticosa* (z5–9) is taller, with slim spikes of violet-mauve flowers. The fragrant false indigo, *A. nana* (z2–8), is a dwarf, rounded shrub with blue-green foliage and sweetly scented lavender flowers.

Anagyris LEGUMINOSAE

Anagyris foetida (z8–11) is the bois puant or stinkwood of Mediterranean regions, so called because the leaves smell horrible when crushed. It can grow to small tree size and relishes a hot place. The yellow, brown-blotched flowers appear early in spring in short spikes.

Anthyllis LEGUMINOSAE

Anthyllis barba-jovis (z8–9), another Mediterranean shrub in the pea family, is one of the most attractive, with silver-gray evergreen, pinnate leaves on tall, upright growth, and primrose-cream flowers in late spring. By contrast, *A. hermanniae* (z6–8) is small enough for the rock garden and very showy when smothered in small yellow, orange-splashed pea flowers.

Aralia ARALIACEAE

Aralia elata (z4) is the Japanese angelica tree, a large suckering shrub with immense, double pinnate leaves borne in ruff-like whorls at the ends of the branches. The large branching sprays of white flowers open in the fall.

Propagate from root cuttings. Less decorative, the ferociously spiny *A. spinosa* (z5), the Hercules' club or devil's walking stick, has greenish-white flowers in summer.

Arbutus ERICACEAE

The strawberry trees are evergreen shrubs or trees valued for their beautiful bark. They are increased from seed, or by grafting on *Arbutus unedo* stock. The Greek *A. andrachne* (z8) has flaking, cinnamon-tan bark and white urn-shaped flowers in spring. It needs protection from frost when young. *A.* × *andrachnoïdes* (z8) is even more beautiful, with rich cinnabar-red stems, and white flowers in fall and winter. The hardier *A. unedo* (z8) is the Killarney strawberry tree, found wild in the Mediterranean region and in southwestern Ireland. It grows to form a small tree with brown, peeling bark, bearing its white pitchers in fall and winter with the ripe, strawberry-like, orange to red fruits from the previous season. 'Rubra' is a selection with pink flowers.

Arctostaphylos ERICACEAE

This largely Californian genus of evergreen shrubs is sadly undervalued, for it includes several beautiful species from the chaparral, whose only fault is that they are often difficult to increase by cuttings and must be planted small. The only exceptions are the dwarf, creeping species such as the pinemat manzanita, *Arctostaphylos nevadensis coloradensis* (z4–7), which forms dense, ground-covering growth to mid-calf height, with glossy leaves

Arbutus × *andrachnoïdes*

and white or pink urn-shaped flowers. The remainder of this list are taller shrubs of great beauty. The heartleaf manzanita, *Arctostaphylos andersonii* (z8–9), grows on graveled slopes, forming a tall, upright shrub, with tan bark and rather yellow-green leaves clasping the stems. The flowers appear early in the season and are followed by sticky fruits. *A. bicolor* (z7–9), the mission manzanita, also grows on hot slopes; its dark, polished green leaves are gray-felted beneath.

Arbutus unedo

Some manzanitas are very gray in leaf, among them *A. canescens* (z7–9), the hoary manzanita, whose young shoots in spring are almost white with down, while the unfurling leaves are velvety silver flushed with pink. It forms a dense, gnarled shrub with mahogany bark and pink flowers followed by rosy berries. *A. glauca* (z8–9) has rounded, gray-green, smooth-textured leaves and deep cinnamon bark; white flowers are followed by heavy bunches of red-brown fruits which give it its common name, big berry manzanita. The downy manzanita, *A. tomentosa* (z8–9), is shrubby in growth, with peeling tan bark and gray leaves with a thick felting on the reverse. *A. tomentosa* and *A. patula* (z6–9), the green manzanita, both have the ability, like the mallee eucalypts of Australia, to regenerate from a basal burl of growth after a fire. The green manzanita is a green-leaved shrub with dark brown bark and fragrant, pink flowers.

A. mariposa (z7–9) has bright pale green young leaves maturing to glaucous-gray and close-mouthed; lavender-pink urns. The bark is as shiny and dark as polished mahogany. *A. viscida* (z7–9) is similar to *A. mariposa*, with bright mahogany-red bark and glaucous-white leaves margined, when young, with lavender-pink. The bright pink flowers on red stems are larger than most. One of the finest manzanitas, *A. pungens manzanita* (z8–9) is also one of the most difficult to increase. It forms an upright shrub with bright chocolate-brown bark and gray-green foliage. The white or blush pitcher-shaped flowers are borne in large, elegant sprays.

Artemisia COMPOSITAE

Artemisia arborescens has silky, silver-gray, divided leaves; it needs a sheltered, sunny place and is rather frost tender (z8–11). 'Faith Raven' is a hardier selection which may be identical with 'Powis Castle' (z5–8), a low, silvery shrub of rounded outline, very tolerant of dry conditions and apparently disinclined to flower, so that it remains neat all season. Both are propagated by soft or half-ripe cuttings, which root more easily than those of *A. tridentata* (z7–9), the big sagebrush of dry areas in the western United States. This spreading, small- to medium-sized shrub has pewter gray, strongly aromatic, wedge-shaped leaves. The silver sagebrush, *A. cana* (z4–8), is a small to medium-sized shrub with softly silvery, aromatic, evergreen leaves, and the threadleaf sagebrush. *A. filifolia* (z5–8) is no less silvery, but the leaves are feathery fine and the whole plant much smaller in growth.

Atraphaxis POLYGONACEAE

Atraphaxis muschketowii (z5–9) revels in dry gravelly soil in full sun and cannot tolerate moist soils. It is thus an ideal plant for cooler dry climates and attractive, too, with its dense, head-high growth of yellow branches, bright tan peeling bark, and pale green leaves. The spikes of pinkish white flowers open in spring.

Atriplex CHENOPODIACEAE

The saltbushes are native to the deserts of the world; tolerant of saline and alkaline soils, some will grow with as little as 3in/75mm of rain annually.

They are silver-white in drought conditions from the salts deposited on the leaf surface, but become grayer with ample moisture. They make good hedge shrubs and are propagated from half-ripe or hardwood cuttings. *Atriplex canescens* (z7–9), the four-wing saltbush, has gray-green, narrow leaves on much-branched, spreading growth. The golden fruits cluster at the end of the branches. Although it tolerates dry conditions, it looks best with adequate moisture. It is very resistant to salt spray. *A. lentiformis* (z8–9), the quail bush, lens-scale, or big saltbush, originates in the deserts of the southwestern United States. It grows slowly in dry areas without irrigation, surviving with no more than $3\frac{1}{2}$in/90mm of annual rainfall, provided the soil is not too poor; it tolerates both heat and cold. The holly-like, blue-gray leaves are borne on slender, sometimes spiny, pale gray branches. *A. l.* ssp. *breweri* has soft, triangular gray leaves and bears heavy clusters of yellow fruit at the tips of the branches in late spring.

A cosmopolitan genus, *Atriplex* is also found in Europe and Australasia. *A. halimus* (z7–9), the tree purslane or European saltbush, is semi-evergreen, with silver-gray leaves. The Australian saltbush, *A. semibaccata* (z8–10), was introduced to California in the 1880s and is now naturalized. It is semiherbaceous and semiprostrate, making excellent ground cover. The leaves are gray-green, the fruits red in the fall.

Aucuba CORNACEAE
Aucuba japonica (z7–10), the spotted laurel, is very handsome in its plain green forms and remarkably tolerant of poor conditions, though it responds to good treatment. The bold evergreen leaves vary in outline from broad to narrow; female plants bear showy red fruits. Cuttings and layering offer means of increase.

Azadirachta MELIACEAE
Azadirachta indica (*Melia azadirachta*) (z8–10), the neem tree or margosa tree, is an evergreen or briefly deciduous, medium-sized tree with pinnate leaves and small, very fragrant, white flowers in clusters in the leaf axils. The tree produces an antiseptic resin used in medicines, soaps and toothpaste; neem twigs are used in Pakistan and India as toothbrushes, and for a variety of medicinal purposes such as healing newly pierced ears (a thin peeled twig is threaded through the lobe).

Baccharis COMPOSITAE
Baccharis halimiifolia (z6–9), the tree groundsel, is a tall shrub with sage-green leaves and white flowers in the fall, very resistant to salt winds. *B. patagonica* (z8–11) is smaller-growing, with evergreen, glossy leaves and inconspicuous off-white flowers in spring. The dwarf coyote brush or chaparral broom from coastal bluffs of California, *B. pilularis* (z8–11), is a creeping green mat, very effective among rocks and suitable for ground cover or erosion control. Male plants are better in the garden, as females shed their cottony fluff of blossom untidily. The chaparral broom needs little water, but is somewhat frost-tender. One of the most versatile is *B. sarothroïdes* (z8–11), the desert broom, rosin bush or broom baccharis from the southwestern United States and Mexico. It makes tall and spreading, cheery green, broom-like growth, the males bearing inconspicuous flowers in fall, the females displaying plume-like buds at branch tips that turn to silky white seeds, all too ready to grow into new plants wherever they fall. Surviving with minimal rainfall and preferring an open soil, it is suitable for massing or screening, or for erosion control.

Bauhinia LEGUMINOSAE

The orchid trees or mountain ebony, trees and shrubs from near-tropical areas, give a spectacular flowering display for most of the year. They have kidney-shaped deeply lobed leaves. *Bauhinia densiflora* (z9–11), from China, has white flowers. The species commonly known as the white butterfly orchid tree is *B. forficata* (*B. corniculata*, *B. candicans*) (z9–11), a small tree forming a wide flat crown and developing gnarled branches with age. The green foliage, glaucous beneath, is lobed to the middle. The flowers open in late spring with a sprinkling of blooms through summer and are borne in clusters that open at night and last until the next day; each narrow-petaled white flower is 4–5in/10–12cm wide. With sufficient summer ripening the tree is somewhat frost-tolerant, shedding its leaves in winter, but it may not flower in colder areas. Though drought-tolerant, it needs moderate irrigation in desert areas. The bright-flowered *B. galpinii* (*B. punctata*) (z9–11), the red bauhinia or nasturtium bauhinia, has brick-red, orchid-like flowers and leaves lobed less than halfway. It forms a sprawling shrub or can be pruned into a small tree or wall-trained as if it were a climber. Native of tropical Africa, it is less hardy than *B. forficata* and has similar irrigation needs. The purple orchid tree or mountain ebony, *B. variegata* (*B. purpurea* of gardens) (z9–11), is a native of India and China, a medium-sized, broad, bushy-crowned tree, often many-stemmed. The flowers are lavender to magenta-purple, or occasionally white, the central petal with darker markings. 'Candida' has white flowers. The mountain ebony normally begins to flower in midwinter while the leaves are still falling, but in prolonged drought the leaves fall before the flowers open so the display is more effective. The Chinese *B. yunnanensis* (z8–11) is fairly frost-resistant; it has blue-green leaves and long hanging racemes of blush-pink flowers streaked with purple.

Bauhinia variegata

Brachychiton STERCULIACEAE

Brachychiton acerifolius (z10–11), the flame tree, is tall with large, thick-textured leaves of variable outline, usually three- to five-lobed. It bears vermilion red-stalked flowers on leafless branches in summer. The extremely drought-resistant *B. populneus* (z10–11), the kurrajong of Australia, is a medium-sized to tall upright, pyramidal evergreen tree, the crown widening with age. The glossy, poplar-like leaves, sometimes three- to five-lobed, rustle in the wind. The small, bell-shaped, yellowish flowers, freckled with brown and shaded with pink within, open in late spring. The kurrajong remains green when all else in the landscape is brown and sere. The Queensland bottle tree or barrel tree, *B. rupestris* (*Sterculia rupestris*) (z10–11), is a large tree with a swollen trunk, thick at the base and suddenly tapering to give the characteristic bottle outline. This stores a reserve of water in a sweet, juicy jelly within the inner bark. The leaves on mature trees are simple, oblong linear to lanceolate, but on young trees are digitate with three to nine long, narrow leaflets. The cream, red-blotched flowers are borne in downy panicles.

Brachyglottis COMPOSITAE

Formerly included in *Senecio*, these are the shrubby daisies chiefly native of New Zealand, ideal for seashore gardens as they will grow in very sandy soils and are tolerant of salt winds. They are evergreen, and many have grayish, white-felted foliage. They can be increased by half-ripe or mature cuttings. One of the most familiar is 'Sunshine' (z9–10), now classed among the Dunedin hybrids. It is an easy, gray-leaved shrub which can be hard-pruned in spring to remain compact, or allowed to bear its cheerful yellow daisies in summer, to be pruned as they fade. It is often still labeled *Senecio grayi* or *S. laxifolius*, which are more or less distinct species now classed as *Brachyglottis*; *B. greyi* (z9–10), one of the parents of the Dunedin hybrids, is seldom seen in gardens, where 'Sunshine' has a virtual monopoly; *B. laxifolia* (z9–10), another parent of the group, is equally elusive in gardens. Another species that enters the hybrid group is *B. compacta* (z9–10), effectively a smaller version of 'Sunshine,' of closer growth, with wavy leaf margins showing the white felting of the underside. The flowers are showy yellow daisies. Another compact, dense shrub in this group is *B. monroi* (z9–10), its gray-green leaves very crimped at the margins and white-felted beneath. It is exceptionally tolerant of coastal winds.

Another group of different aspect, equally resistant to salt winds, is typified by *B. elaeagnifolia* (z9–10), a large, rounded shrub with broad, thick, leathery leaves, dark gray-green above and white- to beige-felted beneath. With age, if not grown in full exposure to sun and wind, it may become rather gangling in habit, displaying fawn, peeling bark. *B. rotundifolia* (z9–10) is similar, though perhaps a little less frost-tolerant, with larger, broader leaves. The much smaller *B. bidwillii* (z9–10) is a very compact, slow-growing shrub, with rounded, very thick leaves of dark gray-green with beige felting beneath. *B. buchananii* (z9–10) has thinner leaves, silvered on the reverse, and grows rather taller.

Broussonetia MORACEAE

Broussonetia papyrifera (z7–11), the paper mulberry, is a shrubby tree with hairy leaves of variable shape, originally from eastern Asia, but naturalized in the United States. Female plants bear showy, rounded heads of orange-red fruits. Half-ripe cuttings with a heel root readily.

BELOW LEFT *Brugmansia* × *insignis*

BELOW RIGHT *Brugmansia* × *candida* 'Grand Marnier'

Brugmansia SOLANACEAE

Formerly included in the genus *Datura*, these include some spectacular flowering shrubs with great hanging trumpets, often deliciously fragrant. They can be raised from cuttings or seed. *Brugmansia arborea* (*B. cornigera*) (z9–11), the angel's trumpet or maikoa, is easily raised from seed and bears its long, fragrant white trumpets even in the first year. *B. suaveolens* (z9–11) has showy white flowers with long-pointed, recurving lobes, giving off a powerful night perfume. The double white 'Knightii,' a form of *B. × candida* (z9), differs from the double form of *B. suaveolens* in the very long drawn-out tips to the flower lobes. *B. × candida* 'Grand Marnier' (z9–11) is a subtle shade of pale apricot, with long, wide-winged trumpets. The variable natural hybrid from the Peruvian Andes, *B. × insignis* (z9–11), is similar to *B. suaveolens*, with longer, white or pink corolla. As its name implies, *B. versicolor* (z9–11) tends to change color as the flowers mature from white to creamy apricot. The odd one out is *B. sanguinea*, less showy, and despite its z9–11 rating rather hardier, than the angel's trumpet type of brugmansia. The light green leaves are velvet-textured, and the long, tubular, hanging flowers are brick-red. Unlike the others it has no scent.

Buddleia LOGANIACEAE

The common butterfly bush, *Buddleia davidii* (z5–9), seems able to grow almost anywhere; it seeds into the crumbling mortar of old walls alongside wallflowers (*Cheiranthus*) and gold dust (*Alyssum*), growing into lusty bushes. In the ground, unpruned, it will reach tree-size and flower from midsummer, or can be cut hard back each year to make long wands of growth. Ordinarily lavender blue, its scented flowers also come in white, red-purple and pink. The flower spikes of *B. fallowiana* (z7–9) are similar, but are set off by wooly white foliage, especially attractive in *B. fallowiana* var. *alba*, in which each tiny floret in the spike is ivory-white with an orange eye. *B.* 'Lochinch' (z6–9) is a hybrid with luminescent gray foliage and ample, deep lavender-blue spikes with honey fragrance.

Wooly pale foliage also belongs to *B. crispa* (z8–9), which has fragrant lilac flowers in cylindrical spikes, combining in soft-toned schemes with *Phlomis italica*, *Lotus hirsutus* and *Lavatera maritima*. It flowers on new growth, but the similar *B. caryopteridifolia* (z8–9) bears its flowers on old wood, as does the tall, bold *B. farreri* (z7–9), in which the large, softly furred leaves are more impressive than the lavender flowers. *B. salviifolia* (z8–9) has wrinkled, sage-like leaves and strongly scented flowers in clusters of muted, mauve-tinged purple, most appealing at close quarters.

The big Chilean *B. globosa* (z7–9) is quite different from the butterfly bushes; it has green leaves and bright orange flowers in spherical clusters. Crossed with *B. davidii*, it has given us *B. × weyeriana* (z6–9), in which the buff-orange flowers are gathered into rounded heads strung along the panicle, diminishing in size toward the apex, to make a gappy spike. Named cultivars vary from a pinkish orange-mauve to delicious and subtle creamy orange, apricot or pale buff. Yolk-yellow to orange is the color of *B. madagascariensis* (*B. nicodemia*) (z9–10), a tall, floppy evergreen with white stems and white-backed leaves. Its hybrid *B. × lewisiana* 'Margaret Pike' (z8–9) also flowers in winter, the honey-scented spikes opening creamy white and slowly aging to deep warm yellow. Its other parent is the winter-flowering *B. asiatica* (z8–9), which has long cylindrical spires of sweetly perfumed flowers. Its fragrance and flowering season – late fall and winter – are the chief attractions of *B. auriculata* (z8–9), which has small gray-backed leaves and stubby cream spikes, and the ability to regenerate from

Caesalpinia gilliesii

the roots if the stems are killed by frost.

Bridging the season between the spring and the high-summer buddleias are two species, each in its way distinct from the typical butterfly bush. *B. alternifolia* (z6–9), left unpruned, develops into a wide sprawling bush of semi-weeping stems, covered from end to end with lavender flowers; grow the silvery-leaved 'Argentea' if possible, for it is pretty all summer in leaf, and prune it to form a weeping standard if you are short of space. The largest in flower is *B. colvilei* (z8–9), which grows tree-like and varies from crushed-raspberry pink to a deep rich crimson in color.

Bupleurum UMBELLIFERAE

Bupleurum fruticosum (z7–10) is a medium-sized evergreen shrub with blunt-ended, blue-green leaves and rounded umbels of yellow-green summer flowers. It is very tolerant of salt winds. Increase from half-ripe cuttings.

Caesalpinia LEGUMINOSAE

Caesalpinia gilliesii (*Poinciana gilliesii*) (z9–11), the yellow or Mexican bird of paradise, is a large, angular shrub, bearing pyramidal clusters of as many as forty cupped, yellow flowers with long red stamens in summer, followed by poisonous seed pods. The elegant foliage is composed of many small leaflets. The bird of paradise needs moderate irrigation in desert conditions, especially during its flowering season, and may become dormant during severe drought. Young plants are less drought-resistant than established ones. *C. decapetala* var. *japonica* (z8–11) is a fiercely spiny plant with arching stems, bright clear green pinnate leaves, and vivid yellow flowers with red stamens in summer. The much more tender *C. pulcherrima* (z10–11), the red bird of paradise, pride of Barbados, or dwarf poinciana, reaches head height or more if not damaged by cold and thrives in the hottest places. It bears its orange-red and yellow flowers through the hottest summer months, amid fresh green, feathery foliage that remains evergreen in warm climates. Though drought-resistant, it appreciates irrigation while in flower.

Calliandra LEGUMINOSAE

Calliandra haematocephala (*C. inaequilatera*) (z10–11), the red powderpuff, forms a small shrubby tree, with pinnate leaves and flowers of which the showy part is the white, red-tipped stamens. The Mexican flame bush, *C. tweedii* (z10–11), is a smaller shrub, with bipinnate leaves and yellow-green flowers of plush texture, enhanced by showy red stamens.

Callistemon MYRTACEAE

The Australian bottlebrushes do well in very dry conditions, but do not relish severe frost. The flowers are assembled into spikes, with long stamens giving a bottlebrush effect. They can be increased by sowing the fine seeds that are held in hard, woody capsules for several seasons, or – less successfully – from half-ripe cuttings. One of the most spectacular is *Callistemon citrinus* (z9–11), the scarlet bottlebrush or lemon bottlebrush, so called because the leaves smell of lemon when crushed. It is a large, spreading shrub, with loose spikes of deep scarlet at midsummer. Though tolerant of a wide range of soils, it may develop chlorosis in limy soils. Once established, it needs little to no watering, even where the annual rainfall is no more than 10in/250mm. 'Splendens' is an old cultivar with especially long filaments of bright crimson-scarlet, flowering over a long season. A newer selection is 'Mauve Mist' with lilac flowers. *C. phoeniceus* (z9–11), known as the fiery bottlebrush or lesser bottlebrush, is similar to *C. citrinus*, but usually of more slender habit. *C. linearis*, the narrow-leaved bottlebrush, though also rated z9–11, is rather more frost-resistant. It grows to about head height and bears long, dense bottlebrushes of rich crimson in summer. *C. subulatus* (z9–11) is a shrubby species, with polished green foliage and long crimson-red flower spikes in summer. The weeping bottlebrush, *C. viminalis* (z9–11), is tree-like, with gracefully pendulous branches, leaves bronzed when young, and bright red-purple to crimson-scarlet bottlebrushes in spring and again in summer. 'Hannah Ray' is semi-weeping, with scarlet flowers. 'Captain Cook' is a selection of low spreading habit, with pinkish-bronze young growths and deep red flowers in summer.

Not all bottlebrushes have scarlet or crimson flowers; some are subtly colored, appealing to quieter tastes. *C. pallidus* (z9–11) has creamy bottlebrush spikes and very attractive young foliage of grayish-pink hazed with silky hairs. The willow-leaved bottlebrush, *C. salignus* (z9–11), is fairly frost-resistant, grows to small-tree size in warm climates, and bears its long bottlebrushes in summer. They are variable in color, often a pretty soft yellow, but sometimes pale pink, red or white. The young foliage is clad in silky hairs, giving it a pink tint and the plant's common name of pink tips. *C. pityoides* (*C. sieberi*) (z9–11), the alpine bottlebrush, is another fairly hardy species, with short yellow bottlebrushes in summer amid thick, close-packed leaves. The green bottlebrush, *C. viridiflorus* (z9–11), has chartreuse-yellow flowers. *C. rigidus* (z9–11), as its name suggests, is a stiff-leaved small tree, bearing its bright red flowers in spring.

Calothamnus MYRTACEAE

Calothamnus quadrifidus (z9–11), the common net bush from western Australia, is a medium-sized shrub bearing one-sided sprays of flowers with deep crimson stamens on the underside of the shoots. It thrives in full sun.

Calliandra haematocephala

Capparis CAPPARIDACEAE

Capparis spinosa (z8–10), the caper bush, is a spiny, small- to medium-sized shrub from dry rocky places in the Mediterranean area, with white flowers, the buds of which, pickled, are the capers of commerce. *C. spinosa* var. *inermis* is an unarmed form with pinkish flowers.

Caragana LEGUMINOSAE

The Siberian pea shrub, *Caragana arborescens* (z3–7), is an exceptionally tough, frost-resistant shrubby tree, with pretty foliage and yellow pea flowers in early summer. 'Lorbergii' is particularly elegant, with thread-like leaves; 'Pendula' is a weeping form. Lesser-known caraganas worth growing in droughty, cold zones include the Maximowicz pea shrub, *C. maximowicziana* (z3–7), similar to the Siberian pea shrub except that it grows low, wide and spiny; the low, suckering littleleaf caragana, *C. microphylla* (z3–7), with dainty grayish leaves and pale flowers; and the dwarf pea shrub, *C. aurantiaca* (z5–7), which has a fountain-like habit and orange-yellow pea flowers all along the slender, arching stems.

Carissa APOCYNACEAE

Carissa grandiflora (*C. macrocarpa*) (z10–11), the Natal plum or amatungula, is a fast-growing, medium-sized shrub, its green, thorny stems set with dense, dark green, semi-succulent, rounded leathery leaves. The fragrant white waxy stars appear throughout the warm season and are followed by edible, dark red fruit. Tolerant of drought once established, the Natal plum can be clipped to form a hedge, or trained to a wall. The cultivar 'Fancy' is particularly good as an espalier, and is free with both flower and fruit. 'Ruby' has red young leaves. Several cultivars are low-growing and compact for low hedges or ground cover: 'Boxwood Beauty,' 'Prostrata' (good ground cover if you trim back any vertical growths), 'Green Carpet' (with smaller leaves), and 'Tuttlei' ('Nana Compacta Tuttlei'), generous with both flower and fruit.

Carpenteria HYDRANGEACEAE/PHILADELPHACEAE

Carpenteria californica (z8–9), the tree anemone, is an evergreen shrub with large, fragrant, white summer flowers enhanced by yellow stamens. Seedlings do not always have well-formed flowers, but named cultivars can be tricky to propagate; one of the best is 'Ladham's Variety.'

Carya JUGLANDACEAE

Carya illinoinensis (z6–9), the pecan, is one of the most drought-resistant hickories, a large tree with bold compound leaves of up to seventeen leaflets and highly prized nuts.

Caryopteris VERBENACEAE

Caryopteris × *clandonensis* (z6–9), sometimes known as blue spiraea though unrelated to the true spiraeas, is a small, soft-wooded shrub with gray-green turpentine-scented foliage topped by a haze of fluffy lavender-blue flowers in summer. Selections such as 'Kew Blue,' 'Ferndown,' and 'Heavenly Blue' have deeper violet-blue flowers than the hardier 'Arthur Simmons.' The seed heads that follow are verdigris-green. Any well-drained soil is suitable, including chalk. To keep the shrub compact, prune it hard back in spring. It can be quickly and easily propagated from softwood or half-ripe cuttings; first-year plants can even be used as fillers to follow early-flowering ephemerals.

Carpenteria californica

Cassia LEGUMINOSAE

The sennas are a large genus of mainly tropical species, with yellow, cupped flowers and pinnate leaves, sometimes thread-fine, as in *Cassia angustifolia* (*Senna alexandrina*) (z10–11), the Alexandrian senna, true senna or Tinnevelly senna, which has green leaves, and vivid yellow flowers in midsummer. *C. artemisioïdes* (*Senna artemisioïdes*) (z10–11), the feather cassia, silvery senna, wormwood senna, or old man senna, is a fast-growing, rounded shrub of medium size, with foliage resembling that of *Artemisia abrotanum*, silver to gray-green and needle-fine. It bears fragrant sulfur-yellow flowers in late winter and early spring. Suitable for an informal hedge, it tolerates periods of drought and has been known to naturalize in semi-desert areas. *C. wislizenii* (z10–11), the shrubby senna, is a small, slow-growing Mexican species from dry slopes and mesas, with minimal water requirements. The rich yellow flowers are borne in summer, amid gray-green, finely divided leaves.

C. didymobotrya (*Senna didymobotrya*) (z10–11) is a spreading, evergreen, medium-sized shrub with pinnate leaves of up to sixteen pairs of leaflets, and bright yellow flowers in long-stalked spires up to 12in/30cm long in summer and fall. The nearly evergreen *C. leptophylla* (z10–11) grows into a small tree with compound leaves and deep yellow flowers. *C. ferruginea* (z10–11) is similar, its leaves with more numerous leaflets – up to twenty pairs – and flowers in long, pendant racemes. The golden wonder, *C. splendida* (*Senna splendida*) (z10–11), is shrubby, the foliage composed of few quite large leaflets. The large flowers are borne in spikes.

One of the hardiest is *C. corymbosa* (*Senna corymbosa*) (z8–11), a name often applied, in cultivation, to *C. candolleana* (*C. obtusa*). It is a medium-sized shrub with pinnate leaves and rich yellow, cupped flowers in small terminal clusters in summer.

Casuarina CASUARINACEAE

A genus of tough desert plants from Australia, resistant to heat, drought, wind, and poor soil; they thrive in an annual rainfall of as little as 10in/250mm. Generally of erect slender growth, older trees are more open than young ones; they are a little reminiscent of tamarisk. What look like needle leaves are actually tiny jointed branchlets; the true leaves are microscopically small. Female plants bear little woody cones. The casuarinas have many functional uses, as wind or shade screens or to stabilize landfill. The she oak, formerly *Casuarina stricta*, is now considered to belong in the genus *Allocasuarina* (see page 25). It is not suitable for wind-shelter. The Australian pine (which is, of course, not a pine at all), *Casuarina cunninghamiana* (z9–11), is the hardiest, growing fast to form dense growth of fine branches with dark green "needles." It is a valuable timber tree. *C. equisetifolia* (z9–11), the horsetail tree, south sea ironwood, or mile tree, grows rather taller and bears its "needles" in whorls.

Catalpa BIGNONIACEAE

Catalpa speciosa (z5–8), shawnee wood, Indian bean, western catalpa, or cigar tree, is native to the United States. It is easily raised from seed and grows rapidly, forming a pyramidal crown. Despite its large, heart-shaped leaves, which give it the look of a tree needing ample moisture, it has only moderate water needs and withstands both heat and cold. However, it needs shelter from wind as the branches are brittle. The white trumpet flowers with yellow-brown or purple markings appear in early to mid-summer and are followed by cigar-like beans.

Ceanothus thyrsiflorus var. *repens*

Ceanothus RHAMNACEAE

The California lilacs, almost all of them natives of California where they are an important component of the chaparral, are among the most valuable shrubs for dry gardens where frosts are not too severe. They seem to be less appreciated in their native regions than in some other places, but their color alone should earn them a place in dry gardens – the great majority bear flowers in shades of blue from smoky lilac to ultramarine, usually opening in spring or early summer. Most are reasonably easy to increase from firm or half-ripe cuttings, though *C. rigidus* can be tricky.

One of the earliest in flower is *C. arboreus* (z9), the felt-leaf ceanothus or Catalina mountain lilac. An evergreen, tree-like species with large, grayish-green leaves, it opens the season as early as late winter. The sky-blue, fragrant flowers are borne in large pyramidal clusters. Selections or hybrids with flowers of richer coloring include 'Trewithen Blue' and 'Ray Hartman.' Several weeks later come the flowers of *C. cyaneus* (z9–10), the San Diego ceanothus, a beautiful but rather temperamental species, drought-tolerant, but resentful of wind and of root disturbance. A tall, even tree-like shrub, it has glossy green leaves and very large sprays of clear blue flowers, opening from deeper buds, from early to late summer. One of the largest in growth is *C. thyrsiflorus* (z8–10), the blue blossom or bluebrush, a bulky evergreen shrub or even a tree, with bold panicles of sky-blue flowers and shining foliage. By contrast, *C. thyrsiflorus* var. *repens* (z8–10) is a spreading shrub, varying from a neat and compact mound to an expansive wide-spreading billow. *C. griseus* (z9–10), the Carmel ceanothus, is another spreader, with pale blue flowers. *C. griseus horizontalis* 'Yankee Point' (z9–10), a form collected from the coastal area of the Monterey peninsula, is a rounded, spreading shrub with bright blue flowers. 'Hurricane Point' is a very wide-spreading, low shrub, not very free with its pale blue flowers.

C. dentatus (z9–10) grows low and wide in the wild, but tends to make a more upright shrub in captivity. Both this and *C. dentatus* var. *floribundus* (z9–10) have neat, small, glandular leaves and massed bright blue flowers.

C. × *lobbianus* (z9–10) is a natural hybrid of *C. dentatus*, forming a tall shrub with bright blue flowers. *C.* × *veitchianus* (z8–10), another natural hybrid of *C. dentatus*, has rich blue flowers. In commerce these names often seem virtually interchangeable. That these hybrids are in cultivation we owe to the nineteenth-century plant collector William Lobb.

Another that tends to grow low and wide in the wild, but to reach up in gardens, is *C. impressus* (z8), the Santa Barbara ceanothus. The tiny, dark green leaves are deeply grooved on the upper surface; the flowers, in the choicest forms, are a deep ultramarine blue. The selection 'Puget Blue' is of naturally more upright growth. The wartleaf ceanothus, *C. papillosus* (z9–10), is an especially attractive tall evergreen, with narrowly oblong, sticky-shiny, dark green leaves textured with little warts on the upper surface. The fragrant, deep sky-blue flowers open in late spring. *C. papillosus* var. *roweanus* (z9–10), the Mount Tranquillon ceanothus or Rowe ceanothus, has even narrower leaves and richer blue flowers. 'Concha' is a selection or hybrid that flowers a little later; the color is a good deep blue.

Not all California lilacs that grow low and wide in the wild forsake their ground-hugging habit in captivity. *C. divergens* (z9–10), the Calistoga ceanothus or Mount St. Helens ceanothus, makes a hummocky carpet of toothed evergreen leaves, half hidden by the deep blue flowers in spring. The wavy leaf ceanothus, *C. foliosus* (z9–10), is another spreader, varying from a low mound to a semi-prostrate mat of polished leaves. The fragrant flowers range in color from smoky to ultramarine blue. *C. foliosus* Austromontanus Group (z9–10) grows still lower and wider. Both need free-draining soil, but prefer to be out of the hottest sun. *C.* 'Italian Skies' (z9–10) is a seedling with *C. foliosus* blood, forming a vigorous, spreading shrub with vivid blue flowers in dense clusters. Some species show a tendency to vary in flower color, such as *C. ramulosus* (z9–10), the coast ceanothus, which makes hummocky mounds bearing powder-blue or white flowers; in *C. ramulosus* var. *fascicularis* they have a distinct honey perfume. The Monterey ceanothus, *C. rigidus* (z9–10), is similar, with wedge-shaped prickly leaves and clusters of scented flowers ranging in color from lilac and violet to pure blue, and white; 'Snowball' is a good white selection.

The coastal *C. gloriosus* (z9–10), the Point Reyes ceanothus, hugs the ground where exposed to sea winds, but is taller, though still comparatively low and wide, in sheltered gardens. The dark green, holly-like leaves set off honey-scented, woodsmoke-blue flowers. Holly-like leaves also belong to *C. jepsonii* (z9–10), the musk bush, a small evergreen shrub with flowers varying from purple, lavender or rich blue to white. *C. prostratus* (z9–10), the squaw carpet or Mahala mats, is a spreading or carpeting evergreen shrub with prickly leaves and bright lavender flowers in spring. It can be short-lived in cultivation. The holly-leaf ceanothus, *C. purpureus* (z9–10), has spreading branches set with holly-like leaves, and silvery buds opening to purple flowers fading to lavender blue, in spring. The town of Hollywood gets its name from these prickly-leaved ceanothus.

In flower the Jim brush, *C. sorediatus* (z9–10), looks like a cloud of wood smoke, for it has rather sparse foliage, glossy on the upper surface and gray beneath, and open, fuzzy flower clusters of pale, smoky-blue blossom, each individual flower held on a slender stalk, contributing to a more airy effect than is usual with Californian lilacs. It grows fairly tall and often has a second season of flower in the fall. Another large species is *C. integerrimus* (z9–10), the deer bush, which flowers in late spring, its open, fuzzy panicles of fragrant flowers ranging in color from white to sky blue or lavender pink.

It is only semi-evergreen. The red-heart or green bark ceanothus, *C. spinosus* (z9–10), is exceptionally drought-resistant, a tall evergreen shrub with palest smoke-gray flowers in open sprays.

Also white-flowered is *C. incanus* (z9), the coast whitethorn, a medium-sized thorny evergreen shrub, with large glossy green leaves, glaucous on the reverse; the young leaves are pale gray on white-bloomed stems, the pearly white flowers held in stiff spikes. *C. megacarpus* (z9–10), the bigpod ceanothus, has evergreen leaves and white flowers in spring. For colder climates there are *C. americanus* (z5–10), the New Jersey tea, a small deciduous shrub with off-white flowers in dense clusters in summer; and *C. ovatus* (z5–10), a small shrub with glossy, toothed leaves, and white flowers, similar to *C. americanus*. *C. velutinus* (z7–10), the tobacco brush, is a rounded, wide-spreading evergreen with highly polished leaves and large, stiff sprays of white flower.

The California lilacs are a promiscuous group, on the whole, and there are many hybrid cultivars available in addition to the natural hybrids already described. Desirable new cultivars include 'Frosty Blue,' a medium-sized shrub with blue, white-frosted flowers, 'Joyce Coulter,' a spreading shrub with long spikes of medium-blue flowers, and the low, spreading 'Blue Mound.' Among older cultivars are 'Autumnal Blue' (z7–9) with pale blue flowers, 'Burkwoodii' (z8–10) in deeper blue, and 'A.T. Johnson' (z8–10) with rich blue blossom, all three flowering in spring and again in the fall. 'Delight' (z8–10) and 'Dignity' are old hybrids with shining foliage and long spikes of bright blue flowers. 'Cascade' (z8–10) is a tall shrub with long, open sprays of soft blue blossom. 'Burtonensis' (z8–10) is very like *C. impressus*, except that its small leaves are almost circular.

Celtis ULMACEAE

The hackberries or nettle trees range from elegant, fast-growing trees to slow-growing shrubs, increased by seed. The Mediterranean hackberry, *Celtis australis* (z6–8), also known as the lote tree or honeyberry tree, is a tall tree with rough-textured leaves and gray, beech-like trunk topped by massive spreading branches. The small, dark fruits are sweet to eat, but self-sown seedlings are apt to appear too freely where they fall. One of the most drought-resistant is *C. pallida* (z6–8), the desert hackberry or spiny hackberry, a medium-sized, slow-growing, thorny shrub from the desert areas of the southwestern United States and northern Mexico. It forms dense thickets, with leaves resembling those of the Chinese elm, becoming deciduous during periods of drought or cold. It will do well without irrigation as long as the annual rainfall exceeds 10in/250mm. The inconspicuous flowers in spring are followed by orange berries popular with birds. *C. reticulata* (z6–8) is known as the netleaf hackberry, western hackberry, palo blanco, or sugar berry. It is less drought-tolerant than the desert hackberry and grows into a craggy tree with pendulous branches and leaves of variable form, distinctly net-veined. Insignificant spring flowers give way to orange to purple berries liked by birds.

Ceratonia LEGUMINOSAE

Ceratonia siliqua (z8–10), the carob, St. John's bread, or locust bean of the eastern Mediterranean, slowly makes a medium-sized, dense, wide-spreading tree, with leathery, very dark green compound leaves. Male plants bear pinkish flowers in spring, the females small red flowers turning to edible, dark, flat pods from which a substitute for chocolate is made; they are also used as animal fodder and are, some say, the "locusts" on which St.

John the Baptist lived while preaching in the desert. Thriving in similar climates to citrus, the carob is tolerant of extreme heat and drought, and provides dense shade.

Ceratostigma PLUMBAGINACEAE

Ceratostigma abyssinicum (z9–10) is a shrubby plumbago with sky-blue flowers in reddish calyces, paler than those of the familiar *C. willmottianum.* Half-ripe cuttings root easily. *C. plumbaginoïdes* (z5–8) is herbaceous, with running roots, and indigo-blue flowers. The foliage turns crimson in the fall. In our garden it is a standby for the dust-dry corners beneath cypresses where no rain ever seems to penetrate.

Cercidium LEGUMINOSAE

Cercidium floridum (*C. torreyanum, Parkinsonia torreyana, P. florida*) (z9–11), the blue palo verde, is the first palo verde to flower in spring. The flowers are yellow, the compound foliage of tiny rounded leaflets blue-green, on a small, spreading, broad-crowned tree branching from low down. Native of the southwestern United States and northern Mexico, it prefers sandy soil and tolerates periods of drought, shedding its leaves as a defense mechanism against cold or water shortage. Like many members of the pea family, it is best raised from seed and planted young, as it transplants badly: scarify the seed, and sow it in deep containers to allow the tap root to form. The little-leaf palo verde, foothill palo verde, or mesa palo verde, *C. microphyllum* (*Parkinsonia microphylla*) (z9–11), is smaller and tougher than the blue palo verde, and differs in its yellow-green leaves and in bearing its yellow flowers later in spring over a long season. It grows slowly (faster where it has plenty of moisture) and develops an irregular rounded crown and multistemmed trunk. The tiny, rounded leaflets drop in periods of drought or cold, and as a further protective mechanism in severe drought, it also sheds its twigs. In the wild it grows in the mesa and rocky foothills, overlapping the range of the blue palo verde. In the garden an open, gravelly soil suits it well, and it needs no irrigation where the rainfall exceeds 12in/300mm annually.

Cercis LEGUMINOSAE

The redbuds have heart-shaped or kidney-shaped leaves and pea flowers in spring. They are all reasonably drought tolerant. They can be raised from seed, but named selections need to be vegetatively propagated. *Cercis canadensis* (z4–9), the redbud, is small and broad-crowned, and needs hot summers to produce its rose-pink flowers in abundance in late spring. In very hot regions it needs protection from the sun in the height of summer. *C. c.* f. *albida* is white. 'Rosea' is brighter pink in flower than the type, *C. c.* f. *mexicana* is more shrubby, and 'Forest Pansy' has purple foliage, in contrast to the usual bright green. The fall color is yellow. Planted in well-nourished, drained soil, it has only moderate water needs. The Chinese redbud, *C. chinensis* (z6–9), is similar to the North American redbud, but more shrubby; the large, heart-shaped leaves are shining green, the flowers bright pink. One of the finest redbuds is *C. c.* 'Avondale,' a recent New Zealand selection which produces masses of deep purple flowers.

 C. occidentalis (z8–9), the western redbud, is shrubby, or occasionally tree-like, with rounded leaves and rosy flowers in spring. The similar *C. reniformis* (z6–9) also grows as a shrub or forms a medium-sized tree, with wide, glossy, kidney-shaped leaves downy beneath, and clusters of pink flowers. Named selections include 'Oklahoma,' with bright reddish-purple

Cercis canadensis

flowers and glossy, leathery foliage, and 'Texas White.' *C. siliquastrum* (z7–9) is the Mediterranean Judas tree, a small tree with heart-shaped leaves and clusters of bright mauve-pink flowers erupting from the branches, and even the trunk, in spring. It flowers in just three or four years from seed. *C. siliquastrum* f. *albida* has white flowers, and 'Bodnant' is an uncommon selection with thundercloud-purple flowers.

Cercocarpus ROSACEAE

The mountain mahoganies are natives of the southwestern deserts of the United States, but several are hardy and evergreen in much colder zones. *Cercocarpus brevifolius* (z5–9) tolerates very dry soils, but looks better in improved soil, growing very slowly to form a small shrub, very similar in aspect to the better-known birch-leaved mountain mahogany, *C. betuloides* (z6–9), a taller shrub, and the beechleaf or alderleaf mountain mahogany, *C. montanus* (z5–9). This last has thick-textured leaves of sculptured perfection, but is only semi-evergreen. The littleleaf mountain mahogany, *C. intricatus*, a small evergreen shrub, is hardier still (z4–9), with narrow polished leaves. It tolerates drought, wind and sun. For an evergreen of larger, even occasionally tree-size, and remarkable hardiness, there is the curl-leaf mountain mahogany, *C. ledifolius* (z4–9). The narrow leaves are bent to one side; the fruits are feathery plumes.

Chamaebatiaria ROSACEAE

Chamaebatiaria millefolium (z6–9) is a small evergreen shrub with aromatic foliage as feathery as an achillea's, and showy white plumes of flower in early summer. It thrives in dry, sandy or stony soil.

Chilopsis BIGNONIACEAE

Chilopsis linearis (*Bignonia linearis*) (z8–10), the desert willow or willowleaf catalpa, grows along dry washes in the southwestern United States and Mexico. It forms a loose shrub or small tree, with an open crown, smooth gray bark, and long pendulous leaves, making it curiously evocative of waterside plantings. The fragrant white, lavender or pink trumpets open over a long season from spring to late summer. Tolerant of heat, cold, drought and wind, the desert willow is the better for occasional deep irrigation. It can be raised from seed to flower in its first year. 'Barranca' is of more upright habit, with rich pink to lavender flowers.

Chionanthus OLEACEAE

Chionanthus virginicus (z4–9), the North American fringe tree, is hardy and easy to raise from seed, a large shrub with bold foliage and white, faintly scented flowers composed of narrow petals, in summer. It is drought-tolerant once established.

× *Chitalpa* BIGNONIACEAE

× *Chitalpa tashkentensis* (*Catalpa bignonioïdes* × *Chilopsis linearis*) (z6–9) is a deciduous small tree with dense ascending branches, and pink to white flowers, up to forty in each erect raceme. 'Pink Dawn' is of spreading habit, and 'Morning Cloud' more upright, with palest pink to white flowers.

Choisya RUTACEAE

Choisya ternata (z7–9), the Mexican orange blossom, is a rounded, aromatic, evergreen shrub of medium size, with polished leaves formed of three leaflets, and fragrant white flowers in spring, often with a late summer repeat. Half-ripe or firm cuttings root readily. Its hybrid offspring 'Aztec Pearl' (z7–9) has long-fingered, elegant foliage, and quite large white flowers with yellow stamens, in spring.

Chorisia BOMBACACEAE

Chorisia speciosa (z9–11), the floss-silk tree, kapok tree, or palo boracho, grows fast and erect at first, then slows to mature as a small- to medium-sized tree. The succulent, spiny trunk is at first slender and bright green, thickening and turning to gray with age. The bright green compound leaves are palmate, with a fan-like outline. Wide, lily-like flowers open in the fall, the petals varying from rose to orchid pink to wine purple, with brown-flecked white centers. Kapok is harvested from the seed capsules. Remaining evergreen with ample irrigation, it tolerates drought, responding by shedding its leaves. *C. insignis* (z9–11), the white floss silk tree, has white flowers, but is otherwise similar.

Cistus CISTACEAE

The sun roses are a chiefly Mediterranean genus of evergreen shrubs indispensable in dry gardens, flowering in summer. Each afternoon the crumpled-silk petals shatter to carpet the ground beneath the shrubs, but a long succession of buds waits to open the next day and the next. Sun roses vary in size from prostrate shrublets to tall shrubs about head high. Half-ripe cuttings are the usual method of propagation, but some, such as *Cistus incanus* ssp. *creticus* and *C. laurifolius*, can be grown from seed for cheap, extensive plantings. All the varieties mentioned below are z8–10.

Now that the yellow-flowered sun roses belong in *Halimium*, cistuses fall into just two colors: white, with or without dark basal patches, or shades of pink from palest dog rose to assertive magenta. One of the finest whites is *C.* × *aguilarii* (*C. ladanifer* f. *latifolius*) a natural hybrid, its long, bright green leaves with crimpled margins; the pure white flowers are large for the genus. 'Maculatus' is more resinous, and the flowers are crimson-blotched. The hardier *C.* × *cyprius* grows fairly tall and has wide white flowers marked

BELOW LEFT *Cistus aguilarii* 'Maculatus'

BELOW RIGHT *Cistus* × *pulverulentus* 'Sunset'

with a red spot at the base of each petal; the foliage turns to leaden gray in cold weather. *C. laurifolius* is the most frost-tolerant of the larger cistuses and is valuable for the ease with which it can be raised from seed to use in massed plantings. The dark, rather blue-green leaves set off clusters of white, yellow-centered flowers. Perhaps the most beautiful in flower is *C. palhinhae*, the St. Vincent cistus, a compact shrub with glossy, resinous, dark green leaves, and large, silky, pure white flowers. If you prefer a cistus with blotched flowers, *C. ladanifer*, the gum cistus or laudanum, is a tall, upright shrub, with narrow, gummily aromatic leaves, and large white flowers, each petal with a deep red basal blotch.

There are some pretty sun roses of low, spreading growth, ideal for hot, sunny banks. *C. salviifolius* has creamy white, yellow-centered flowers; 'Prostratus' has trailing stems that will follow the contours of the ground or drape over a wall. The appealing *C. × dansereaui* (*C. × lusitanicus*) is usually seen in its prostrate form, 'Decumbens,' which bears large white flowers with a small blood-red blotch at the base of each petal. A size or two larger is *C. × hybridus* (*C. × corbariensis*), a spreading shrub ideal for covering banks, with pink buds opening to ivory flowers. In dry, poor soils the foliage deepens to bronze and copper with the onset of winter. *C. × florentinus* is a dependable, pleasant ground-covering hybrid, of spreading, knee-high growth, with green leaves and white, yellow-eyed flowers. For very informal settings there is *C. hirsutus*, which has white flowers freely borne in clusters, and hairy dark green foliage.

The free-seeding *C. incanus* ssp. *creticus* is aromatic with resin and bears flowers of rose-pink to near magenta, varying also in leaf from gray to green. The foliage of *C. albidus* is very white-wooly, contrasting with flowers of soft lilac pink, on compact growth. For ground-covering qualities similar to those of *C. × hybridus*, *C. × skanbergii* is a pretty hybrid with narrow, gray-green leaves and abundant small flowers of dog rose pink. The habit of *C. parviflorus* is similar, but its flowers are larger; the true plant is seldom seen, with hybrids such as 'Grayswood Pink' usually standing in for it. It is a low, spreading shrub with gray-felted leaves and clear pink flowers. *C. × pulverulentus* (*C. crispus* × *C. albidus*) is another of spreading habit, with grayish foliage and bright pink flowers; 'Sunset' has flowers of vivid magenta, brightest of all the sun roses; all these are unblotched. The blotched pink cistus *C. × purpureus* is more upright in habit, with large, rose-pink flowers, each petal bearing a deep chocolate-maroon blotch at the base.

Cistus hybrids of garden origin include 'Peggy Sammons,' which has gray-green leaves on upright stems, and flowers of clear pink, and 'Anne Palmer,' a pretty but less frost-resistant soft pink. 'Paladin' is one of the most beautiful of white-flowered hybrid cistus, with large flowers set off by sticky-shiny, dark green foliage.

Citrus RUTACEAE

The species of *Citrus* and allied genera are mainly evergreen spiny shrubs or small trees originating in southern and southeastern Asia and the Malay peninsula. Few wild forms are cultivated today, as selection has given superior fruiting qualities. Typically, they have deep glossy green foliage and delectably fragrant flowers in spring. Commercially the many varieties of citrus are grown in orchards; in the garden they can be grown as lawn or patio specimens, in the open ground, or in large containers. The chief restriction on their cultivation is cold, though extreme heat may cause the fruitlets to drop. The species mentioned here are all z9–10 unless otherwise shown.

Hardiest of all are those grown as ornamentals: the calamondin, sour orange and bouquet orange are generally hardy to 23F/−5C, and may survive short spells down to 18F/−8C. Fruiting varieties, when mature, may survive 23F/−5C, but at temperatures below 30F/−1C, the fruit is damaged. Despite this, they may survive in unlikely places: at Salcombe on the southwestern coast of England, a Seville orange tree survived for over two hundred years, and during the mid-nineteenth century oranges, citrons, lemons and limes all ripened successfully there and were reported as "equal, if not superior, to any brought from abroad" (*Illustrated London News*, March 1, 1856).

The hardiest of the fruiting citrus is the kumquat, then grapefruit, tangerines (mandarins and tangeloes), sweet oranges, lemons (sensitive to 30F/−1C), and limes – the most cold-sensitive as they are tropical plants needing heat and high humidity. As important as the temperature is how often cold spells occur and how long they last.

In very hot, exposed areas, protect the young trunks against sunburn, and wrap them against cold in winter. Irrigation is essential in desert areas if the fruits are to ripen successfully. Plant young trees in a hollow, with a berm to retain water. Where the soil is highly alkaline or saline, give a long, slow soak in winter, to wet the soil to a depth of 6ft/1.8m and leach the salts away from the root zone.

× *Citrofortunella microcarpa* (× *C. mitis*) is the calamondin, calamondin lime, or sour acid mandarin, a small columnar or rounded tree. The numerous small orange fruits are very ornamental. *Fortunella margarita*, the kumquat, varies from a small shrub to a medium-sized tree, and has small oval or rounded fruit ripening in winter, with a sweet skin and tart flesh making excellent conserve. 'Nagami' is a common cultivar; *F. japonica* is the round kumquat, of which 'Meiwa' is the best for eating.

Citrus aurantium, the sour orange, Seville orange, bitter orange or bigarade, was brought to the New World by Spanish settlers. It is a wild species of vigorous, spiny growth, with white, waxy flowers in spring, their powerful fragrance floating on the air. The fruits ripen in the fall and remain on the tree through winter. *C. aurantium* 'Bouquet,' the bouquet orange, or bouquet de fleurs, is more restrained in growth, clad with foliage to the ground, and bears showy, fragrant flowers followed by yellowish fruit suitable for marmalade. *C. × paradisi*, the grapefruit, is one of the easiest to grow. The best fruit is said to come from plants grown in desert conditions. Pink varieties include 'Redblush' and 'Ruby Red'; 'Marsh' is a yellow, acid and nearly seedless variety. 'Golden Special' has large, juicy, yellow fruits. The fruits are ripe from fall to spring, when they are at their best. The fullest flavor develops in hot summers.

C. reticulata is the tangerine or mandarin. It comes in many forms, including the 'Clementine,' or Algerian tangerine, as well as those known as 'Fairchild,' 'Kara,' and 'Kinnow,' which must be the kinnoo of Pakistan. They all have a spreading habit. The fruits ripen from fall to midwinter, often only in alternate years. *C. × tangelo* (*C. reticulata* × *C. paradisi*) is similar in habit to the tangerine. 'Mineola' is a large-fruited variety of good flavor, easy to peel, ripening in late winter to early spring. 'Orlando' is less vigorous but more cold tolerant, with yellow-orange fruit in winter, a regular heavy cropper. Neither is self-fertile.

The sweet orange, *C. sinensis*, is classified into four groups based on fruit character (navel and blood) and geographical ancestry (Spanish and Mediterranean). 'Arizona Sweets,' a Valencia type, grows well in desert conditions and is one of the easiest for non-commercial growers. 'Valencia'

× *Citrofortunella microcarpa*

Citrus limon

itself, which ripens early to late spring, produces medium-sized fruit for eating or juicing. 'Diller' is the hardiest; it bears small seedy fruit good for juicing, ripe in early winter, on a small tree. 'Trovita' is a California cultivar, vigorous, tolerant of heat and cold, and a dependable cropper of thin-skinned fruit ripe in early spring. 'Washington' is a navel variety, successful in warm interior valleys of California, but not so good in desert areas and unsuccessful in sandy soil. It bears abundant flower but sheds much of its fruit, which ripens in winter. 'Robertson' is a navel of similar but smaller growth, ripe two to three weeks earlier. 'Shamouti' is a small cultivar grown on dwarf rootstock; the 'Jaffa' orange, developed in Palestine, bears large crops of big seedless fruit. Blood oranges such as 'Sanguinella,' 'Ruby Blood' and 'Moro' are best for desert conditions; their fruit ripens in late spring.

The fastest-growing citrus is *C. limon* (z10), the lemon, distinctly frost-tender and best grafted on rough lemon rootstock. 'Meyer' (*C. limon* × *C. sinensis*) is hardier, but is banned in some places as it hosts citrus quick decline (a virus disease). Where it can be grown, it is valued for its very aromatic, juicy fruits. 'Lisbon' forms a dense thorny tree, the fruits ripening in the fall; pick them early to avoid frost damage. 'Eureka' is the standard market fruit, borne all year round on a similar but smaller, more open tree. The lemon-citron hybrid 'Ponderosa' (*C. ponderosa*) produces giant bumpy fruits with a thick skin and mild flavor, on open angular growth of medium height; it fruits when young. *C. aurantiifolia*, the lime, is the most tender citrus, a large, spiny bush. Varieties include the 'Key,' 'Mexican' or 'West Indian' lime, and the Persian lime. 'Bearss' is a seedling of the Persian lime said to be as hardy as the lemon, with yellow, seedless, very acid, aromatic fruit. 'Indian Lime' is a lime-lemon cross.

Cneorum CNEORACEAE

Cneorum tricoccon (z9–11), the spurge olive, is an evergreen shrub from the Mediterranean, with narrow, obovate leaves, small yellow flowers and russet fruits, useful in sunny, dry places, but not showy.

Cocculus MENISPERMACEAE

Cocculus laurifolius (z9–11), the laurel-leaf cocculus or laurel-leaf snailseed (so called on account of the seed pods which are coiled like snail shells), is an evergreen shrub which can be kept to about head height, or allowed to develop into a small tree when it will slowly form a dense, wide canopy over a leaning trunk. It is a native of warm temperate regions of southern Japan and the Himalayas. The bold, dark green, laurel-like leaves are shed in spring as the new growths appear. The laurel-leaf cocculus needs an acid soil with free drainage and moderate to ample irrigation if grown in desert conditions.

Colutea LEGUMINOSAE

The bladder sennas are undemanding shrubs with pinnate leaves, showy pea flowers, and inflated, bladder-like seed pods in the fall. Seeds and half-ripe cuttings are easy means of increase. *Colutea arborescens* (z6–8) is a large strong-growing shrubby tree, with yellow flowers. It naturalizes readily where suited. The more compact but equally vigorous *C.* × *media* (z6–8) has grayish foliage and warm yellow flowers. A similar self-contained color scheme belongs to *C. orientalis* (z6–9), a rounded shrub with glaucous foliage and coppery yellow flowers. *C. persica* (z7–9) is a large shrub from Kurdistan, with pinnate leaves and yellow flowers.

Comptonia MYRICACEAE

Comptonia peregrina (z3–6), the sweet fern, is a low-growing, suckering shrub with aromatic leaves resembling the fronds of spleenwort. Small brown catkins appear in spring. It needs lime-free conditions, but with this proviso is equally happy in peaty or in dry, sandy soils. It is increased by root cuttings or division.

Conradina LABIATAE

Conradina canescens (z6–8), a native of sandy coastal pinelands in the southeastern United States, is a low-growing shrub with grayish leaves and lilac flowers. The rosemary-like *C. verticillata* (z5–8) has aromatic needle leaves and clusters of pink flowers.

Convolvulus CONVOLVULACEAE

Convolvulus cneorum (z8–9), the silver bush morning glory, is a silvery-silky, evergreen shrub from the Mediterranean, bright as polished platinum under the midday sun but moonlight-pale as dusk falls, and decorated with wide, white funnels opening all summer from pink, scrolled buds. It resents the combination of wet and cold in cool temperate winters, but also dislikes intense heat in summer, especially if the nights are hot. Propagate from half-ripe cuttings.

Cordyline AGAVACEAE

Cordyline australis (z8–11), the cabbage tree, is a palm-like tree at first forming a rosette of sword leaves, but with age developing a tall, slender trunk with branching crown, each branch topped by a tufted mass of foliage. The wide, branching sprays of fragrant, ivory-cream flowers open

Cordyline australis

45

in spring. For extra color there are purple- or red-leaved forms: *C. australis* Purpurea Group and named selections. Seed of purple-leaved plants gives a range of leaf colors from milk chocolate to rich purple; selections can be grown from sections of a main stem. *C. indivisa* (z9–11) has much broader, gray-green blades, at first forming stemless rosettes, but with age developing into a branching tree with massive tufts of foliage.

Coronilla LEGUMINOSAE

Coronilla valentina (z9–10) is a small pretty shrub with glaucous green leaves and canary-yellow, apricot-scented flowers. *C. v.* ssp. *glauca* (z9–10) grows larger, and has bluer leaves and bright yellow pea flowers; 'Citrina' is enchanting, with pale lemon flowers; 'Variegata' has bright flowers among cream and blue-gray leaves. All can be raised from half-ripe cuttings.

Cytisus LEGUMINOSAE

The brooms are variable. Typically yellow pea-flowered, they also come in white and bright or parti-colors. They range in size from tiny shrublets to large, leafy, bulky shrubs. Most root easily from half-ripe cuttings.

One of the smallest is *Cytisus ardoinoi* (z6–8), a miniature shrub with bright yellow flowers in spring. Prostrate or creeping brooms include *C. decumbens* (z6–8), which bears yellow flowers in spring. *C. demissus* (*Chamaecytisus hirsutus*) (z6–8) is almost as prostrate, and bears disproportionately large yellow, brown-keeled flowers in spring. The tiny *C. procumbens* (z6–8) is a prostrate shrublet with yellow flowers in spring. One of the prettiest is *C. × kewensis* (z6–8), its almost prostrate, spreading branches thickly set with cream pea flowers in spring. Of more upright growth are *C. × beanii* (z7–8), a shrublet with vivid yellow flowers in spring, and the rather taller *C. supinus* (*Chamaecytisus supinus*) (z7–8), a variable

Cytisus battandieri

small shrub with large yellow flowers from midsummer on. Slightly taller again is *C. purgans* (z6–9), which bears its fragrant yellow flowers in spring. *C. nigricans* (z6–8) is valued for its late flowering season, the long spikes of yellow flowers opening in late summer. These last three all grow to around waist height.

C. purpureus (*Chamaecytisus purpureus*) (z6–9), the purple broom, is a pretty shrub with low, arching branches, sparsely leafy, and lilac-purple flowers in spring. It has a white form, *C. p.* f. *albus*. So does the larger Warminster broom, *C. × praecox* 'Warminster' (z7–9), which has arching, mounded stems smothered in heavily fragrant, cream flowers in spring. 'Albus' is the white form; 'Allgold' is a rich yellow selection; 'Hollandia' has pale cream and cerise flowers; and the related 'Zeelandia' is cream, lilac and pink. Brooms that are naturally white include *C. albus* (*Chamaecytisus albus*) (z6–8), of upright growth, with abundant small white flowers in late spring; and the white Spanish broom, *C. multiflorus* (z7–8), which has abundant small, white flowers in spring on upright stems. The much more tender *C. supranubius* (z9–10), the Tenerife broom, is like a small *Spartium* in growth, with fragrant, blush-white flowers in spring.

The common European broom is *C. scoparius* (z6–8), a generally erect, green-stemmed shrub with showy, large yellow flowers in spring. It is the parent of many named cultivars with flowers of varying colors. *C. battandieri* (*Argyrocytisus battandieri*) (z8–9), from Morocco, is a large shrub with laburnum-like foliage, silver-gray with a coating of silky hairs and cones of densely packed, bright yellow, pineapple-scented flowers in summer. A delicious fragrance also belongs to *C. canariensis* (*Genista canariensis*) (z9–10), the florists' 'Genista fragrans,' a native of the Atlantic isles, with spikes of yellow flowers on green, leafy branches in spring. It can grow large if not cut back by frost. (This last and *C. scoparius* are noxious weeds in Australia, where all brooms can become weedy.)

Dalea LEGUMINOSAE
The indigo bushes are natives of dry and desert areas of western North America and Mexico, with compound leaves. Tricky to transplant, they are best raised from seed and planted out while small. *Dalea schottii* (z8–10) is spiny, with spikes of dark blue to purplish flowers in summer. The smoke tree, *D. spinosa* (z8–10), is a spiny shrub or small tree, with ash-gray foliage and stems, and short spikes of violet-purple flowers.

Delonix LEGUMINOSAE
Delonix regia (z10–11), the flamboyant, royal poinciana or gul mohr tree of the Indian subcontinent, is a tree with ferny, doubly pinnate leaves and brilliant vermilion scarlet flowers in spring and summer.

Dendromecon PAPAVERACEAE
Dendromecon rigida (z9–10), the tree poppy, grows on hot, gravelly slopes in California. It is a slender, evergreen shrub of medium height, with bluish, willow-like leaves and shredding bark. The satiny, fragrant, clear yellow poppies appear over a long summer season. *D. r.* ssp. *harfordii* (z9–10) differs in its green foliage. Root cuttings offer a means of increase.

Desmodium LEGUMINOSAE
Desmodium elegans (*D. tiliifolium*) (z7–10) is a small, soft-wooded shrub with upright stems and trifoliate leaves, bearing abundant soft lilac pea flowers in airy sprays in summer. It can be divided for increase. The larger *D.*

Dendromecon rigida

Diospyros kaki

yunnanense (*D. praestans*) (z9–11) has scandent stems and handsome large, rounded silvery-silky leaves. The purple flowers are borne in crowded racemes in late summer. It is propagated from cuttings.

Diospyros EBENACEAE

Diospyros kaki (z8–9), the Chinese persimmon, date plum, or kaki, is a large shrub or small tree with orange-yellow, edible fruits. It is decorative as well, with bold, polished leaves richly colored in the fall. It can be raised from seed. The North American persimmon or possum wood, *D. virginiana* (z5–9), forms a tree with a wide crown, craggy bark, and bright fall tints from the dying leaves.

Dodonaea SAPINDACEAE

Dodonaea viscosa (z9–10), the hopbush, hopseed bush, or switch-sorrel, grows rapidly to form a large shrub if given enough moisture, but remains more compact in dry soils. The narrowly oblanceolate leaves are borne on slender stems; the insignificant flowers appear at the end of winter and are followed by winged, hop-like seeds in late spring. *D. viscosa* Purpurea Group is less frost resistant, and being seed-raised varies in intensity of leaf color; 'Saratoga' is a cutting-grown cultivar that is consequently dependably purple.

Ebenus LEGUMINOSAE

Ebenus cretica (z9–10) is an evergreen subshrub from rocky places and cliffs in Crete. The fingered leaves are gray with silky hairs when young, and the bright pink pea flowers are borne in cylindrical spikes.

Elaeagnus ELAEAGNACEAE

Elaeagnus angustifolia (z3–8), the oleaster or Russian wild olive, is an excellent substitute, visually, for the true olive in cold or windy areas, though it sheds its leaves in the fall. It is a small, angular, often spiny tree, sometimes remaining shrubby. The narrow, willow-like leaves are silver-gray, and the small, yellow-cream flowers opening in spring are intensely fragrant. They are followed by small, inedible olive-like fruits. The oleaster will grow in areas where the rainfall is no more than 12in/300mm annually without irrigation, except in desert heat when it needs occasional deep watering; it does not thrive where the winters are warm. The silver berry, *E. commutata* (*E. argentea*) (z2–6), has broader leaves of brilliant silver coloring, on suckering stems up to head height. The fragrant flowers are followed by small, silvery, ovoid fruits. The leaves drop in the fall. Like the Russian olive it can be increased by layering. *E. multiflora* (z6–8) is a large, spreading, deciduous shrub with leaves silvered beneath, bearing fragrant flowers in spring and dark red fruits in summer. The fall olive, *E. umbellata* (z3–8), is a big, spreading, deciduous shrub with apple-green leaves silvered beneath, sweetly scented flowers in late spring, and small, decorative orange fruits in the fall. It too can be layered.

The evergreen *E. × ebbingei* (z7–10) has large, dark gray-green leaves, silvery when young and remaining silvered on the reverse with pale scurf. It makes a fine shelter planting, withstanding salt winds. 'Gilt Edge' has the leaves boldly margined with yellow, and 'Limelight' shows a central splash of gold. They need to be increased from cuttings. One of the parents of the Ebbing silver berry is *E. pungens* (z7–10), a vigorous evergreen becoming large in time, with glossy green leaves covered on the underside with pale scurf. The fragrant flowers open in the fall. 'Maculata' is a popular selection on account of its bright daffodil-yellow variegations; shoots that revert to green need to be cut out.

Encelia COMPOSITAE

Encelia farinosa (z9–10), the brittle bush, incienso, or white brittle bush, is a soft-wooded shrub from the southwestern United States and northern Mexico. Citrus will also grow wherever it thrives. The fragrant resin it exudes was used as chewing-gum, analgesic and incense by the early Spaniards. Fast-growing, forming a low, wide-spreading mound, it has gray-green to whitish triangular leaves, densely packed on shrubs growing in good conditions, but sparse in cold or harsh climates. It bears yellow daisies in spring. A light sandy or gravel soil with free drainage suits the brittle bush, which needs no irrigation where the rainfall exceeds 10in/250mm annually.

Ensete MUSACEAE

Ensete ventricosum (*Musa ensete*, *M. arnoldiana*) (z10–11), the Abyssinian banana, from the Ethiopian highlands, forms a trunk-like but not woody stem, and has wide, bright green paddle leaves with crimson midribs on long arching stalks. 'Maurelii' has red-tinged leaves. The foliage is damaged by wind and burned by strong sun or light frost. A light rich soil suits it best; it copes with desert conditions, but needs irrigation.

Encelia farinosa

Ephedra EPHEDRACEAE

The virtually leafless ephedras or joint firs are not for those who want brightly colored flowers; but they are characterful plants that give an evergreen effect, and are both hardy and drought-resistant. *Ephedra distachya* (z5–8) grows into a mass of jointed, slender, olive-green stems of less than waist height, but with a much wider spread; *E. d.* var. *helvetica* (z4–7), from high altitudes in the Swiss Alps, is a beautiful plant with shorter stems even more densely tangled, of grayish cast. Gerard's joint fir, *E. gerardiana* (z5–8), is similar to *E. distachya*, but with shorter, thicker joints; it is rather shorter in growth. *E. intermedia* (z5–8), the blue joint fir, has very upright, blue-toned stems.

Eriobotrya ROSACEAE

Eriobotrya japonica, the loquat, Japanese plum, or Japanese medlar, is a small- to medium-sized tree, with bold, even coarse leaves, forming an umbrella-like crown on a single or several stems when mature. The fuzzy white flowers, held in wooly, cream clusters in the fall and winter, are followed by small, pear-like, edible fruits in late spring in warm-winter areas. It is hardy in z9–11 for fruit, and down to z8–11 if grown only for foliage. The largest, most striking leaves are borne by non-fruiting trees. Unfortunately, like some other members of the family Rosaceae, it is susceptible to fireblight. Once established, it tolerates periods of drought. The bronze loquat, *E. deflexa* (*Photinia deflexa*) (z9–11), is a smaller, more refined shrub, sensitive to excessive heat or wind. The young growths are covered in rusty fur; the large, oblong, evergreen leaves have coarse serrate margins. The white flowers are followed by small inedible fruits.

Erythrina LEGUMINOSAE

The coral trees all have trifoliolate leaves, and most have spiny stems. *Erythrina caffra* (z10–11), the Cape kafferboom, coral tree, lucky bean tree or koraalboom, is a slow-growing, thorny, semi-evergreen, multistemmed tree with vermilion, or occasionally cream, pea flowers in racemes, opening in spring. The dwarf kafferboom, *E. humeana* (z9–11), forms a small tree, its leaves white with long hairs. The pea flowers are followed by scarlet seeds. The naked coral tree, *E. coralloïdes* (z9–11), is a small, spiny tree with triangular leaflets; the red flowers are borne on bare branches. *E. crista-galli*, the cockspur tree, is a soft-wooded shrub with rich scarlet, waxy pea flowers in large racemes in summer. Careful deadheading will encourage it to flower two or three times a year in warm climates. As a shrub it is hardy in z9–11, but with a protective winter mulch will behave like a herbaceous plant in z8–11, regenerating from the roots. *E. × sykesii* (z10–11) is striking, with its blue-green leaves and vivid orange flowers.

Eucalyptus MYRTACEAE

The eucalypts have long since shed their image as koala bear fodder to become among the most familiar trees in areas with Mediterranean or even warmer, drier climates. Over eighty species had already been introduced to California by 1900, of which around twenty have proved very successful. All are evergreen; most are remarkably drought- and heat-tolerant, and grow rapidly, but they can be poor neighbors, with their hungry, invasive roots. Some have flaking or peeling bark that sheds litter near the tree. Until established, they appreciate deep periodic irrigation, but thereafter will grow well without extra water where the rainfall exceeds 10in/250mm annually. Their tolerance of cold varies greatly, depending not only on the

Eriobotrya japonica

species in question but also the provenance: trees from higher altitudes are hardier than low-altitude specimens; horticulturalists in Britain gather seed from their home-grown specimens to extend the range of those that will stand British winters. As a general rule, eucalypts with colored flowers are less frost-resistant than those with white or cream flowers.

Of those with colored flowers, *Eucalyptus calophylla* (z9–11) 'Rosea' is one of the hardiest; its flowers are pink, and its foliage is glossy dark green. The type itself has cream flowers. One of the most striking is *E. ficifolia* (z9–11), a small graceful tree with brilliant cinnabar-red flowers, or sometimes white or pink, borne in large sprays amid polished, pointed green leaves. The pink, crimson or scarlet form of *E. leucoxylon*, known as 'Rosea' (z9–11), is generally considered hardier than *E. ficifolia* in the Mediterranean area. 'Purpurea' has purple flowers, and like 'Rosea' is rather smaller than the type. *E. leucoxylon* itself (z9–11), the white ironbark or yellow gum, has pendulous branches and rounded, dark gray-green juvenile foliage, very rich in essential oil; the mature leaves are the same color, but change shape to long, slender, slightly curved blades. The smooth whitish bark is shed in flakes revealing pink, yellow or bluish inner layers. It is tolerant of heat, wind, drought, and heavy or rocky soils, but is not very frost-resistant. The red ironbark or pink ironbark, *E. sideroxylon* 'Rosea' (z9–11), is a tree of narrow, open habit, which grows fast, usually maturing as a small tree, but sometimes reaching considerable size. The slender, dark brown trunk is deeply fissured, revealing the red inner bark. The foliage, which is very narrow in the juvenile state, is in varying shades of gray-green, and the flowers are hanging clusters of creamy pink to deep pinkish-crimson, opening from fall to spring; dark-toned leaves are usually matched by darker flowers. The red ironbark tolerates high heat and poor or shallow soils, but is at its best in light soil with deep periodic irrigation.

E. erythrocorys (z10–11), the red cap gum or illyarrie, grows fast but remains small, with roots less greedy than most. Virtually all eucalypts respond well to hard pruning, but this is especially suited to growing as a shrub or small, multistemmed tree. It has tan to ivory bark, and long, narrow, bright green leaves. The showy yellow, brush-like flowers open from scarlet capped buds from fall to spring. The rose mallee, *E. rhodantha* (z10–11), is naturally shrubby. The long slender stems are set with silvery, rounded, perfoliate (stem-clasping) leaves. It bears a long, almost continuous succession of large, rose-red pompon blooms. It is reasonably frost-tolerant, but in very dry areas needs some irrigation.

Despite its vernacular names, which might suggest colored flowers, the red gum, river red gum, or Murray red gum, *E. camaldulensis* (*E. rostrata*) (z9–11), has white blooms. It is a tall, fast-growing tree, with pendulous branches and long, slender, thin-textured green leaves. The trunk has smooth bark, flaking to show patches of tan to light gray. *E. citriodora* (z9–11), the lemon-scented gum, is a tall, graceful, fast-growing tree, with a smooth-barked, pinkish-white, slender trunk, and narrow green leaves which release an aroma of lemon when crushed. The flowers are white. One of the all-round hardiest eucalypts is *E. microtheca* (z10–11), the coolibah tree or flooded box, tolerating heat, drought and poor soil, as well as the wide variation between day and night temperatures characteristic of desert regions, but not suited for frosty areas. It grows rapidly, but does not become very tall. The bark of young trees is white to gray, the leaves light gray-green and as narrow as ribbons, the flowers white. *E. rudis* (z10–11), the desert gum, is a very drought-resistant, medium-sized tree with sickle-shaped prominently veined leaves and white flowers. The bark is rough, dark gray, persistent on the trunk, but smooth and shedding above. Where a smaller eucalypt is needed, the choice might be *E. spathulata* (z10–11), the narrow-leaved gimlet or swamp mallee, a barely frost-tolerant species, usually forming a small- to medium-sized, multistemmed shrub with white flowers. The narrow leaves are bright green.

A characteristic of several eucalypts is the striking difference between the juvenile and adult foliage. In *E. cinerea* (z9–11), the spiral eucalypt, mealy stringybark, Argyle apple, or ash gum, the mature leaves are gray-green and willow-like, but in the juvenile stage they are ovate to orbicular and very blue-glaucous, giving rise to the alternative name silver dollar. It is a tree of moderate growth, with cream flowers. One of the most frost-resistant of this type is *E. gunnii* (z9–11), the cider gum, which has blue-glaucous, almost circular juvenile leaves. It can be kept low and in the juvenile state by annual hard pruning, or allowed to develop to a tall tree with narrow, blue-green adult foliage and small cream flowers. The spinning gum, *E. perriniana* (z9–11), earns its name from the blue-white, semi-circular juvenile leaves which are joined at the base to surround the stem, and with time become loose, spinning around the stem in the wind. The flowers are ivory-cream and the adult leaves narrowly blunt-ended, with glaucous coloring. It is a fairly frost-resistant species, growing to medium size. *E. polyanthemos* (z9–11), the silver dollar gum, silver dollar tree, or red box, is a medium-sized, white-flowered tree of moderate to fast growth, often asymmetrical in outline, the crown spreading with age, the snakeskin bark covering the whole tree. The rounded juvenile leaves are brown-green to gray-green with a silver cast, becoming more pointed in the adult stage. The selection 'Polydan' is more symmetrical and lacks the very rounded juvenile foliage; it is not so drought-tolerant. The silver mountain gum or money tree, *E. pulverulenta* (z9–11), is now very rare in the wild, but well established in cultivation. It is a small, fast-growing tree. The juvenile foliage is shining glaucous-white, heart-shaped to rounded, clasping the stem; the adult leaves are slender and pointed. The white bark is smooth and silky; the flowers are white. The silver mountain gum is reasonably frost-tolerant, but dislikes wind.

E. globulus (z9–11) is often grown from seed in areas where the winters are too severe for it to survive, for it has bold, very blue juvenile foliage, white-glaucous beneath. Where it survives, it grows to a large tree with white flowers; in California, it can reach 40–43ft/12–13m in little over three years from seed, while older trees, cut right back, grow again to 100ft/30m in six to eight years. A tree of more modest size with striking foliage is *E. cordata* (z10–11), the heart-leaved silver gum, which tolerates wind. It has blue-gray, heart-shaped leaves, smooth white or green bark, and ivory-cream flowers. *E. glaucescens* (z9–11), the tingiringi gum, has white-glaucous juvenile leaves, while even the adult foliage, when first emerging, is glaucous or flushed with pink. It is a tall, fast-growing tree with green bark maturing to white, and cream flowers.

Eucalypts suited to rather colder climates include several from high altitudes in their native haunts, as suggested by such names as snow gum or mountain gum. *E. coccifera* (z9–11), the Tasmanian snow gum, is a medium-sized tree with purple-backed juvenile leaves, aromatic like peppermint, and long, slender, glaucous mature foliage. The flowers are white. The bark flakes to show gray and white patches. *E. dalrympleana* (z8–11), the mountain gum, is another frost-resistant eucalypt with bright young shoots of coppery pink or scarlet, gray-green leaves, and many-colored patchwork bark: tan, cream and buff-pink. It grows rapidly to a

Eucalyptus pauciflora ssp. *niphophila*

considerable size and bears white flowers. The alpine snow gum, *E. pauciflora* ssp. *niphophila* (z8–11), is a very frost-resistant eucalypt of moderate growth, with large, scimitar-shaped, gray-green or silvery leaves on orange stalks, patchwork bark of gray, cream and olive-green, and ivory flowers. *E. pauciflora* (z8–11) itself, the snow gum or cabbage gum, is almost as frost-tolerant as the alpine snow gum and has even bolder, green juvenile foliage. The bark is patched with white and gray, the flowers are white.

The small-leaved gum, *E. parvifolia* (z8–11), is another cold-tolerant eucalypt, with small leaves, feathery-fine when in the juvenile state, and gray or brown bark. Unlike most species, it will even grow in chalk soils. It forms a medium-sized tree with white flowers. *E. nicholii* (z9–11), Nichol's willow-leaf peppermint or narrow-leaved black peppermint, is an exceptionally graceful and pretty, fast-growing small tree, the crown spreading with age. The pendulous branchlets are set with thread-fine, hanging, blue-green to purplish leaves smelling of peppermint when crushed. The white flowers are insignificant.

E. urnigera (z9–11), the urn gum, gets its name from the urn-shaped seed capsules that follow the cream flowers. The adult foliage is polished green, the bark patched with many colors. A fast-growing, medium-sized tree, it is reasonably frost-tolerant. *E. viminalis* (z8–11), the manna gum, grows upright, with long pendulous branches eventually spreading to form a dome-shaped crown. The dense, pendulous leaves are light gray-green and rather soft-textured. The gray bark sheds constantly to reveal the shiny white underbark. The manna gum tolerates arid, poor soil, though it needs winter moisture, and is moderately frost-resistant. The ivory-cream flowers are borne almost continuously.

Eucommia EUCOMMIACEAE

Eucommia ulmoïdes (z5–7), the gutta percha tree, is the only hardy tree known to produce rubber latex. It forms a small- to medium-sized tree with bold, glossy leaves. If a leaf is picked and torn in half, and the two halves gently separated, the latex will harden into almost invisible threads so that the lower half seems to hang unconnected to the upper.

Eumorphia COMPOSITAE

Eumorphia canescens and *E. sericea* (z9–11) are small South African subshrubs with silky-silvery needle leaves and soft pink or white daisies. Soft or half-ripe cuttings root easily.

Euonymus CELASTRACEAE

Euonymus fortunei (z5–9) does well even in very dry areas with some irrigation. It is a very hardy, evergreen climber or trailer; 'Vegetus' is more of a sprawling mound, very free with its orange-seeded fruit in the fall. The larger *E. japonicus* (z7–9) is exceptionally tolerant of extremes of drought, heat and poor soil, and is fairly frost-resistant. It is a bulky evergreen shrub, much used in coastal areas and equally happy in sun or shade. Both these evergreens root well from half-ripe cuttings.

Euphorbia EUPHORBIACEAE

Euphorbia acanthothamnos (z8–10) is a small spurge from rocky places in Greece. In spring it is bright green with foliage, but as the dry season continues, it sheds its leaves to leave only a spiny skeleton. *E. spinosa* (z8–9) is like a slightly larger version of *E. acanthothamnos*. They are entirely different from the familiar shrubby spurges of the Mediterranean region, which form bulky, spreading mounds. *E. characias* (z7–8) has thick stems and narrow, dark blue-green leaves; the subspecies and varieties differ chiefly in their inflorescences. *E. characias* ssp. *characias* has narrowly cylindrical inflorescences composed of green bracts around dark brown glands, while ssp. *wulfenii* has more open spires of brighter, acid-yellow bracts, lacking the dark "eye." Var. *sibthorpii* is very handsome, with airy columns of chartreuse-yellow, and glaucous foliage. In all these, as spring approaches, the stems that will flower bend like shepherds' crooks, turning upright as the flowers open. Cut the flowered stems out at the base as soon as they fade. *E. dendroïdes* (z8–9) is taller and less frost-resistant, a native of dry, rocky cliffs by the Mediterranean. Its stout yellow stems, set on the upper half with narrow blue-gray leaves, bear lime-yellow flowers.

The most colorful spurges are only for virtually frost-free climates. *E. fulgens* (z10–11), the scarlet plume, is a small Mexican shrub with narrow, drooping leaves and bright scarlet flowers on arching branches. 'Purple Leaf' has deep plum-purple foliage and orange flowers. *E. pulcherrima* (z9–11), the poinsettia, Christmas star, painted leaf or Mexican flame leaf, is a winter-flowering shrub of medium size, with lobed leaves and insignificant flowers set off by showy vermilion bracts. There are also cream- and pink-bracted forms.

Euryops COMPOSITAE

This genus of shrubby South African daisies with bright yellow flower heads is easily propagated from half-ripe cuttings, so that more tender species can be used even in cool climates, overwintered as young plants under cover. *Euryops abrotanifolius* (z9–10) has thready green foliage resembling *Artemisia abrotanum*, while *E. pectinatus* (z8–10) has hairy, finely cut foliage, green in moist soils, attractively gray in hot, dry conditions. *E. chrysanthemoïdes* (z9–10) has dissected green leaves and yellow daisies. Smaller are *E. acraeus* (z8–10), a dwarf shrub with platinum-white needle leaves to set off its bright daisies, and *E. virgineus* (z9–10), a small, spring-flowering shrub with tiny crowded green leaves.

Fallugia ROSACEAE

The apache plume, *Fallugia paradoxa* (z4–8), is an all-year shrub with snowy white, rose-like flowers in spring, neat foliage, and pink feathery plumes of seed clusters that endure until the following spring. Set it with shrubby potentillas, caraganas, the antelope bitterbrush (*Purshia*), hippo-phaë and buffaloberry (*Shepherdia argentea*) for a trouble-free planting of shrubs that will stand drought, wind, cold and sun.

× *Fatshedera* ARALIACEAE

× *Fatshedera lizei* (z7–10) is a cross between *Fatsia japonica* and a form of the Irish ivy, *Hedera hibernica*. It forms a loose shrub with large leathery, evergreen leaves. Only in desert conditions does it need moderate to ample irrigation.

Fatsia ARALIACEAE

Fatsia japonica (z7–10), the Formosa rice tree, paper tree or Japanese aralia, is a large, bulky shrub with bold, palmate, glossy green leaves, each "finger" with an undulate margin. The ivory-white, ivy-like heads of flowers appear in the fall. Sometimes grown as a house plant in cold areas, it is quite frost-resistant and creates a lush feel even in dry gardens. However, in desert conditions it does need occasional to ample watering. It is increased by half-ripe to firm cuttings.

Felicia COMPOSITAE

Felicia fruticosa (*Diplopappus fruticosus*, *D. fruticulosus*) (z10) is a small shrub with abundant mauve daisies in late fall and winter. The shrublet *F. filifolia*, known as *Diplopappus filifolius*, is more of a trailer, ideal for draping over walls or banks. Both are easy from soft or half-ripe cuttings.

Ficus MORACEAE

The figs are important trees for climates where frosts are light or unknown. They can be increased by cuttings. A characteristic tree of the Mediterranean regions is the common fig or edible fig, *Ficus carica* (z7–10), which makes large, somewhat shrubby growth, or can be trained to tree form. It is very decorative in leaf. The first crop of figs sets with the emerging leaves to ripen at midsummer; in cold areas the second crop may not ripen before the fall frosts, when the leaves drop. 'Black Mission' ('Mission') is a good choice for low zones and is the best landscape tree; 'Brown Turkey' is more suitable for cooler areas. In desert regions the fig should be given deep, widely spaced irrigation.

Other species with evergreen foliage make handsome trees for frost-free climates. *F. benjamina* (z10–11), the weeping fig, benjamin tree, or weeping Chinese banyan tree, is an evergreen tree of moderate growth, with an open, irregular crown. The wavy-margined, glossy leaves are dark green. Mature plants produce decorative but inedible orange figlets. The weeping fig tolerates both desert heat and low humidity, but is damaged by even light frost. The Indian laurel, *F. microcarpa* (*F. retusa*, *F. nitida*) (z10–11), also called Malay banyan, Chinese banyan, or glossy-leaved fig, is a

Ficus benjamina

good shade tree, forming a dense rounded crown. It is much used in California and Mexico in parks and plazas. These figs are drought-tolerant, but need moderate to ample water in desert regions.

Fraxinus OLEACEAE

Fraxinus uhdei (z8–10), the evergreen ash, shamel ash, or Mexican ash, is a fast-growing upright tree, narrow in outline when young, developing a broad crown with age. The almost evergreen leaves are formed of five to nine long-stalked, long and narrow, toothed leaflets. The petal-less flowers are borne in large panicles. It can be easily raised from seed. 'Majestic Beauty' is more truly evergreen and is a fast shade-maker with larger leaves than the type, needing occasional deep irrigation in summer in desert regions. The velvet ash, *F. velutina* (*F. toumeyi*) (z9–10), grows very rapidly to medium size, with an open irregular crown. The leaflets are velvet-textured and turn yellow in fall. 'Modesto' makes a more symmetrical tree, while 'Rio Grande,' the fantex ash, has large, darker green leaves resistant to sunburn and is a very vigorous, drought-tolerant tree. Once established it needs only occasional deep irrigation in desert areas.

Fremontodendron STERCULIACEAE

Both the fremontodendrons form large, evergreen shrubs with wide-spreading branches. The green, fig-shaped leaves are backed with a felting of rusty hairs which also coat the stems; these hairs can be a severe irritant to the eyes and nose. The flowers are satin-textured cups of rich yellow with waxy hearts. In the wild fremontodendrons grow on hot, gravelly slopes and are summer-dormant; in gardens they must have similar conditions, as in moist soils they grow fast, but die soon. *Fremontodendron californicum* (z9–10) has pure yellow flowers, while *F. mexicanum* (z10–11) has larger, flatter, deeper yellow flowers marked with red-gold on the exterior. The hybrid between the two species, 'California Glory' (z9–10), has the broad petals of the Californian parent, but inherits the wider saucer shape of the Mexican; it is the most frost-resistant.

Gardenia (RUBIACEAE)

Gardenia augusta (*G. jasminoïdes*) (z8–10), the Cape jasmine, is reasonably drought-tolerant and can even be grown in desert gardens, but needs ample water and increased humidity to do well there. Some of the South African species, such as the white, very fragrant *G. thunbergia* (z9–10), are less dependent on soil or atmospheric humidity and are a better choice for very dry climates.

Geijera RUTACEAE

Geijera parviflora (z9–11), the wilga or Australian willow, is a graceful small weeping tree, resembling a eucalyptus in slender green leaf, though it is neither a willow nor a eucalypt. The creamy flowers are insignificant. The wood is hard and fragrant.

Genista LEGUMINOSAE

This genus of brooms is well suited to dry gardens (although they are not recommended for rural areas in Australia, where they become weeds). Many are almost leafless, but their green stems give them an evergreen appearance. They vary from prostrate or small shrubs to open airy trees. Seed or half-ripe cuttings offer means of increase. The most tree-like is *Genista aetnensis* (z8–10), the Mount Etna broom, an open-canopied tree

Fremontodendron 'California Glory'

that casts the lightest of shade, for the branches are almost leafless. In early summer the abundant, bright yellow pea flowers open. Similar, but rather more shrubby, are *G. cinerea* (z8–9), a tall shrub with almost leafless branches wreathed in fragrant yellow pea flowers in summer; and *G. tenera* (*G. virgata*) (z8–9) with yellow fragrant flowers in summer.

The dyer's greenweed, *G. tinctoria* (z5–7), is a small shrub which bears long, slender spires of yellow flowers over a long summer season. 'Royal Gold' is free-flowering, and semi-prostrate 'Flore Pleno' is bright with double flowers. Ideal for a low barrier, *G. hispanica* (z8–9), the Spanish gorse, is a low, wide-spreading, prickly green mound bearing cheery yellow flowers in early summer. *G. lydia* (z8–9), a Syrian species, also forms mounds, but of a different character, its outline built up from interlacing, arching green stems. The yellow flowers open in early summer. Smaller still is *G. sagittalis* (z7–9), a dwarf shrub with broadly winged, procumbent branches, and yellow flowers at midsummer. *G. sericea* (z8–9) is a small shrub with yellow flowers in early summer. The smallest is *G. pilosa* (z6–8), ideal for covering dry banks, for it spreads to form a dense prostrate mat of stems set with tiny green leaves and sprinkled generously with yellow flowers in summer. Quite unlike the other species is *G. monosperma* (*Retama monosperma*) (z9–10), a fragile shrub with rush-like stems and silvery young growths, bearing fragrant white flowers in early spring.

Gleditsia LEGUMINOSAE

Gleditsia triacanthos (z4–9), the honey locust, sweet locust, or honey shuck, is a large, fiercely thorny tree, extremely elegant in leaf, with its many small, bright green leaflets. The thornless form, *G. t. f. inermis*, is a good choice for gardens. The honey locust comes into leaf late, so is well suited to areas where late spring frosts are common. 'Sunburst' has golden green foliage, brightest as the new leaves unfurl, while 'Rubylace' has red-purple young growths. 'Moraine' is a fast-growing, spreading selection, though outstripped by 'Shademaster,' which will make a fair-sized tree in as little as six years. The more compact 'Imperial' has a symmetrical outline and is clad in dense foliage. All color in the fall and bear striking long, glossy, dark brown seed pods. They are tolerant of air pollution, heat, and wind, and resist drought once established, but give young plants plenty of water.

Grevillea PROTEACEAE

This large Australian genus contains some very appealing shrubs suited to dry climates; a few are reasonably frost-resistant, and many more need frost-free conditions. All are evergreen. They can be grown from half-ripe cuttings; the silk oak, *Grevillea robusta* (z9–11) is easy from seed and often seeds itself in gardens. It is a tree of erect, columnar or pyramidal habit, fast-growing when grown in deep soil, and capable of growing to 45m/150ft, though in desert conditions it does not attain this size. It has handsome silky, ferny foliage and bears buff-orange flowers in dense clusters in spring on short, leafless branches of the old wood; these are attractive to birds and bees. Though evergreen, it may shed its leaves in cold weather. Sadly, it is very susceptible to Texas root rot. In youth it needs irrigation and is very sensitive to frost, but when established it tolerates drought and some frost.

Other grevilleas likely to be encountered in cultivation are of much more modest size, varying from small- to medium-sized shrubs. *G. alpina* (z9–11) is a small shrub with close-set, dark green, broadly needle-shaped leaves and flowers usually red, but occasionally yellow or pink. One of the more frost-hardy species is *G. juniperina* f. *sulfurea* (z9–11), which has fresh green needle leaves and spidery, pale yellow flowers. In growth it varies from a sprawling mound to an upright shrub. The rosemary-leaved grevillea, *G. rosmarinifolia* (z9–11), is a medium-sized shrub with dark green needle leaves and crimson claw flowers. 'Jenkinsii' with rose-red flowers, is a more compact selection. *G. lanigera* (z9–11) is similar to the rosemary-leaved grevillea, with pink and cream or green and cream flowers; cultivars such as the more compact 'Canberra Gem,' with waxy crimson-pink flowers, may be hybrids between the two.

G. aspleniifolia (z9–11) has fern-like foliage, and bold spikes of crimson and green flowers in one-sided racemes on tall, bushy growth; 'Robin Hood' is a fine selection. *G. thyrsoïdes* (z9–11) is a small shrub with red flowers in dense, one-sided clusters, and fern-like foliage. The leaves of *G. thelemanniana* (z9–11), a parent of *G.* × *semperflorens*, are soft and thread-fine, and the thin-clawed flowers are pink and yellow-green. *G.* × *semperflorens* (z9–11) is a charming medium-sized shrub with the same fine, silky foliage, and spidery flowers of warm buff-yellow tipped with pink and chartreuse.

Griselinia CORNACEAE

Griselinia littoralis (z8–10) is a handsome large, bulky evergreen shrub, which may even grow to a medium-sized tree if suited. Its fairly large, apple-green leaves are smooth and soapy in texture. Very tolerant of coastal wind, it makes a good wind shelter or can be clipped as a hedge. It moves well even when quite large. Firm or half-ripe cuttings root slowly. *G. lucida* (z8–10) has larger leaves of the same fresh spring-green coloring and thick, smooth texture, but does not grow as large.

Hakea PROTEACEAE

Hakea laurina (z9–10), the pincushion or sea urchin tree, is often cultivated on the French and Italian rivieras. It is a handsome tree with eucalypt-like leaves, and crimson pincushion heads studded with creamy styles. It is easy to grow from seed and tolerant of drought, poor soil and salt winds.

× *Halimiocistus* CISTACEAE

Bigeneric hybrids between *Halimium* and *Cistus*, these are small evergreen shrubs for dry, sunny places. Like their parents, they bear flowers that shatter the day they open, with a succession of buds opening day after day. They are increased by half-ripe cuttings. × *Halimiocistus* 'Ingwersenii' (z8–9) is a gray, hairy shrub with white flowers, and × *H. revolii* (z8–9) has grayish leaves and white or creamy yellow, yellow-eyed flowers of silken texture. The low, wide-spreading × *H. sahucii* (z8–9) is remarkably frost-tolerant, and very appealing with its narrow, dark green leaves and squarish, pure white flowers. The beauty of the group is × *H. wintonensis* (z7–9), a fickle thing, taller than the others, with larger gray-wooly leaves and large white flowers zoned at the center with crimson-maroon and yellow. 'Merrist Wood Cream' is even lovelier, with the same contrasting bands on petals the color of thick fresh cream.

Halimium CISTACEAE

Whereas *Cistus*, and the bigeneric × *Halimiocistus*, are chiefly pink- or white-flowered, *Halimium* offers several charming yellow-flowered sun roses for dry, bright places. *Halimium atriplicifolium* (z9–10) is a small evergreen shrub with silvery felted, rhomboidal leaves and large, bright yellow silken flowers on hairy stems. It has a more spreading habit than *H. halimiifolium* (z8–10), which has narrow, gray leaves and yellow flowers, the petals marked with a small black spot at the base. *H. commutatum* (*H. libanotis*) (z8–10) is a small, slender, needle-leaved shrub with clusters of yellow flowers. *H. umbellatum* (z8–10) is similar to *H. libanotis*, but has white flowers. Prettier than these is *H. ocymoïdes* (z8–10), silver-gray in leaf, with clusters of coppery red buds opening to bright yellow flowers, each petal marked with a black basal blotch. 'Susan' is a named selection. *H.*

Halimium atriplicifolium

lasianthum (z8–10) is a fairly frost-hardy, wide-spreading shrub with gray-felted leaves and wide clear yellow flowers, marked with chocolate basal blotches in *H. l.* ssp. *lasianthum*, unstained in *H. l.* f. *concolor*.

Halimodendron LEGUMINOSAE

The salt tree, *Halimodendron halodendron* (z3–8), is a native of dry salt lands in Siberia, but happy in any dry soil in the garden. Except in flower it looks rather like the sea buckthorn, *Hippophaë rhamnoïdes*, being a tall shrub of silver-gray cast, with spiky branches. In spring the lavender pea flowers open. It is difficult both to propagate (try seed) and to transplant, but otherwise has few fads.

Haplopappus COMPOSITAE

Haplopappus coronopifolius (*H. glutinosus*) (z9–10) is a dwarf evergreen subshrub with narrow, dark green leaves and yellow daisy flowers in summer, ideal for growing on a bank, among rocks, or in a dry wall.

Helianthemum CISTACEAE

The rock roses (z6), a tribe of dwarf evergreen shrublets, are well suited to dry soils in sunny places. They come in a range of flower and leaf colors and in sizes varying from those that are small enough for modest rock gardens to wide-ranging kinds able to cover a square yard or more of soil. Half-ripe cuttings are quick and easy.

Helichrysum COMPOSITAE

The helichrysums are a very varied group, even without the shrubby, often heath-like antipodeans which have been returned to the genus *Ozothamnus*. They range from tiny alpine plants to sizeable shrubs. The usual method of increase is cuttings.

Some of the most familiar are the so-called curry plants, their name deriving from the aroma of the silvery foliage. *Helichrysum fontanesii* (z8–9) is a low, silver-needled shrub, *H. italicum* (z8–9) another, with very silvery needle leaves and clusters of yellow button flowers in summer. *H. i.* ssp. *serotinum* is similar, with a very strong, persistent aroma of cheap curry powder. *H. plicatum* (z8–9) is also of the curry plant type, with very long, silver needle leaves. They are valued for their comparative frost-hardiness, but if you cannot do with the curry smell, choose *H. splendidum* (z8–9), a low mound of a shrub with broad, three-veined silver-gray leaves and yellow flower heads in winter.

H. petiolare (z9–10) is decidedly frost-tender, but much used as summer bedding, for it grows rapidly and has a characteristic spraying outline, or can be trained into a miniature "tree" by staking a leader to a cane. It is a soft-wooded shrub with heart-shaped, gray-felted leaves and cream flower heads. The yellow-leaved 'Limelight' is susceptible to scorching if too dry or sun-baked; 'Variegatum' has gray and cream leaves. They are at their best in deep but very well-drained soil; in shallow soils they suffer during very hot spells, but during winter they are easily damaged by frost unless growing in dry soil. *H. populifolium* (z9–10) is as white-felted as *H. petiolare*, but has larger, more pointed leaves shaped like an aspen's.

Some of the smaller helichrysums are good rock garden plants. *H. bellidioïdes* (z8–9) is a dwarf subshrub with slender, prostrate, rooting stems, tiny gray leaves, white-wooly on the reverse, and white everlasting daisies. *H. orientale* (z8–9) is a dwarf, soft-wooded shrub with very wooly, gray-white leaves and ivory-cream flowers on white-felted stems.

Hibiscus MALVACEAE

Hibiscus rosa-sinensis (z9–10) does very well in moderately hot, dry climates, but survives desert heat only with assistance from deep irrigation. It flowers only when the atmospheric humidity is high enough, so that in the hottest areas of the Mediterranean, it blooms in spring and fall, not during summer. It is not suitable for frosty climates. The large flowers come in a range of colors from white and pink to crimson, yellow or soft orange. *H. sinosyriacus* (z8–10) is more frost-resistant, though even it needs a warmer and more sheltered place than *H. syriacus*. Its large flowers are very beautiful, often marked with crimson feathering at the center. *H. syriacus* (z6–9) has smaller flowers, ranging from white to blue or crimson. It comes into leaf very late, and in areas where the summers are short it may not manage to open its flowers before the fall frosts.

Hibiscus rosa-sinensis

Hippocrepis LEGUMINOSAE

Hippocrepis emerus (*Coronilla emerus*) (z7–9), the scorpion senna, is a graceful shrub with compound leaves and bright yellow pea flowers over a long summer season. The seed pods that follow resemble a scorpion's tail.

Hippophaë ELAEAGNACEAE

Hippophaë rhamnoïdes (z4–7) is an almost indestructibly hardy tall shrub with narrow, silver-gray leaves. If male and female plants are grown together, the females bear showy, bright orange berries which remain long on the branches, as they are unappetizing to birds. Sow the seeds to make more plants, which are easy to sex even at the seedling stage, for the axillary buds of male plants are very prominent, especially in spring, whereas the shoots of female plants are quite smooth.

Hymenosporum PITTOSPORACEAE

Hymenosporum flavum (z9–11) is an evergreen tree forming a narrow crown, with dark leaves, and very fragrant jasmine-like flowers opening ivory-white and maturing to warm yellow.

Hypericum GUTTIFERAE

Hypericum 'Hidcote' (z6–9) is an immensely popular flowering shrub, with aromatic leaves and large yellow flowers over a long summer to fall season. It can be allowed to grow unchecked to head height or more, or cut almost to the ground each spring to keep it neat. It is sometimes classed as *H. patulum* (z7–8). Closely related is *H. beanii* (z7–8), a small shrub with arching branches and cupped yellow flowers.

    H. frondosum 'Sunburst' (z6–8) is a fine selection of a North American native, a small shrub with sea-green leaves and bright yellow summer flowers with showy stamens. The broombrush, *H. prolificum* (z4–8), is a small, slow-growing shrub with peeling bark, narrow leaves and clusters of yellow flowers. *H.* × *moserianum* (z7–9) is a dwarf shrub with arching red stems and large yellow flowers with red anthers. *H. olympicum* f. *minus* (z6–8) is even smaller, a delightful miniature with glaucous foliage and yellow flowers. 'Sulphureum' is enchanting with its pale lemon blooms.

    The St. John's worts can be raised from seed or cuttings.

Hyssopus LABIATAE

Hyssopus officinalis (z6–9) is a small aromatic subshrub with narrow green leaves and blue-purple flowers. White or pink-flowered forms are also known. Cuttings root easily.

Iberis CRUCIFERAE

Iberis sempervirens (z5–9) is a dwarf, spreading shrublet with very dark green foliage as a foil for stark white candytuft flowers in spring. It can be seed-raised, but named cultivars must be grown from cuttings.

Ilex AQUIFOLIACEAE

Ilex aquifolium (z7–9), the common holly, is a handsome evergreen shrub or small tree, tolerant of a wide range of climatic and atmospheric conditions including air pollution. If plants of both sexes are growing together, females bear showy red berries in winter. There are a great many cultivars with differing leaf forms or variegations. One of the few hollies tolerating desert heat is *I. cornuta* 'Burfordii' (z7–9), though it appreciates shade during the afternoon. It will survive with moderate to little irrigation once established. The type, by contrast, will survive only in high zones of desert. *I. vomitoria* (z7–10), the yaupon or cassina, a native of the southern United States, does well in desert areas, providing it receives moderate irrigation. 'Pride of Houston' is a selection of medium size and erect, loose-branching habit. Two dwarf cultivars that are drought-tolerant once established, and make good low hedges, are the very compact 'Stoke's Dwarf,' and the similar but slightly taller 'Nana.'

Indigofera LEGUMINOSAE

The indigos are dainty shrubs with attractive pinnate foliage and racemes of pea flowers in shades of pink or rose-purple, borne over a long season. Most can be cut back hard in spring to flower from midsummer. They are

Jacaranda mimosifolia

increased by cuttings. *Indigofera amblyantha* (z7–9) is a medium-sized shrub with clear pink flowers throughout the summer; *I. potaninii* (z7–9) is very similar, with shrimp-pink flowers over a long season, and *I. pseudotinctoria* (z7–9) is similar again, with racemes of clear pink flowers. The spreading *I. hebepetala* (z8–9) has bicolored flowers, rose-pink with a rich crimson standard (the large, uppermost petal). *I. decora* (*I. incarnata*) (z7–9) is a small shrub with long spires of rosy pink flowers with pale standards. The bright pink flowers of *I. kirilowii* (z5–8) are rather hidden in long, leafy sprays. *I. dielsiana* (z6–9) is a small, open-growing shrub with slender upright spikes of pale pink flowers. The foliage of *I. heterantha* (*I. gerardiana*) (z7–9) is especially dainty; the flowers are bright rose-purple. *I. cylindrica* (z9–10) is a slender, half-woody shrub, with dense, many-flowered racemes. The similar *I. frutescens* (z9–10) is more muscular, and the flower spikes are looser.

Jacaranda BIGNONIACEAE
Jacaranda mimosifolia (*J. ovalifolia*) (z9–11) grows rapidly to form a medium-sized tree in virtually frost-free climates. The elegant foliage drops in late winter, new leaves emerging at or just before flowering time. The flowers are typical bignonia trumpets in large sprays, normally lavender-blue, sometimes white or orchid pink, borne freely only in hot climates. An open, sandy soil is most suitable; occasional deep irrigation during summer is helpful in desert areas. *J. acutifolia* (z9–11) is a small tree with compound, ferny foliage and blue-mauve trumpet flowers. The true species is rare in cultivation; plants so labeled are usually *J. mimosifolia*.

Jasminum OLEACEAE
Many jasmines are climbers, and even the winter jasmine, *Jasminum nudiflorum* (z6–10), could be so classed, for it is a scrambling shrub with trifoliate leaves, bearing scentless, bright yellow flowers on the bare green stems in winter. It is very hardy and flowers well even in shady places. Cuttings root easily.

Justicia ACANTHACEAE
Justicia brandegeeana (*Beloperone guttata*) (z9–10), the shrimp plant, rattle-snake plant, or false hop, is a small evergreen shrub that is almost continuously in flower during the warm season. The showy part of the flower consists of the overlapping bracts forming long spikes; the small true flowers are white. Typically, the bracts are copper-colored; in 'Yellow Queen' they are chartreuse. *J. spicigera* (z9–10), the Mexican honeysuckle, desert honeysuckle, or firecracker plant, is a dependable soft-wooded shrub for desert climates, with softly furry leaves on erect stems. Clusters of orange-red tubular flowers, popular with birds, are borne most freely in spring. *J. californica* (z10–11), the chuparosa, is similar but sparser in growth, with bright red tubular flowers. It is very frost-tender.

Koelreuteria SAPINDACEAE
Koelreuteria bipinnata (z7–10) is an elegant small tree with large pinnate leaves and yellow flowers, followed by red, lantern-like seed pods, more showy than the brown pods of *K. paniculata* (z5–9), the golden rain tree, which has pinnate leaves and yellow flowers freely borne only in hot climates. Bladder-like fruits follow, and the leaves turn to yellow in the fall. The seeds of both species germinate readily to make new plants that grow fast and soon reach flowering maturity.

Justicia brandegeeana

Justicia spicigera

Lantana camara

Kolkwitzia CAPRIFOLIACEAE

The beauty bush, *Kolkwitzia amabilis* (z5–8) is a fine large shrub with pinkish-tan young growths soon smothered beneath countless small foxglove-like flowers of clear pink with a creamy yellow throat. The leaves may turn yellow or red to purple in the fall. If the shrub is pruned into a multistemmed small tree, it reveals its peeling, brown bark. It is very easy to propagate from cuttings and tolerant of drought. Some forms are shy-flowering; to be sure of abundant bloom, choose the cultivar 'Pink Cloud.'

Lagerstroemia LYTHRACEAE

Lagerstroemia indica (z7–9), the crape myrtle, is a slow-growing, small deciduous tree, often multistemmed, which can be trained to a single trunk. The smooth gray bark flakes to reveal the pinkish inner layers. The glossy foliage is bright green, bronzed when young, and colors brightly in the fall. The ample clusters of crimson, white, purple or pink, crepe-textured flowers appear with the hot season and are followed by rounded seed capsules which remain at the branch tips during winter; new plants can easily be raised from seed. The crape myrtle thrives in heat, but needs shelter from wind. It does best in a deep soil, though it is remarkably drought-tolerant, needing occasional deep irrigation in saline or alkaline soils. There are many named cultivars, vegetatively propagated, from which individual colors can be chosen.

Lantana VERBENACEAE

Lantana camara (z9–10), the bush lantana, shrub verbena, or yellow sage, provides intermittent color all year on a medium-sized shrub, sometimes rather prickly. The many-colored flowers are orange to yellow or orange changing to red, pink or white. There are several named cultivars selected for color, but they are generally less tolerant of severe drought. The bush lantana is barely frost-tolerant, but easily replaced as cuttings root so quickly (and hence has become a noxious weed in Australia and some other warm areas). *L. montevidensis* (*L. sellowiana*) (z9–10) is a little more frost-tolerant. Known as the trailing lantana, weeping lantana, or lavender lantana, it is a South American native, naturalized in warmer areas of the United States and Australia. It is constantly in flower during hot weather, its verbena-like, lavender flower clusters borne among small, prickly, gray-green leaves. The slender stems root as they go, to give the shrub an almost indefinite spread, or they may climb through neighboring branches. The trailing lantana tolerates heat and periods of neglect, becoming dormant during severe drought, but recovering as soon as it is watered.

Larrea ZYGOPHYLLACEAE

Larrea tridentata (z8–10), the creosote bush, greasewood, or guamis, survives where the annual rainfall is as little as 3in/75mm. It appears to have developed two survival mechanisms: shedding its foliage as water becomes scarce, and deterring other plants from growing too close and so competing for scarce moisture. In spring or during the wet season, the foliage is bright green, becoming yellow-green or dark olive-green in the dry season. A shrub of medium height, the creosote bush grows rapidly when water is available and slowly in drought conditions; it is resistant to great heat and some cold, but is soon killed by excess moisture. The yellow flowers appear mainly in spring, with a scattering at other seasons; small white, fuzzy seedheads follow. Resin forms in tiny droplets on the branches, and the foliage has a pungent fragrance most pronounced in wet weather.

Laurus LAURACEAE

Laurus nobilis (z8–10), the sweet bay or Grecian laurel, is a typical aromatic, large evergreen shrub of the Mediterranean, tolerant of drought, but apt to scorch in very hot, exposed desert sites. Increase by ripe cuttings.

Lavandula LABIATAE

Lavandula angustifolia (*L. spica*, *L. officinalis*) (z6–9), lavender, is a small aromatic Mediterranean shrub with more or less gray leaves and narrow spikes of fragrant flowers. Several selections have been named, including white- and pink-flowered variants: 'Munstead' with narrow leaves, greener than most, and flowers nearer to blue, and 'Hidcote,' with thin gray-green leaves and deep violet-purple flowers. Half-ripe cuttings root quickly and easily. *L. latifolia* (z8–9) is similar to *L. angustifolia*, with very gray leaves. Forms of lavandin, *L. × intermedia* (z6–9) include the Dutch lavender (also known as *L. spica* 'Vera'), a strong-growing shrublet with rather broad, very gray leaves, and very fragrant, rather pale flowers in long spikes. The old English lavender also belongs here, together with cultivars such as the stout 'Grappenhall.'

L. *stoechas* (z8–9) has narrow, powerfully aromatic leaves and cockaded dark purple flower heads. The soft-wooded *L. lanata* (z7–9) has strongly aromatic, white-wooly leaves and pale violet flowers. Unusually, *L. viridis* (z8–9) has green needle leaves, and four-sided, tapering heads of small flowers in green bracts, topped by a pale jade cockade. Finely cut silvery foliage belongs to *L. pinnata* (z8–9) and to *L. dentata* (z8–9), from the Iberian peninsula, which has spikes of lavender-blue flowers topped by a

Lavandula dentata

small terminal bract, and gray, toothed leaves. It is a fairly substantial plant ideal for hedges, with a long flowering season, and one of the most drought-resistant. *L. stoechas* and *L. pinnata* are weeds in Australia.

Lavatera MALVACEAE

Lavatera arborea (z8–10), the tree mallow, is a coarse-leaved shrub with purple-red flowers, well-suited to dry, coastal gardens. It is easily raised from seed. Far superior as a garden plant is *L. maritima* (*L. bicolor*) (z8–10), a soft-wooded shrub with vine-shaped, gray-velvet leaves, and wide mallow flowers of palest glacier mauve brought to life by a crimson-madder central blotch and veinings; the green calyx peeps between the bases of the petals to add the final piquant touch to a beautiful plant with its own self-contained color scheme. Propagate from half-ripe cuttings.

Leptospermum MYRTACEAE

An Australasian and Indonesian genus of heath-like shrubs, all well suited to dry, drained soils, but not tolerant of chalk. Propagation is by cuttings; *Leptospermum scoparium* (z9–10) self-sows where suited. This, the manuka or tea-tree of New Zealand and eastern Australia, is a variable species ranging from dwarf mounded shrublets to large shrubs or even small trees. The tiny needle leaves may be green, bronzed, coppery purple, or grayish; the hawthorn-like flowers are typically white, but vary to pink and crimson, with double-flowered cultivars available in all colors. One of the most famous is 'Nichollsii,' which has dark bronze-purple foliage and carmine flowers. Many other leptospermums would be worth trying in dry gardens; one of the most distinct, and known to be drought-tolerant, is *L. rotundifolium* (z9–10), a medium-sized evergreen shrub of weeping habit, with rounded leaves, and pale pink-mauve, hawthorn-like flowers.

Lespedeza LEGUMINOSAE

The bush clovers are handsome, late-summer flowering shrubs of medium size, with trifoliolate leaves and long sprays of small pea flowers weighing the branches into graceful arches. *Lespedeza bicolor* (z5–8) has bright magenta-purple flowers, and *L. thunbergii* (z6–8) has massive panicles of rose-purple flowers, spectacular cascading down over silvery foliage. *L. t.* 'Gibraltar' is a new U.S. selection with rose-purple flowers and a pleasing fountain-like growth habit. Half-ripe cuttings root easily.

Leucadendron PROTEACEAE

Leucadendron argenteum (z10–11), the silver tree, is a dense-crowned, intensely silver-leaved tree from South Africa, which revels in dry, sunny places. It can be grown from seed, but take great care to prevent the seedlings from damping off.

Leucophyllum SCROPHULARIACEAE

Leucophyllum frutescens (*L. texanum*) (z9–10), the Texas ranger, ceniza, or barometer bush, grows slowly above head height in mild climates, but only half that in desert areas. The rounded, gray-felted foliage on silvery purple branches becomes green and almost succulent in wet weather, and except at the branch tips is shed during severe drought. The Texas ranger is tolerant of quite hard frost, but needs heat to produce its rosy lavender, bell-shaped flowers, which usually open after the summer rains in very dry climates. It will stand extreme heat, but cannot tolerate heavy or damp soils, which makes it unsuitable for regions with cool, wet winters.

Ligustrum OLEACEAE

Privets, often associated with messy, root-greedy hedges or unpleasant-smelling flowers, are not all of this stamp. Some, such as *Ligustrum amurense* (z3–8), the Amur privet, are exceptionally tolerant of difficult conditions. This is a large shrub similar to *L. ovalifolium*, the common hedging privet. Others are garden-worthy by any criteria. *L. japonicum* (z7–10), the waxleaf privet or Japanese privet, is an evergreen shrub of dense, compact habit, which grows to medium size if unclipped, or can be clipped back. The leathery, polished, dark green foliage is rather like that of a camellia. Large sprays of slightly fragrant white flowers open in summer. 'Silver Star' is a slower-growing cultivar with cream marginal variegation. 'Texanum' is a fine form of *L. japonicum*, with larger leaves, pale when young and maturing to very dark green, and fragrant white flowers. Even more beautiful is *L. lucidum* (z8–10), the Chinese privet, an indispensable tree or large shrub for dry or desert gardens wherever the winters are mild enough for it to thrive. Left to grow unclipped, it forms a small- to medium-sized round-headed evergreen tree, with dark, glossy green, pointed oval leaves. The large sprays of white flowers open in late spring in hot desert areas, but not until late summer or fall in cooler climates. Once established, the Chinese privet will tolerate periods of drought.

Lonicera CAPRIFOLIACEAE

The shrubby honeysuckles include two "workhorse" species in *Lonicera nitida* (z7–9), a small-leaved evergreen small shrub of dense habit, often used for hedging because of its willingness to grow even from slips stuck in the ground where the hedge is to be, but needing frequent clipping; and *L. pileata* (z6–8), another evergreen standby, with spreading branches, small bright green leaves, and translucent violet berries. It tolerates quite dense shade and makes useful cover for difficult places. The winter-flowering *L. fragrantissima* (z5–9), a medium-sized, semi-evergreen shrub of rather untidy habit, is valued for its small but deliciously fragrant, cream flowers opening during late winter and spring. Red berries follow in late spring. *L × purpusii* (z5–9) is a hybrid of *L. fragrantissima*, with larger cream flowers.

Lotus LEGUMINOSAE

Lotus berthelotii (z10–11) forms a cascade of trailing stems set with soft, silver needle leaves; large, claw-like flowers of coppery crimson form a startling contrast. *L. maculatus* is similar, but with tawny yellow flowers. *L. sessilifolius* (*L. mascaensis* of gardens) (z10–11) is another trailing, soft-wooded shrublet, its white stems set with platinum-bright needle leaves; the small, vivid lemon pea flowers, which may be tipped with tawny red like those of the "egg and bacon plant," are held in little clusters. The small, upright *Lotus hirsutus* (z8–11), which used to be known as *Dorycnium hirsutum*, is a small, soft-wooded shrub with silky silvery, trifoliolate leaves, and clusters of pink-white pea flowers followed by polished, oblong, bronze seedheads. It can be increased from seed or cuttings.

Lupinus LEGUMINOSAE

The tree lupine, *Lupinus arboreus* (z8–10), from California, is an ideal "filler" for new gardens, a fast-growing, loose-habited shrub with green, fingered leaves, and spikes of sweetly scented flowers, usually in some shade of yellow from primrose to lemon, occasionally white or soft violet. It is easy from seed and not too tricky from cuttings. Appealing though it is, it is outclassed by the silvery-leaved shrubby or subshrubby California lupines.

Lotus berthelotii

Lupinus arboreus

L. albifrons (z8–10) is a medium-sized shrub with short spikes of creamy or lavender flowers maturing to violet-blue. *L. chamissonis* (z8–10) is a small, branching shrub with small, silky-silvery, palmate leaves, and short airy spikes of hazy, lilac-blue and ice-white flowers, and *L. ornatus* (z8–10) also has silken, silvered leaves beneath spires of blue and white flowers.

Lycianthes SOLANACEAE
Lycianthes rantonnetii (*Solanum rantonnetii*) (z10–11) is a small, soft-wooded shrub with long-pointed, wavy-edged leaves, violet potato flowers with a yellow central pointel appearing over a long season, and scarlet fruits.

Lysiloma LEGUMINOSAE
Lysiloma thornberi (*L. microphylla* var. *thornberi*) (z8–11), the feather bush of southern Arizona and northern Mexico, is a fast-growing shrub or small tree with finely dissected green foliage. The abundant puffball clusters of creamy white flowers appear in spring with the new leaves. The feather

bush is tolerant of drought and great heat, but barely frost-resistant. It needs no irrigation if the rainfall exceeds 10in/250mm annually.

Maclura MORACEAE

Maclura pomifera (z5–9), the Osage orange, is a small- to medium-sized tree with thorny branches and large yellow fruits on mature female trees. The leaves turn yellow in the fall. It can be used as a hedge and is increased from seed.

Magnolia MAGNOLIACEAE

Magnolia grandiflora

Magnolia grandiflora (z7–9), the southern magnolia or bull bay, is surprisingly drought-tolerant even in desert conditions, though here it will need occasional deep irrigation to leach out soil salts. It makes a small tree in the desert, but can become very bulky in more favorable climates. 'Exmouth,' a popular cultivar with leaves russet-felted beneath, flowers at an early age. 'Majestic Beauty' is a very large-growing cultivar, and 'Samuel Sommer' rapidly reaches a large size, while 'Saint Mary' remains compact. 'Edith Bogue' (z6) is probably the hardiest cultivar. In cool climates the wonderfully fragrant flowers, like wide cups of cream suede, begin to open from summer on, while in hotter areas the flowering season starts in spring.

Mahonia BERBERIDACEAE

The mahonias are evergreen shrubs, most with spine-edged leaves and yellow flowers. Some are quite easy from cuttings, but the beautiful California species can be tricky. The Oregon grape, mountain grape, or holly mahonia, *Mahonia aquifolium* (z5–8), is fairly drought-resistant, but dislikes extreme heat and if grown in desert areas must have shade. The bright yellow flowers are followed by showy blue-black fruits. Another of suckering tendencies is *M. repens* (z6–8), a small shrub forming a low carpet of matte green leaves. 'Rotundifolia' has spine-free sea-green leaves and showy clusters of yellow flowers. Of the small mahonias perhaps the most appealing is *M. nervosa* (z6–8), a slowly suckering shrub forming mats of hard prickly leaves, dark green in summer and flushed with mahogany in cold weather.

The much taller, more bulky *M. japonica* (z7–8) is a handsome large shrub with pinnate leaves, each leaflet rather like, and as spiny as, a holly leaf. The arching sprays of yellow flowers appear in winter and are fragrant of lily-of-the-valley. *M. × media* (z7–9) unites *M. japonica* and the tall, rather frost-tender *M. lomariifolia*. The result is a group of hybrids with the showy yellow candle-clusters of the second parent, but hardier. There are many named cultivars, most of which are barely scented. Of similar character is *M. fortunei* (z8–9), an erect shrub of medium size with very narrow matte green leaves and slim spikes of bright yellow flowers.

The finest of the Californias is *M. fremontii* (z9–10), which grows on hot, desert-facing slopes. It has narrow-leafleted, spine-edged, twisted, intensely blue-glaucous foliage and yellow flowers. *M. trifoliolata* var. *glauca* (z8–9) is a Texas and Mexico species with stiff, spiny, gray-blue leaves composed of three leaflets, and yellow flowers followed by red fruits.

Medicago LEGUMINOSAE

Medicago arborea (z9–10), the moon trefoil, is a tall Mediterranean shrub with clover-like, semi-evergreen leaves, and a long season of yellow pea flowers, followed by curled seed pods like snail shells.

Murraya paniculata

Melia MELIACEAE

Melia azedarach (z8–10), the chinaberry, bead tree, or pride of India, is a deciduous tree which grows rapidly to medium size and can be easily raised from seed. The deep green foliage is doubly pinnate and ruffles elegantly in the breeze; it turns yellow in the fall. The small, fragrant, lavender to purple flowers are borne in loose sprays in spring, followed by the clusters of yellow, bead-like fruits which last all winter. 'Umbraculifera,' the Texas umbrella tree, has an erect trunk and regular radiating branches making a dome-like crown. The bead tree is susceptible to Texas root rot.

Melianthus MELIANTHACEAE

Melianthus major (z9–10) is a magnificent foliage plant with large, pinnate leaves composed of toothed, glaucous-blue leaflets. In cool climates it may behave as an herbaceous plant, losing its top growth but regenerating from below ground each spring; where not cut back by frost, it is evergreen, growing to head-height or more; overwintered stems bear spikes of maroon flowers in spring amid the unfurling jade-green new leaves.

Michelia MAGNOLIACEAE

Michelia doltsopa (z9–10) is a small- to medium-sized evergreen tree, with bold, glaucous-backed leaves and very fragrant white flowers like small magnolias, opening from large buds clad in golden-brown fur. 'Silver Cloud' is a fine selection with larger creamy flowers and brighter golden buds. The banana bush, *M. figo* (z7–9), has smaller, polished, dark green leaves and small flowers, dowdy in their purple-brown coloring, but powerfully fragrant of ripe bananas – or of pears.

Mimulus SCROPHULARIACEAE

The California musks are soft-wooded shrubs of the chaparral, with narrow, resinous green leaves and monkey-faced flowers, easily propagated by half-ripe cuttings. *Mimulus aurantiacus* (z9–10) has apricot-buff flowers; *M. puniceus* (z9–10) is similar, but its flowers are coppery crimson.

Morus MORACEAE

Morus alba (*M. bombycis*) (z5–8), the white mulberry, is the Chinese tree traditionally used to feed silkworms. It is heat-tolerant and does well with little irrigation, even in the desert, so long as the soil is deep. Like other mulberries, it is easily propagated, even quite large hardwood cuttings rooting readily.

Murraya RUTACEAE

Murraya paniculata (*M. exotica*) (z10–11), the orange jasmine, orange jessamine, satinwood, or Chinese box, is a shrub or small tree, with compound glossy leaves and deliciously fragrant white flowers borne in several bursts throughout the year.

Musa MUSACEAE

The bananas are not woody plants, but perennials. However, the leaf sheaths form a trunk-like stem, giving them the appearance of huge-leaved trees. *Musa acuminata* (z9–11) is a Chinese banana with blue-green paddle leaves and flower clusters showy with red, leathery bracts. Many edible bananas are forms of this; 'Dwarf Cavendish' is perhaps the most famous. The plantain, *M. balbisiana* (z10), is one parent of a group of hybrids of which *M. acuminata* is the other; collectively known as *M.* × *paradisiaca* (z9–

11), they include some forms commonly called banana and others called plantain. They form clumps of slender, succulent "trunks" with the leaf stalks rising spiral-fashion from the base. The thin-textured paddle leaves are bright green and may be as much as 24in/60cm wide and 8ft/2.4m long on larger plants. *M. × paradisiaca* will grow rapidly in frost-free climates and needs shelter from wind to protect the great leaf blades from tearing. The flowers are borne from midsummer to the fall. Bananas need ample moisture in desert gardens, but in less severe conditions are drought-tolerant in deep, enriched soil. Even a touch of frost damages the leaves, but mulched roots survive several degrees of frost. I know of a plant of *M. acuminata* that has survived several winters in a Swiss garden.

Myoporum MYOPORACEAE
Myoporum insulare (z9–11), the boobyalla, is a tall shrub or small tree with thick-textured, gland-speckled, lance leaves, and white, purple-spotted flowers followed by blue-purple fruits. The ngaio, *M. laetum* (z9–11). quickly forms a round-headed tree with bright green, semi-succulent, pointed evergreen leaves, freckled all over with minute translucent oil glands. The flowers are white spotted with purple. Half-ripe cuttings root easily. The much smaller *M. parvifolium* (z9–11) is an evergreen, prostrate shrub with narrow, semi-succulent leaves and clusters of small, fragrant flowers, white or pink freckled with purple, followed by small purple fruits.

Myrica MYRICACEAE
Myrica cerifera (z7–9), the wax myrtle, is an evergreen shrub or small tree equally tolerant of damp and dry soils. The wax covering the fruits is aromatic and has been used to make fragrant candles. The bayberry, *M. pensylvanica* (z3–7), is a hardy shrub with aromatic leaves which fall late to reveal many tiny, ash-white fruits. The seeds of both germinate freely.

Myrtus MYRTACEAE
Myrtus communis (z8–9), the true myrtle or Greek myrtle, is an aromatic Mediterranean evergreen shrub or small tree, very tolerant of neglect and able to withstand drought once established. It is very resistant to Texas root rot. The white flowers with their showy central puff of stamens are fragrant. *M. c.* var. *tarentina* is a more compact, slow-growing variety with tiny leaves, ideal for hedging. 'Variegata' has white-margined leaves, and 'Flore Pleno' has double flowers. It was the tradition, at one time, for brides to carry a sprig of myrtle in their bouquets, rooting it like a conventional cutting so that the living plant symbolized the growing love within the family.

Nandina BERBERIDACEAE
Nandina domestica (z7–9), the heavenly bamboo or sacred bamboo of Japan, is neglect- and drought-proof, and very resistant to soil-borne diseases. It grows slowly to medium size; some forms spread by underground roots. The bold, compound leaves on erect unbranched stems are often bronzed in winter, while the new growths are fresh green. In hot climates sprays of white flowers open in spring, followed by long-lasting red berries. Selections include 'Compacta,' the even smaller 'Pygmaea,' and 'Nana Purpurea' with deep red foliage. 'Firepower' has bright cream, orange and red winter foliage. 'Harbor Dwarf' is very low-growing and spreads by underground runners. Cuttings represent a surer method of increase for all forms of the sacred bamboo.

Myrtus communis

Nerium oleander

Nerium APOCYNACEAE

Nerium oleander (z8–10), the oleander or rosebay, is a first-rate shrub for hot climates, tolerant of heat, drought and a wide variety of soils, and easy to root from cuttings. There are many cultivars, providing a choice of colors and a range of sizes, from compact dwarf shrubs to tall, quick-growing kinds which can be trimmed to reveal gnarled trunks. The most vigorous cultivars can make a head-high hedge in three years. The long, narrow, dark green leaves set off flowers of red, pink, salmon, yellow or white, single or double – the singles displaying the propellor outline characteristic of the family, the doubles less elegant, but often more showy – and sometimes scented. The whole plant is poisonous, and even the smoke from burning twigs is noxious.

Nicotiana SOLANACEAE

Nicotiana glauca (z9–10), the tree tobacco or mustard plant, is a shrubby tobacco of tall, open habit, with large, smooth, brightly glaucous-blue leaves and stems to set off sprays of small, tubular, soft yellow flowers. Propagation may be by seed or cuttings.

Olea OLEACEAE

Olea europaea (z8–10), the olive, probably originated in Asia Minor, but has been grown for thousands of years in the Mediterranean region. A very long-lived tree tolerant of heat, drought and poor soil, it forms in time a gnarled trunk and wide crown. The leathery, narrow, gray-green leaves are silvery white beneath. Clusters of tiny yellowish flowers are followed by the edible fruits which ripen in the fall. The first olives to be seen in the United States were those planted by Franciscans at the San Diego mission in the eighteenth century. There are several cultivars, including those such as 'Fruitless' and 'Swan Hill' which are grown purely for their decorative qualities. 'Cipressino' ('Pyramidalis') is one of the most suitable for cool climates. 'Manzanillo' is both attractive and a good fruiter. 'Mission' is taller and more compact, with smaller fruits, while 'Ascolana' bears large fruit and those of 'Sevillano' are even larger. 'Barouni' is especially heat-tolerant. The best fruits result from hot summers and a slight winter chill of a degree or two of frost for about three months. Named cultivars must be vegetatively propagated from cuttings; if this is not a concern, new plants can be grown from seed. *O. europaea* ssp. *africana* (*O. verrucosa*), the shrubby olive, is a first-rate hedge or screening plant, densely clad to the ground with small, narrow, dark gray-green leaves. It will tolerate drought and neglect as long as the rainfall is over 10in/250mm annually.

Olneya LEGUMINOSAE

Olneya tesota (z8–10), the desert ironwood, palo-de-hierro, or tesota, is a native of deserts in warm winter areas of California, Arizona and northern Mexico. A medium-sized to large shrub, it grows slowly, forming a naturally low-branching outline with a gray trunk and thorny lower branches. The gray-green foliage is finely divided, giving it from a distance the aspect of an olive tree. Orchid-pink pea flowers are borne in clusters in summer. The desert ironwood is very heat- and drought-resistant, preferring a sandy or gravel soil and full to reflected sun.

Osmanthus OLEACEAE

Osmanthus fragrans (z8–10), the sweet olive, fragrant olive, tea olive, or sweet osmanthus, has pervasively fragrant flowers, typically white, but pale orange in *O. f.* f. *aurantiacus*. The flowers are used in China to perfume tea. The evergreen, polished, dark green leaves are handsome all year. The sweet olive grows slowly to medium size and needs protection from the hottest desert sun. It is increased by cuttings or layering.

Othonna COMPOSITAE

Othonna cheirifolia (*Othonnopsis cheirifolia*) (z8–10), a North African sub-shrub, has spoon-shaped, glaucous-blue leaves set in close fans on trailing stems. Short-rayed yellow daisies often appear in winter.

Ozothamnus COMPOSITAE

These heath-like shrubs have been shuffled in and out of the genus *Helichrysum* by taxonomists, and may still be found under that name in nursery catalogs. One of the less heath-like is *Ozothamnus antennaria* (z9–10), a branching, upright shrub with leathery, pale green leaves, and white flowers in summer. *O. coralloïdes* (z8–10) is a dwarf, gnarled shrub with silver-green whipcord branches patterned with the white felty margins of the appressed scale-like leaves. The flower heads are yellow. The whipcord stems of *O. selago* (z9–10), a dwarf, branching shrublet, are set with pointed, scale-like leaves thinly rimmed with the white felting of the reverse. *O. ledifolius* (z9–10) is a hummocky, low, wide-spreading shrub with close-set, narrow green leaves, yellow with sticky resin beneath, and tight clusters of whitish flowers opening from coppery red buds. The whole plant is aromatic, with a fragrance like stewed prunes.

Taller species with needle leaves include *O. diosmifolius* (z9–10), an upright shrub with linear leaves and white flower heads tinged with pink, and two oft-confused species: *O. rosmarinifolius* (z9–10), an upright, heath-like shrub with green needle leaves, and clusters of white flowers opening

Ozothamnus ledifolius

from crimson-red buds; and *O. thyrsoïdeus* (z9–10), which has almost everlasting white flower heads, and dark green needle leaves. 'Silver Jubilee' is a selection of *O. rosmarinifolius* with gray foliage.

Pachysandra BUXACEAE

The Allegheny spurge, *Pachysandra procumbens* (z5–9), is a dwarf, creeping subshrub with broad, toothed leaves, narrowing to a long petiole. The greenish-purple flowers with pale stamens are borne in close-packed spikes in spring. *P. terminalis* (z5–8) is more decidedly evergreen, with diamond-shaped, toothed leaves at the ends of the stems. The greenish-white flowers appear early in spring. Both can be increased by half-ripe cuttings.

Pachystegia COMPOSITAE

Pachystegia insignis (*Olearia insignis*) (z9–10) grows in the wild on hot, sun-baked cliffs in New Zealand. It has thick-textured leaves, green or bronzed on the upper surface and gray- or beige-felted beneath, and large, solitary white daisies on long stems. In habit it varies from a medium-sized spreading shrub to a compact miniature known as var. *minor*. Selected forms can be grown from cuttings.

Parkinsonia LEGUMINOSAE

Parkinsonia aculeata (z9–11), the Mexican palo verde, Jerusalem thorn, or ratama, is a fast-growing, small thorny tree with smooth yellow-green bark, ideal for quickly creating light shade. In warm-winter areas it is evergreen, the leaves composed of tiny leaflets along a long midrib; the leaves drop during hot, dry spells. In late spring and early summer, it puts on a tremendous show of yellow flowers. It needs no irrigation where the rainfall exceeds 10in/250mm annually. The Jerusalem thorn can be propagated by seed, which germinates quickly and grows fast.

Paulownia SCROPHULARIACEAE

Sometimes known as the foxglove tree, *Paulownia tomentosa* (z5–9) is a medium-sized deciduous tree with bold, velvety foliage and violet-purple, foxglove-shaped flowers in upright panicles, opening from buds formed in the fall. Unsuitable where late spring frosts are common, *P. tomentosa* does well in climates where long hot summers provide well-ripened wood to survive the winter. It can be increased by seed or by root cuttings.

Philodendron ARACEAE

Philodendron bipinnatifidum (*P. selloum, P. johnsii*) (z10–11) is a giant shrubby member of a chiefly climbing genus, forming a large shrub with immense, long-stalked, heart-shaped leaves divided and subdivided into many segments. It produces edible fruit.

Phlomis LABIATAE

The Jerusalem sage and its relatives are Mediterranean and Asiatic shrubs with whorls of hooded flowers in spiky calyces. The Mediterranean species especially are found in the driest areas where few other shrubs persist. The most typical of the region is *Phlomis fruticosa* (z8–9), the Jerusalem sage, which has grayish, wooly foliage, and whorls of bright yellow flowers in spiky frills. *P. lanata* (z8–9) is a compact shrub with smaller, more densely felted, darker gray-green foliage than the Jerusalem sage, and yellow flowers. In both of these, the foliage has a slightly yellowish cast, more pronounced in *P. chrysophylla* (z9–10), a low, spreading evergreen with broad yellow-green leaves and clear yellow flowers in widely spaced whorls. By contrast, the net-veined leaves of *P. longifolia* (z8–9) are bright green. This is a small- to medium-sized shrub with whorls of yellow flowers like those of the Jerusalem sage. One of the hardiest is known as *P. anatolica* or *P.* 'Lloyd's Variety' (z8–10), a compact shrub with gray-green felted leaves and deep yellow flowers.

Some species have pink flowers instead of the more familiar yellow. *P. italica* (z9–10) is a suckering, soft-wooded shrub with white-wooly foliage and pink flowers, while *P. purpurea* (z8–9) has narrow, gray-felted foliage, white beneath, and whorls of rose-purple flowers. There is also a pure white form. The easterly *P. cashmeriana* (z8–10) has wooly, gray-green leaves and whorls of lilac-pink flowers. All can be propagated from cuttings.

Paulownia tomentosa

Photinia ROSACEAE

Photinia × *fraseri* (z7–9), the red leaf of the southern United States, popular for its bright red or copper young growths, is surprisingly drought-tolerant and will even cope with desert conditions, surviving periods of neglect, but not looking its best unless irrigated. The Chinese photinia, *P. serratifolia* (*P. serrulata*) (z8–10), is not so tolerant of desert heat, but is drought-resistant in less extreme climates. Photinias are propagated by cuttings of half-ripe, or – slowly but surely – nearly mature sideshoots.

Phygelius SCROPHULARIACEAE

Phygelius aequalis (z8–9) is a soft-wooded South African shrub of small to medium size, with curved trumpets of muted buff-pink, yellow in the throat and touched at the lobes with scarlet. There is a delightful butter-yellow form. Its hybrids with the brighter Cape figwort, *P. capensis* (z8–9), range in color from soft yellow 'Moonraker' through clear red 'Pink Elf' and 'Salmon Leap' to dusky pink 'Winchester Fanfare,' 'Devil's Leap' and 'African Queen.' Cuttings root very easily, and seed may produce some interesting results; the yellow *P. aequalis* comes virtually true.

Physocarpus ROSACEAE

Physocarpus opulifolius (z3–7), the nine bark, is a tough and easy but rather undistinguished, medium-sized deciduous shrub with three-lobed leaves and modest white, pink-tinged flowers at midsummer. Cuttings root with great ease.

Pistacia ANACARDIACEAE

The mastic tree or lentisk of the Mediterranean region is *Pistacia lentiscus* (z9–10), a large evergreen shrub or small tree which, like many natives of the maquis, thrives in dry conditions. *P. atlantica* (z9–10), the Mount Atlas pistache, Mount Atlas mastic tree or Algerian pistache, is a neat, slow-growing tree of medium size, forming a rounded to pyramidal outline. The compound green leaves are evergreen in mild areas, but are shed in winter in cool climates. Once established, it is very tolerant of heat, wind and drought. Like others in the genus, it produces resin. The Chinese pistache, *P. chinensis* (z7–9), is similar to the Mount Atlas pistache, but grows larger except in poor soils, and is less drought-tolerant. It is deciduous, the polished leaves often turning scarlet in the fall. Female trees produce long bright red fruits aging to purple-blue. It is best to remove the pulp from the seeds before sowing them to hasten germination. The more tender *P. terebinthus* (z9–10), the Cyprus turpentine tree, is a large shrub or small tree with shining green, aromatic, pinnate leaves and small red to maroon-

Pistacia chinensis

purple fruits. The genus is also represented in the New World: *P. texana* (z9–10), the American pistachio or lentisco, is a medium-sized Texas tree, with pinnate leaves and reddish fruits.

Pithecellobium LEGUMINOSAE
Pithecellobium flexicaule (*Ebenopsis flexicaulis*) (z9–10), the Texas ebony, is a small tree of characteristic outline, the twig structure forming a wide crown over an erect gray trunk. The green leaves are thorny at the base and are shed in cold winters. Fragrant, creamy yellow catkin-like flowers are borne in dense clusters in spring, followed by long brown pods. The Texas ebony tolerates periods of drought and thrives in heat.

Pittosporum PITTOSPORACEAE
From this chiefly Australasian genus, many of which are tolerant of drought and of sea winds, here is a selection which suggests their diversity. *Pittosporum crassifolium* (z9–10), the karo, is a large evergreen shrub or small tree with thick-textured, leathery, dark green leaves, white-felted on the reverse. The small flowers are deep maroon-purple. It fits equally comfortably into formal or informal settings, while *P.* 'Garnettii' (z9–10),

an evergreen shrub with thinner leaves variegated with white and spotted with pink, especially in cold weather, looks its best in gardened rather than naturalistic plantings. *P. phillyreoïdes* (z9–10), the willow pittosporum or narrow-leaved pittosporum, is a graceful, slow-growing, small evergreen tree of slender, erect habit, with long trailing branches and very narrow, gray-green leaves. Tiny yellow flowers are borne along the branches in spring, followed by strings of pea-sized, orange-yellow fruits. A familiar shrub in the Mediterranean area, often bravely flowering despite apparent complete neglect, is *P. tobira* (z8–10), the tobira, Australian laurel, or Japanese mock orange. It is a slow-growing, eventually large shrub with polished, dark green leaves in whorls, and showy cream flowers powerfully scented like orange blossom, followed by blue-green berries with orange seeds. 'Variegatum' is more compact, while 'Wheeler's Dwarf' is ideal for small spaces or low hedges. The species can be propagated from seed, but cultivars must be vegetatively increased.

Platanus PLATANACEAE

Platanus × *hispanica* (*P.* × *acerifolia*) (z5–8), the London plane, is a large deciduous tree with flaking bark, bold palmate leaves, and rounded flower clusters hanging long on the branches, disintegrating the following spring into invasive fluff. It is quite unsuited to small spaces, but is a handsome park tree, which can be increased by hardwood cuttings. The California sycamore or aliso, *P. racemosa* (z8–9), is a large tree with thick-textured leaves of variable outline, downy beneath.

Plumbago PLUMBAGINACEAE

Plumbago auriculata (z9–10), the Cape plumbago or leadwort, is a scrambling shrub with clusters of pure pale blue flowers over a long season, the perfect emollient for the strident magenta of bougainvillea. Drought-tolerant in mild climates, it needs a moist soil in desert heat.

Plumeria APOCYNACEAE

Plumeria rubra (z10–11), the frangipani, is amazingly easy to grow in dry soils or wet, rich soils or poor, demanding only a frost-free climate. The thick, milky-sapped stems root fast and easily. To these qualities the frangipani adds bold foliage and waxy flowers of characteristic propellor shape opening from scrolled buds; they are endowed with an intoxicating fragrance. They may be crimson, pink, soft yellow or white. *P. rubra* f. *acutifolia* has white, yellow-throated flowers, *P. r.* f. *lutea* is yellow flushed with red on the reverse. *P. alba* (z10–11), the West Indian jasmine, has yellow, white-eyed flowers.

Poncirus RUTACEAE

Poncirus trifoliata (*Aegle sepiaria*) (z5–9), the Japanese bitter orange, is a slow-growing, medium-sized shrub with thick green, very spiny stems and trifoliolate leaves. The large, white, orange-blossom flowers are fragrant and open in spring. The miniature oranges that follow are green, ripening to yellow.

Populus SALICACEAE

Some poplars are tolerant of drought in cool climates, but although used in desert areas they need irrigation to do well in extreme heat. The aspen and the white poplar are valuable trees in very cold zones. *Populus alba* (z4–8), the white poplar or abele, is a large, suckering tree with leaves of variable

Potentilla 'Elizabeth'

shape, white-felted on the reverse and turning yellow in the fall. The quaking aspen or quiverleaf, *P. tremuloïdes* (z1–6), is a small- to medium-sized tree with pale yellowish bark and fine-toothed leaves. For warmer climates there is the Fremont cottonwood, *P. fremontii* (z7), a tall tree with large, triangular, glossy leaves. *P. f.* var. *wislizenii* (*P. deltoïdes* ssp. *wislizenii*), the valley cottonwood or Rio Grande cottonwood, has larger yellow-green leaves. Increase by hardwood cuttings.

Potentilla ROSACEAE

Potentilla fruticosa (z3–7) is a dwarf to small deciduous shrub with many cultivars; leaves vary from green to silver, and the strawberry-like flowers range from white to deep yellow, tangerine and orange-scarlet, with clear pink as a recent introduction. It is very hardy and ideal for dry gardens in cold climates; half-ripe cuttings root quickly.

Prosopis LEGUMINOSAE

The mesquite or algarrobo of North and South America are spiny deciduous shrubs that can easily be trained to make small, multistemmed trees with spreading crowns, fast-growing where there is ample moisture and taking on picturesque twisted forms in dry climates. Extremely tolerant of drought, thanks to their very deep tap roots, they are ideal for warm deserts and hot interior climates, providing summer shade. The leaves are composed of many small leaflets; the yellow catkin-like flowers in spring are followed by edible beans, the pinole of Mexico. Their drawbacks are their invasive roots (in Australia and some other warm areas the mesquite has become an aggressive weed), and their litter from the flowers in spring, seed pods in summer, and leaves in the fall. Like other tap-rooted plants they are best raised from seed and planted small from containers. *Prosopis juliiflora* (z10–11), is a very variable South American native, often forming a large shrub, occasionally a tall tree. The creamy yellow flowers are borne in short spikes. *P. spicigera* (z10–11) is an Arabian species well suited to desert conditions, searching out moisture with its immensely long tap root. It is very like *P. juliiflora*, though rather taller, with curved, red-brown pods. The velvet mesquite or Arizona mesquite, *P. velutina* (*P. juliiflora velutina*) (z8–11), has soft gray-green foliage composed of small leaflets and forms a craggy shrub.

The Chilean mesquite, *P. chilensis* (z10–11), is semi-evergreen, especially in mild areas. Young trees are sometimes armed with enormous white, woody thorns. A hybrid offered in U.S. nurseries as a South American hybrid is not the same as *P. chilensis*; it is vigorous, forming a wide crown, and has deep green deciduous foliage. *P. glandulosa* var. *glandulosa* (z10–11), the honey mesquite or Texas mesquite, has bright green leaves with larger leaflets than other species, and with its weeping outline forms a picturesque tree that grows large in favorable conditions. The Argentine mesquite, *P. alba* (z10–11), is very fast-growing, and the almost evergreen leaves are blue-green. One of the smallest is *P. pubescens* (z10–11), the screwbean mesquite or tornillo, a small deciduous shrub.

Prunus ROSACEAE

Some of the wild plums or laurel cherries of North America are suited to dry areas. *Prunus americana* (z5–9), the wild plum or sloe, is a large shrub or tree, often thorny, with white flowers and yellow or red fruits. For milder areas, *P. caroliniana* (z7–10), the Carolina laurel cherry, mock orange, or wild orange, is a refined small tree of upright habit, with glossy, dark green, narrow foliage clothing the branches to the ground. The small white flowers in clusters are followed by gleaming black, dryish fruits. Old World species that tolerate drought include the almond and peach. *P. dulcis* (z6–9), the almond, is a familiar sight throughout the Mediterranean, thriving in deep, well-drained soils and reveling in the summer heat. The white or very pale pink flowers (deeper pink in some cultivated varieties) appear very early in spring. The peach, *P. persica* (z6–9), is a small tree with pale pink flowers followed by juicy, velvet-coated fruits. Wild forms such as the vineyard peach of Switzerland seem to be able to tolerate neglect. In complete contrast to these small trees, *P. prostrata* (z6–8), the rock cherry, is a low, spreading, gnarled shrublet with bright pink flowers in spring.

Punica PUNICACEAE

Punica granatum (z9–10), the pomegranate or granada, is a native of southern Asia, long cultivated in the Mediterranean and brought by the Spanish to the New World. It is a large deciduous shrub with small shiny leaves, bronzed when unfurling, bright green in summer, and golden in autumn. The flowers are usually red, but may also be pink or white. Juicy, many-seeded red to bronze fruits are borne by single-flowered kinds, but not by the doubles such as 'Alba Plena,' 'Double Red' or 'Mme. Legrelle,' a double with cream flowers striped red. 'Nana,' a perfect miniature, produces single orange-red flowers and small red inedible fruits; it is nearly evergreen in warm climates and flowers when tiny. Fruiting cultivars include 'Wonderful,' with large, orange-red flowers, and 'Sweet,' with paler, less acid fruit. The pomegranate stands hot winds, drought, saline soils, intense sun and – provided the wood is well ripened by a long sunny summer – cold winters. It is resistant to Texas root rot and will grow without attention where the annual rainfall exceeds 10in/250mm. Where suited it self-sows; to propagate named cultivars, take half-ripe cuttings.

Purshia ROSACEAE

The antelope bitterbrush, *Purshia tridentata* (z7–8), is a semi-evergreen, medium-sized shrub which positively dislikes moisture in the soil. The tiny leaves are blue-green, contrasting with single yellow flowers.

Prosopis glandulosa var. *glandulosa*

79

Robinia hispida

Pyrus ROSACEAE

Pyrus kawakamii (z8–10), the evergreen pear, is a shrub or medium-sized tree, often thorny, with white flowers and rounded fruits.

Quercus FAGACEAE

From the Mediterranean region come such diverse species as *Quercus coccifera* (z8), the kermes oak, a typical maquis shrub with small, evergreen, holly-like leaves, slow-growing and compact, and the massive *Q. ilex* (z8–9), the evergreen oak or holm oak, which makes a large tree tolerant of adverse conditions including periods of drought and desert heat, but at its best where there is ample winter rain. It is a bad neighbor, casting a dark shadow and shedding leaves and scurf, but is valued for its tolerance of salt winds. It can be clipped to shape. *Q. suber* (z9–10), the cork oak of southern Europe and North Africa, is the tree from which bark is harvested for cork. It is a slow-growing, medium-sized evergreen tree, with tooth-edged leaves, polished dark green above and gray-felted beneath.

Q. agrifolia (z8), the California live oak, resembles the holm oak, *Q. ilex*, but is a much smaller, slow-growing tree, with black bark and shining green leaves. The shrub live oak, *Q. turbinella* (z5–9), is the climax tree of the chaparral region of Arizona, where it grows with mountain mahogany and little else. It is a thicketing, medium-sized to large shrub with evergreen, fiercely armed, holly-like leaves that open red-tinged, turning glossy chartreuse-green before developing to blue-bloomed maturity. The bear oak, *Q. ilicifolia* (z4–8), announces its leaf style in its botanical name, which means holly-leaved; the leaves are evergreen and spiny, on a small, shrubby tree that produces an abundance of acorns. The dwarf chinquapin oak, *Q. prinoïdes* (z5–8), is a rounded small shrub with many-lobed leaves, tolerant of adverse conditions including drought.

One of the best for desert regions is *Q. virginiana* (z8–10), the southern live oak, which copes even with hot interior valleys with periodic irrigation and is tolerant of periods of drought once established. It is a fast-growing, large, spreading tree with nearly horizontal branches at maturity, and dark shiny green leaves with white-wooly reverse. For cooler dry areas, there is the blackjack oak, *Q. marilandica* (z6–9), a medium-sized tree which develops an open crown of gnarled branches; the lobed, leathery leaves are glossy dark green above and brown-felted beneath.

Rhaphiolepis ROSACEAE

Rhaphiolepis indica (z8–11), the Indian hawthorn, is a small evergreen shrub, with narrow leaves and loose sprays of pink flowers over a long season. *R. × delacourii* 'Springtime' has deeper pink flowers and tawny young growths. The slightly taller *R. umbellata* (*R. ovata*) (z8–11) has broader, thick-textured, leathery leaves and fragrant white flowers in clusters. All can be propagated by seed or half-ripe cuttings.

Rhus ANACARDIACEAE

The sumacs are grown chiefly for their attractive foliage; some display vivid autumn colors. Handle them with care, for some have irritant sap. Root cuttings offer an easy means of increasing the sumacs, and seed can be sown if available. The stag's horn sumac, *Rhus hirta* (*R. typhina*) (z4–8), is a gaunt, spreading small tree or large shrub, often with invasively suckering tendencies. The thick branches are covered when young with dense tawny fur. The large pinnate leaves develop brilliant autumn colors of orange, scarlet and crimson-purple, amid which female plants bear showy crimson fruit clusters. Also for colder climates, *R. aromatica* (z4–9), the fragrant sumac, lemon sumac or polecat bush, is a small deciduous shrub with aromatic foliage and small, yellowish flowers in showy clusters in spring. The dwarf sumac or mountain sumac, *R. copallina* (z5–9), is a small- to medium-sized shrub with glossy, pinnate leaves coloring vividly in the fall amid the showy red clusters of fruit.

For warmer zones, there is *R. ovata* (z9–11), the sugarbush, which originates in the chaparral belts of California, Arizona and Mexico. It grows slowly to form a large, lush-foliaged shrub of rounded habit, with leathery, rich green leaves folded at the midrib and curved, with reddish, wavy margins and red petioles. Deep red flower buds in short spikes form in autumn, opening to creamy flowers in spring. Other similar large, shrubby sumacs are *R. choriophylla* and *R. virens*, both native to higher elevations of the deserts of the Southwest, suitable for low deserts with a little extra water. Their deep green compound leaves have a waxy texture. *R. lancea* (z9–11), the African sumac, is a native of arid areas of South Africa, and does well in dry areas in the southwestern United States. It forms a small evergreen tree with a flat-topped crown casting dense shade. The foliage is dark green, the fruits red or yellow.

Robinia LEGUMINOSAE

The locusts and acacias all have attractive ferny foliage and racemes of pea flowers; some have spiny stems, and many spread by suckers, which offer a straightforward means of increase. Their branches tend to be brittle, so that shelter from wind is desirable. Among shrubby acacias are *Robinia hispida* (z5–8), the rose acacia, a medium-sized, suckering shrub with deep rose flowers, and the similar *R. fertilis* (z5–8), which has narrower leaflets and smaller rose-pink flowers. *R. × margaretta* 'Pink Cascade' ('Casque Rouge,' 'Purple Crown') (z4–8) unites *R. hispida* and *R. pseudoacacia*, the result a medium-sized, freely suckering shrub with abundant, large pink flowers. 'Idaho' has pink flowers and is of more compact habit. *R. kelseyi* (z5–9) is a pretty shrub or small tree with especially elegant foliage, sharp spines at the leaf nodes, and slightly fragrant, lilac-pink flowers. Larger again is *R. × ambigua* 'Decaisneana' (z4–8), a medium-sized tree with large sprays of pale pink flowers. The black locust or false acacia, *R. pseudoacacia* (z4–8), is a fast-growing tree of medium to large size and suckering habit, with white flowers very attractive to bees.

Rosa rugosa 'Pink Grootendorst'

Romneya PAPAVERACEAE

The matilijas have dissected, blue-gray foliage and large, fragrant, white, silky poppies with a bold central boss of yellow stamens. They can be hard to establish, but spread freely once settled and can be increased by root cuttings. *Romneya coulteri* (z8–10) typically has smooth buds, while *R. c.* var. *trichocalyx* is distinguished by its bristly, rounded buds. 'White Cloud' has larger flowers and gray leaves.

Rosa ROSACEAE

Rosa pimpinellifolia (*R. spinosissima*) (z4–9), the Scotch rose or burnet rose, is a small, suckering shrub, forming dense thickets of slender, upright stems set with innumerable small bristles and spines. The tiny leaves are in proportion to the little white or pale pink, deliciously fragrant flowers which appear early in the season. A native of coastal sand dunes in northern Europe, it is very tolerant of dry soils. Variants of hybrids with single or double flowers of various colors are known, including a charming

Rosa rugosa 'Roseraie de l'Haÿ'

double white. *R. p.* 'Grandiflora' (*altaica*) (z4–9) has larger creamy white flowers on taller growths. The ramanas rose, *R. rugosa* (z2–8), grows on sandy seashores in Japan. It is a more muscular shrub than the burnet rose, with very prickly, stout stems and bold, crinkled foliage, bright shining green above, turning corn-gold in the fall. The wide, fragrant flowers appear in almost unbroken succession from late spring to autumn; typically rose-purple, they may also be white or pale pink. Double-flowered garden variants include 'Pink Grootendorst,' magenta 'Roseraie de l'Haÿ' and white 'Blanc Double de Coubert.' 'Fru Dagmar Hastrup' is a low-growing cultivar with clear pink flowers. All the singles produce large scarlet hips among the later flowers.

Rosmarinus LABIATAE

Rosmarinus officinalis (z8–9) is one of the finest low-growing plants for arid climates, commonly a spreading shrub of irregular habit with aromatic needle leaves, white beneath and green to gray-green above. The flowers are typically pale blue, but cultivars have deeper blue flowers, or pink or white. 'Lockwood de Forest' is similar in appearance to *R. × lavandulaceus*, with richer blue flowers and paler foliage. 'Benenden Blue' ('Collingwood Ingram') has gracefully arching branches, very narrow dark green leaves, and bright blue-violet flowers. Other bright blue flowered cultivars are 'Severn Sea' and the rather tender, broad-needled 'Tuscan Blue.' 'Miss Jessopp's Upright' forms, until middle-aged spread catches up with it, a neat upright pillar set with pale blue flowers in spring. *R. × lavandulaceus* (z8–9) is a prostrate rosemary forming wide mats of aromatic evergreen foliage, with blue flowers in spring. Rosemaries are drought-tolerant and heat-resistant, and easily propagated by cuttings.

Rubus ROSACEAE

Rubus pentalobus (*R. calycinoïdes* hort.) (z7–9) is a creeping evergreen shrub with rooting stems, and lobed, crinkled, glossy green leaves, pale-felted beneath. The white flowers are half hidden by the leaves. The much larger and more rumbustious *R. tricolor* (z7–8) has long, trailing and rooting stems covered with red-bristles, polished dark green leaves with white reverse, and white flowers.

Ruscus RUSCACEAE

Ruscus aculeatus (z7–9), the butcher's broom, is a small evergreen shrub forming impenetrable thickets of stout, erect, green stems. The "leaves," which are in fact cladodes or modified stems, are spine-tipped and closely packed on the upper parts of the stems. Tiny flowers are followed, on female plants, by showy scarlet-red berries. The butcher's broom will grow even in dense shade and can be divided if new clumps are needed.

Ruta RUTACEAE

Ruta graveolens (z5–9), rue or herb of grace, is a small, strongly aromatic evergreen shrub, with finely divided blue-green leaves and small bright yellow flowers. 'Jackman's Blue' is a selection with particularly bright blue foliage, perpetuated by cuttings.

Salix SALICACEAE

A few willows, usually thought of as waterside plants, are tolerant of dry soils. They can be propagated from cuttings, even of quite large stems. *Salix cinerea* (z2–6), the gray sallow, is a large shrub with leaves gray beneath and

Salvia officinalis

catkins on the bare branches in spring. Though not particularly beautiful, it is an almost indestructibly tough tree, useful for reclaiming waste land. The goat willow or great sallow, *S. caprea* (z5–8), is a large shrub or small tree with oval leaves, gray beneath, on stout stems. On the leafless branches in early spring, male plants bear showy yellow catkins, often called palm, and females have smaller silvery catkins like silky fur, earning the name pussy willow. For much smaller spaces there is the creeping willow, *S. repens* (z5–7), a small shrub occasionally growing to head height, sometimes of low, spreading habit. The slender stems are set with small gray leaves, silvery beneath, especially in *S. r.* f. *argentea*.

Salvia LABIATAE

Salvia greggii (z7–9) is one of the most successful of the shrubby Mexican sages in dry climates. It has small aromatic leaves and magenta-pink flowers. There is a white form, a pretty peach-pink, and variants with redder flowers, such as 'Furman's Red.' *S. leucantha* (z10) is a small shrub with its own self-contained color scheme of narrow, gray-green leaves and arching spikes of velvet-plush, white and lilac flowers. The common sage of the Mediterranean region, *S. officinalis* (z6–9), is an evergreen, aromatic shrub used in cooking, but also very ornamental with its low spreading habit and gray-green leaves. 'Purpurascens' has gray-purple foliage, and 'Icterina' is variegated green and gold. A narrow-leaved form with a different aroma and good spikes of violet-purple flower is now classed as *S. lavandulifolia*. All are easily grown from cuttings.

Sambucus CAPRIFOLIACEAE

Sambucus caerulea var. *neomexicana* (*S. c.* var. *arizonica*, *S. c.* var. *mexicana*) (z7–9), the Mexican elderberry, is a rather coarse shrub, useful in desert gardens, for it is summer deciduous and winter green. With irrigation, it grows fast to small tree size. In common with other elders, the wood is light and rather brittle; the bright green leaves hold until the onset of hot weather. The flat clusters of white flowers are also borne during the cooler months. The berries ripen in summer and make excellent jelly or wine. If grown in desert conditions, it appreciates moderate irrigation during winter, but needs much less while summer-dormant. Propagation is not difficult by cuttings or seed.

Santolina COMPOSITAE

Santolina chamaecyparissus (z7–9), the lavender cotton of Spain and northern Africa, tolerates drought, heat, wind and poor soil. It has intensely silvery, tight-packed foliage, and bright yellow button flowers in summer. It can be clipped hard back in spring each year to keep a neat mounded outline. *S. c.* var. *nana* is a naturally dwarf variant. *S. pinnata* (z7–9) is similar, with looser, greener leaves and creamy flower heads; *S. p.* ssp. *neapolitana* has gray, very feathery foliage, and lemon-yellow flower heads, and 'Sulphurea' is paler in flower, while 'Edward Bowles' has creamy primrose flowers. *S. serratifolia* (z7–9) is an uncertain name applied to a gray-silvery lavender cotton with looser foliage than *S. chamaecyparissus*. Another species sometimes encountered in gardens is *S. rosmarinifolia* ssp. *rosmarinifolia* (z7–9) (more familiar by the name *S. virens*) which has thready, green foliage and bright yellow flower heads; 'Primrose Gem' is a very pretty selection with paler flowers. *S. r.* ssp. *canescens* (z7–9) has gray-silver foliage. The green-leaved santolinas are less tolerant of fierce sun than the gray and silver species. Half-ripe cuttings of all the cotton lavenders root easily.

Santolina rosmarinifolia ssp. *rosmarinifolia*

Sapindus SAPINDACEAE

Sapindus drummondii (z6–9), the soapberry of the central United States and northern Mexico, is a small tree with robinia-like leaves and large, full sprays of tiny cream flowers in summer.

Sapium EUPHORBIACEAE

Sapium sebiferum (z8–10), the Chinese tallow tree, is a small tree with broad, pointed leaves turning yellow or bright red in the fall, and narrow spikes of greenish flowers followed by fruits with large white seeds. Their waxy coating is used to make candles in China.

Sarcococca BUXACEAE

The sarcococcas are known as Christmas box because of their winter flowering season. They are shade-lovers and will tolerate very dry conditions if not sun-baked. They can be increased by division or cuttings. One of the most attractive is *Sarcococca hookeriana* (z6–8), a small, thicket-forming evergreen shrub, with elegant, narrow foliage on erect stems, often set off by dark petioles, and tiny pinkish-cream, honey-scented flowers in winter. *S. h.* var. *digyna* is especially appealing with its dark maroon stems. *S. h.* var. *humilis* (*S. humilis*) (z6–8) is shorter in growth and more widely suckering, with glossy, pointed, dark green leaves and tiny fragrant flowers. The more tender *S. ruscifolia* (z7–8) is taller and larger in leaf; its fruits are red, not black.

Schinus ANACARDIACEAE

Schinus molle (z9–11), the pepper tree of South America, is a graceful small tree with half-weeping branches and dark green leaves composed of narrow resinous leaflets. The unshowy clusters of yellow flowers are followed by bright pink "peppercorns" in summer on female plants. The pepper tree can be allowed to grow unchecked, when it will develop a rough-barked trunk, or can be cut back to near ground-level every year to form a multistemmed tree. It is at its best in dry areas, needing occasional deep irrigation in extreme desert conditions. The Brazilian pepper tree or Christmas-berry tree, *S. terebenthifolius* (z9–11), is a small- to medium-sized tree with a wide dense crown of interlaced branches, naturally branching low down so that it needs training to form a trunk. The shining, dark green leaves are pinnate and set off the clusters of red fruits borne in late fall and winter by female trees. It needs similar treatment in desert areas.

Senecio COMPOSITAE

Senecio cineraria (z8–9) is the name decreed – until the next revision, at least – for the familiar silvery gray, felt-leaved plant often raised from seed to use in summer bedding schemes in cool climates. It is in fact a small, soft-wooded shrub that survives even cool winters if not subject to excessive wet. The leaf form varies from very finely feathered to the broad-lobed 'Cirrus.' Cuttings root readily, and several seed strains come virtually true. The equally silvery *S. vira-vira* (*S. leucostachys*) (z8–9) is a scandent, soft-wooded shrub with finely divided, comb-like leaves, and sprays of ivory flower heads that make their own gentle contribution to a plant that has the knack of weaving through its neighbors without oppressing them.

Shepherdia ELAEAGNACEAE

The buffalo berries are tough, undemanding shrubs with grayish leaves, tolerant of coastal winds and dry, stony soils. *Shepherdia argentea* (z2–7) is a

Sarcococca hookeriana
var. *humilis*

slow-growing, sometimes spiny, medium-sized shrub with silvery scaly leaves and scarlet fruits borne only by female plants. The soapberry, *S. canadensis* (z2–7), is spineless, with leaves silvery-scurfy beneath.

Sideritis LABIATAE

Sideritis candicans (z8–9) is a small shrub with thickly white-wooly, triangular leaves and long spikes of yellow, rust-tipped flowers in summer.

Simmondsia BUXACEAE

Simmondsia chinensis (z10–11), the jojoba, coffee bush, goat nut or deer nut, is a desert native from the southwestern United States, Baja California and Mexico. It is the source of jojoba oil, a substitute for spermwhale oil. Forming a dense rounded shrub of medium size, it has oval, gray-green, leathery or almost succulent leaves. It is tolerant of drought and neglect, provided the annual rainfall exceeds 10in/250mm.

Sophora LEGUMINOSAE

The sophoras are a cosmopolitan and varied genus of perennials, shrubs and trees, often doing well in dry areas. *Sophora japonica* (z5–8), the Japanese pagoda tree, is a medium-sized to large tree with robinia-like foliage and ivory-white flowers in large sprays in late summer. It does not flower freely, if at all, in cool climates where the summers are dull, but is very generous in hotter areas. There is a variant with lilac flowers. Fragrant violet-blue pea flowers belong to *S. secundiflora* (z8–9), the mescal bean, Texas mountain laurel, or frijolito, an evergreen shrub or small tree with glossy green, pinnate leaves, which bears its flowers in early spring, followed by woody silver-gray pods which split in late summer to show bright red, inedible beans. It is tolerant of heat, drought, wind and poor soil. *S. arizonica* (z8–9), the Arizona mescal bean or mountain laurel, which grows on dry, rocky hillsides, is similar, though smaller and very slow-growing, the deep green leaves silver beneath. *S. gypsophila guadalupensis* (z9–10), the Guadalupe mountain laurel or mescal bean, is a low, wide-spreading shrub with larger flowers.

The antipodean sophoras have yellow, claw-like flowers. *S. microphylla* (z9–10) is a shrub with zigzag stems and evergreen, drooping, pinnate leaves, developing as it matures into a small tree as many as forty pairs of tiny leaflets to each leaf. The flowers are bright yellow. *S. prostrata* (z9–10) is perhaps a permanently juvenile form of this, synonymous maybe with 'Little Baby,' a low shrub with densely interlaced stems. The kowhai of New Zealand, *S. tetraptera* (z9–10), is a large shrub or small tree similar to *S. microphylla*, but with fewer leaflets to each leaf, and larger, rich yellow flowers followed by winged seed pods like strings of beads.

Sparmannia TILIACEAE

Sparmannia africana (z10–11), the African hemp, has very large velvety, pale green leaves, and clusters of white flowers with yellow stamens.

Spartium LEGUMINOSAE

Spartium junceum (z8–10), the Spanish broom, is a tall, open shrub, with green, rush-like stems, and large, almond-scented, golden-yellow pea flowers in summer and fall. It can be cut back hard each spring, or allowed to billow free, as it does to such effect on dry waste banks and roadsides in its native land and as a garden escape. It is a fast-growing shrub and is easily raised from seed, but it is an undesirable weed in Australia and some other warm areas.

Styrax STYRACACEAE

Styrax officinalis (z9–10), the gum storax, is a Mediterranean shrub or small tree yielding an aromatic resin used as incense. The flowers are white bells, larger than those of the Asiatic snowbells, which are not drought-tolerant. The seeds, used to make rosaries, can be sown to make more plants.

Sutherlandia LEGUMINOSAE

Sutherlandia frutescens (z9–10) is a South African shrub of medium to large size, with gray-green, pinnate leaves and coppery scarlet to terracotta pea flowers in summer, followed by bladder-like seed pods. It is easily raised from seed.

Symphoricarpos CAPRIFOLIACEAE

The snowberry, *Symphoricarpos albus* (z4–7), is a small, thicket-forming, deciduous shrub with tiny flowers followed by clusters of large, soft, pure white fruits. It will grow almost anywhere and can be increased by division.

Tamarix parviflora (T. tetrandra var. *purpurea)*

S. × *chenaultii* (z5–7) is more of a garden shrub, with blush-white berries flushing to rose-purple on their exposed sides. Another of garden value is *S.* × *doorenbosii* (z6–7), which comes in various cultivars: 'Erect,' upright and narrow, with bright rose-pink berries; 'Magic Berry,' low and wide, with deep pink fruits; 'Mother of Pearl,' a low shrub weighed down by the quantity of palest pink to white fruits; and stiff, upright, white-berried 'White Hedge.'

Tamarix TAMARICACEAE

Tamarix aphylla (z8–10), the tamarisk, athel tree or athel salt cedar, a native of the deserts of North Africa and the Middle East, is a deep-rooted tree which can endure great heat, hot winds, drought and very saline soil, making it an ideal shade-provider for difficult areas. Fast-growing to tree stature, it has long, slender, jointed branchlets which look like gray-blue needle leaves; the true leaves are minute scales. The grayest plants are those growing in hot, dry conditions in alkaline soils. In summer the branch tips bear plumes of dusty pink to creamy flowers. The salt cedar, *T. africana* (z9–10), bears its feathery pink flowers in spring.

Several of the European and Near Eastern tamarisks are suitable for quite cold climates and are tolerant of coastal winds. *T. gallica* (z6–9), a native of southwestern Europe, forms a large spreading shrub or small tree, with blue-green foliage on dark branches; the clouds of pink flowers open in summer. *T. parviflora* (*T. tetrandra* var. *purpurea*) (z6–9) is a large shrub or small tree with purple-brown branches and bright green foliage; the feathery plumes of deep pink flowers are borne in spring. *T. tetrandra* (z6–9) is a large, open shrub with green foliage on dark branches, and long sprays of pink flowers in spring. One of the most attractive is *T. ramosissima* (z3–8), which has paler, glaucous foliage, amid which the abundant pink flowers open in summer; it can be hard-pruned in spring to remain compact, or allowed to develop freely into a large shrub or small tree. 'Pink Cascade' is a selection with bright pink flowers, and 'Rubra' is deeper pink. All the tamarisks can be propagated from hardwood cuttings.

Teucrium fruticans

Templetonia LEGUMINOSAE

Templetonia retusa (z9–10) is a medium-sized evergreen shrub with deep green leaves and rich coral-scarlet pea flowers in winter and early spring.

Teucrium LABIATAE

Teucrium × *lucidrys* (*T. chamaedrys* Hort.) (z6–9), the wall germander, is an aromatic, soft-wooded shrublet, with creeping roots, neat foliage and lilac-pink flowers in summer. It tolerates poor soil, heat, wind, drought and cold. More beautiful but less frost-resistant, *T. fruticans* (z7–9) from southern Europe and North Africa is a small shrub giving a silvery gray effect on account of the fine white felt covering the stems and undersides of the leaves. The flowers are pale blue and open over a long summer season. 'Azureum' is a beautiful selection with richer blue flowers. Half-ripe cuttings are easy to root. The tiny *T. subspinosum* (z9–10) is a spiny shrublet with gray-blue foliage and mauve-pink flowers.

Thevetia APOCYNACEAE

Thevetia peruviana (z10–11), the yellow oleander, be-still tree, or lucky nut, is a large shrub or small tree from tropical America. It has polished, dark green, narrow leaves densely clothing the stems, and yellow to buff-apricot flowers in clusters from summer to fall. 'Alba' has white flowers. It thrives in the desert heat with ample water and will do tolerably well with moderate or widely spaced irrigation when established.

Thryptomene MYRTACEAE

Thryptomene saxicola (z9–10) is a small, dark green, heath-like shrub from Western Australia, with white or pink flowers.

Tibouchina MELASTOMATACEAE

Tibouchina multiflora (z10–11) is a medium-sized shrub with four-angled, winged stems, and large, five- to seven-nerved leaves of velvety texture, gray and hairy beneath. The attractive violet flowers are borne in large clusters. *T. urvilleana* (*T. semidecandra*) (z9–11) has similar foliage, and large, flat, royal purple blooms opening from red buds over a long summer to autumn season.

Ugni MYRTACEAE

Ugni molinae (*Myrtus ugni*) (z9–11), the Chilean guava, is a small, evergreen shrub with dark, glossy green leaves, and waxy pale pink bell flowers in spring, followed by brown-purple, aromatic fruits. Cuttings root easily.

Ulex LEGUMINOSAE

Ulex europaeus (z7–9), the common European gorse, is a ferociously spiny shrub of medium size, forming dense clumps of green branches set with rich yellow, coconut-scented flowers in spring and early summer, with a scattering of blooms at almost any season (hence the saying "when the gorse is out of bloom, kissing's out of fashion"). It is useful cover for dry, poor soils, and a fine coastal plant. However, it can become a fire hazard as the tinder-dry branches ignite explosively with the least spark. 'Flore Pleno' is a better choice for gardens, as its double flowers produce no seed; it must be propagated from cuttings.

Umbellularia LAURACEAE

Umbellularia californica (z9–11), the California laurel, California bay or headache tree, is a large, powerfully aromatic evergreen shrub with pale bright green leaves and insignificant yellowish flowers. It can be increased by seed or cuttings.

Vauquelinia ROSACEAE

Vauquelinia californica (z8–9), the Arizona rosewood, is a slow-growing, medium-sized to large shrub, with dark green, leathery, long slender leaves similar to those of the oleander. The minute cream flowers are held in wide, flat clusters in summer. The Arizona rosewood can stand fierce sun, poor soil and hot winds, and copes with complete neglect as long as it has a minimum annual rainfall of 12in/300mm. *V. angustifolia* (z8–9) is similar with very narrow, serrated leaves.

Vella CRUCIFERAE

Vella pseudocytisus (z8–10) is a curious small shrubby crucifer with little rounded, bristly, gray-green leaves, and sprays of little yellow flowers.

Viburnum CAPRIFOLIACEAE

Viburnum lentago (z2–8), the sheep berry, is a large, vigorous shrub or small tree with glossy dark green leaves turning scarlet and crimson in the fall, and creamy flowers followed by blue-black fruits like little damsons. It can

88

be increased by layering. The Ichang viburnum, *V. ichangense* (z6–8) is a compact, medium-sized shrub with abundant small heads of flowers followed by showy, long-lasting red fruits. One of the most dependable viburnums for milder climates is *V. tinus* (z8–9), the Mediterranean laurustinus, a large, evergreen shrub of dense, rounded habit, with very dark leaves and flat clusters of white flowers opening from pink buds from late fall to spring. An excellent coastal plant that also does well in shade, in desert conditions it needs moderate to ample irrigation. Little known, but worth garden space, *V. suspensum* (z8–9) is a medium-sized evergreen shrub with shining green leaves, and fragrant pink flowers in flat clusters in spring, followed by round red fruits.

Vinca APOCYNACEAE

Vinca major (z7–9), the greater periwinkle, is a creeping, stem-rooting evergreen shrublet with large blue flowers. It will survive almost anywhere, even in dark, dry shade, and though in desert conditions it will, if neglected in times of drought, turn brown, it soon recovers completely when watered. The lesser periwinkle, *V. minor* (z4–9), is a smaller, choicer, less invasive shrublet with blue flowers, also known in white or plum-purple forms, single or double.

Vitex VERBENACEAE

Vitex agnus-castus

Vitex agnus-castus (z6), the chaste tree, monk's pepper tree, hemp tree or sage tree, is a shrub or small tree with a single or many stems, and a spreading crown. A native of southern Europe, it has naturalized in warm areas of the United States. It will do well in desert conditions, where unless irrigated it remains shrubby; with only moderate irrigation it grows fast to tree stature. The dark green leaves are formed of five to seven narrow leaflets; the long, slender spikes of flower are held above the foliage from early summer to fall. Ordinarily lilac-blue, it also comes in pink and white: 'Rosea' and 'Alba.' It does not bloom freely where the summers lack sun. *V. negundo* (z8–10) is a large shrub with looser, more open sprays of lavender flowers in summer and early fall; *V. incisa* (*V. n.* var. *heterophylla*) (z8) has attractive, deeply cut foliage.

Xylosma FLACOURTIACEAE

Xylosma congestum (*X. racemosum*, *X. senticosum*, *Myroxylon senticosum*) (z8–10) is a large shrub or small tree that can be trained almost as you like. The glossy, bright green, pointed, tooth-edged leaves are bronzed when young; the flowers are insignificant. It is drought-tolerant once established.

Ziziphus RHAMNACEAE

Ziziphus jujuba (z7–9), the Chinese date, or the ancient lotus plant, is a large deciduous shrub with a characteristic twiggy structure of angular, spiny branches, suckering from the base to form thickets of stems. It has deep roots to search out any moisture and tolerates drought, heat, cold and alkaline soil. The fine-textured, glossy green leaves form shimmering waterfalls of foliage, and turn golden in the fall. The insignificant yellow flowers, borne in late spring and early summer, are followed, in hot summer areas, by brown, fleshy, edible fruits. Basal suckers form groves. 'Inermis' is an unarmed selection. *Z. spina-christi* (z9–11), Christ's thorn or crown of thorns, is an Arabian and Near Eastern evergreen shrub valued for its edible fruits and as a good hedge. It is very slow-growing and deep rooted.

Conifers

OPPOSITE ABOVE This seedling
Norfolk Island Pine (*Araucaria
heterophylla*) will grow with time
into a tall tree, but the tiered
structure of its branches remains
into maturity, making it one of
the most distinctive of conifers
for warmer climates.

OPPOSITE BELOW The wide
crown of the Mediterranean
Pinus pinea earns it the name
umbrella pine. Spiky agaves and
the fleshy pads of prickly pear
contribute to a typical dry-
landscape planting.

Every climate has its characteristic trees, and many of them are conifers.
The rugged Scots pine (*Pinus sylvestris*), and many junipers, are valuable
drought-resistant evergreen trees and shrubs for cold climates. The Tuscan
plains would seem very different without the slender dark flames of the
Italian cypress (*Cupressus sempervirens*), while the Côte d'Azur would be
unrecognizable without its umbrella pines (*Pinus pinea*), and the warmer
regions of the Costa del Sol without the Norfolk Island pine (*Araucaria
heterophylla*). California has its Monterey cypress (*Cupressus macrocarpa*), a
wind-contorted grotesque on the coastal bluffs, but a noble, almost cedar-
like tree inland, and its bigcone pine (*Pinus coulteri*) with dramatic cones.

Some say that conifers are dull. But even among this list of drought-
tolerant conifers, there is a great variety of silhouettes, leaf types (from tiny
appressed scales to long, graceful needles) and colors. Disregarding the
many conifer cultivars with colored foliage, the variety of shades is wide,
from the gray-blue of the Arizona cypress to the rich bronze of *Microbiota*'s
winter garb, via many shades of green.

Abies PINACEAE
Most of the silver firs demand deep, moist soil, but there are a couple of
drought-tolerant and hardy species. *Abies concolor* (z4–7), the white fir, is a
tree of formal outline with rich green needles, while the white subalpine fir,
A. lasiocarpa var. *arizonica* (z5–6), has a narrow crown and needles of a
bluish cast more appropriate to the group name "silver fir."

Afrocarpus PODOCARPACEAE
Afrocarpus gracilior (*Podocarpus gracilior*) (z9–10), the African fern pine, is an
elegant tree with willow-like leaves and fine, flaky bark. It grows to a
comparatively modest 60ft/18m, a mere pygmy compared to *A. usambarensis* (*Podocarpus usambarensis*) (z10), that reaches as much as 200ft/60m in its
native habitat – which it shares with the mountain gorilla. The
comparatively slender branches are set with linear leaves.

Araucaria ARAUCARIACEAE
Araucaria bidwillii (z9–11), the Australian bunya-bunya, grows slowly to
80ft/24m, forming in maturity a dome-shaped tree with horizontal
branches drooping at the tips, and dark green leaves, sharply pointed in the
juvenile state; the small, ovate mature leaves grow in overlapping spirals.
The cones are like large pineapples. It is only moderately drought-
resistant, especially when young. It is hardy to 25F/ − 4C, becoming more
frost-tolerant in maturity. It cannot compare in beauty of form with *A.
heterophylla* (*A. excelsa*) (z9–11), the Norfolk Island pine, a tall tree with
symmetrical, near-horizontal branches forming tiers of dark green foliage.

Cedrus deodara

Cedrus PINACEAE

Cedrus deodara (z8–9), the deodar, is a beautiful tree, extremely elegant in youth and of stately habit, with semi-pendant branches, in maturity. In dry climates it grows slowly, and its dark green needles are shorter than in areas where it has ample moisture. Selected cultivars, especially those raised from Afghan or Kashmiri seed, are hardy to z6–8. *C. libani* ssp. *atlantica* (z6–7), the Atlas cedar, is a large tree, fast-growing where there is plenty of moisture but slower in dry conditions, and displaying a characteristic horizontal branching structure at maturity. The short needles are green or gray-green; in some forms, classed as the Glauca Group or blue cedars, they are glaucous-blue. The Atlas cedar is now regarded as a subspecies of the cedar of Lebanon. Cedars should be given a good start in enriched soil if they are to thrive.

Cupressus CUPRESSACEAE

Cupressus arizonica (z7–9), the Arizona cypress, is a variable tree which, in its best forms, such as 'Gareei' or 'Blue Ice,' has silvery to blue-green foliage. It is of medium size and pyramidal form. A light dry soil suits it best, and it needs no additional irrigation where the annual rainfall exceeds 16in/375mm. If overwatered, it may outgrow its root system and blow over; if left unwatered through severe, extended drought, it becomes susceptible to bark beetles, which may even kill it. It is not in any case long-lived. The Monterey cypress, *C. macrocarpa* (z8–9), varies from a stunted, gnarled tree in full coastal exposure on its native California headlands to a massive, tall tree in sheltered inland areas, where it develops a spreading, almost cedar-like habit. It is not very stable in shallow soils. In complete contrast is the Italian cypress, *C. sempervirens* (z8–9), much grown in arid parts of southern Europe, where the narrow, dense 'Stricta' adds its characteristic strong vertical, dark accent to the Mediterranean or Tuscan landscape. A light dry soil suits it best; it needs regular irrigation to establish, but thereafter is very drought tolerant and stands heat well.

Juniperus CUPRESSACEAE

Most junipers are very tolerant of dry soils and periods of drought, and some are even suitable for desert gardens, provided they receive afternoon shade in low-altitude hot valleys; occasional deep irrigation may be needed, but you should allow the soil to dry between soakings. Forms of *Juniperus chinensis* (z4–9) and of *J. sabina* (z3–7) are especially suitable, as are the *J.* × *media* group (z3–7), hybrids between these two species. These alone provide a choice ranging from large shrubs or small trees such as *J. chinensis* 'Kaizuka,' by way of shrubby types such as *J. sabina* 'Arcadia,' to the prostrate 'Buffalo' with bright green, soft feathery branches, or the familiar 'Tamariscifolia.' *J. horizontalis* (z4–9) and its cultivars are also drought-resistant.

Microbiota CUPRESSACEAE

Microbiota decussata (z3–7) is a dwarf, spreading, juniper-like shrub found wild in a single valley in eastern Siberia, but now widely established in cultivation. It has green, scale-like leaves turning russet brown in winter.

Pinus PINACEAE

Some pines do well in the heat of the desert, but need regular deep irrigation even when established. In less hostile climates, they will tolerate dry acid soils, and some, such as *Pinus mugo* and *P. nigra*, are suitable for thin

Cupressus arizonica

soils over chalk. The needles of pines come in bundles of differing numbers according to species. Pines are best raised from seed.

Ranging from the polar regions to the tropics, pines dominate the vegetation in many regions of both the Old and New Worlds; many come from Mexico, such as *P. ayacahuite* (z8–10), a beautiful five-needle pine with pale, glaucous-green foliage and long cylindrical cones. *P. cembroïdes* (z5–9), the pinyon or Mexican nut pine from rocky foothills of Arizona and Mexico, makes a small, round-headed tree. Its needles are normally in threes, whereas those of *P. edulis* (z5–8), the Rocky Mountain pinyon or nut pine, are in twos. The Rocky Mountain pinyon grows slowly, forming a small irregular tree with a flat to rounded crown. The nuts of both the Mexican nut pine and the Rocky Mountain nut pine are edible. *P. monophylla* (z6–9), the single-leaf pinyon pine, is a small, hardy, and drought-resistant tree of high rocky foothills from Idaho to Mexico.

From California and the southwestern United States comes *P. aristata* (z5–7), the bristlecone pine, a small, slow-growing, extremely long-lived five-needle pine with bristly-spiny cones. The western populations are now classed as *P. longaeva*, of which the oldest living specimens are over 5,000 years old. *P. coulteri* (z8–10), the bigcone pine, grows on dry, rocky slopes in California and Baja California. Of moderate growth, with spreading lower branches, it is resistant to heat, drought and wind. The long, bluish-green needles are held in threes; the cylindrical cones are as much as 14in/35cm long. *P. sabiniana* (z8–10), the digger pine, grows on dry slopes in the California foothills and is very resistant to drought. It is a three-needle pine with blue-gray foliage and edible nuts, forming an open crown of thin, whippy branches. *P. torreyana* (z8–10), the Torrey pine or soledad pine, is a gnarled tree on its native California coast and Santa Rosa Island. It does well in desert gardens and grows rapidly to 60ft/18m, keeping a regular candelabra outline if sheltered from wind. The stiff, gray-green to dark green needles are held in fives.

Some pines from the eastern United States are also suitable for dry gardens. For cold areas *P. banksiana* (z2–6), the jack pine, is a tree or gnarled shrub with needles in pairs, suitable for dry or moist soils, but not chalk. *P. strobus* (z3–8), the Weymouth pine or white pine, is widespread in northern and northeastern North America and much planted on the southern English coast. It is a large, fast-growing tree, conical at first and developing a rounded crown in maturity. The needles, in bundles of five, are glaucous green. *P. rigida* (z4–7), the northern pitch pine, grows to 60ft/18m or more, with stiff, spreading, dark green needles in threes. *P. echinata* (z6–9), the short-leaf pine, yellow pine or long-tag pine from the eastern United States, has dark, blue-green needles in pairs. It grows to 100ft/30m or more. *P. virginiana* (z6–8), the scrub pine of the eastern United States, is a small tree with short, paired, stiff needles. It does not thrive on thin chalky soils, but tolerates drought in acid soils.

Japan is the home of several pines suitable for dry soils. *P. densiflora* (z4–7), the Japanese red pine, is a two-needle pine with dense, dark foliage and reddish young bark, similar to the Scots pine. *P. parviflora* (z5–7) is the Japanese white pine, a small tree with deep blue-green needles in fives, growing to a picturesque outline. *P. thunbergii* (z5–8), the Japanese black pine, is another species that readily forms a picturesque outline, with spreading branches and dark green needles in pairs. It does not thrive in very hot desert gardens, but tolerates drought in cooler areas.

Further west, the Himalayan foothills and the near-deserts of the northern Indian subcontinent provide still more pines suitable for dry gardens. *P. eldarica* (*P. brutia* ssp. *eldarica*) (z7–9), the Quetta pine or Eldar pine, is from a region that experiences extremes of temperature both hot and cold, and severe drought. It resembles *P. halepensis*, the Aleppo pine, but is much more cold-hardy. *P. roxburghii* (z9–10), the chir pine or Indian longleaf pine, grows in the Himalayan foothills, where it forms a slender pyramid in youth, spreading outward at maturity, when it is usually around 85ft/26m tall. The long, bright green needles are in bundles of three. It is related to the geographically distant *P. canariensis* (z9–10), the Canary Island pine, which grows rapidly to its mature height of 60–80ft/18–24m, with a narrow silhouette and long, dark bluish-green needles in bundles of three.

Several Mediterranean and southern European pines do well in dry conditions similar to those of their native regions. *P. halepensis* (z8–10), the Aleppo pine, Mediterranean pine, or Jerusalem pine, is recommended as the best pine for desert gardens. It grows fairly rapidly to a height of 30–50ft/9–15m, with a rounded or irregular, billowing crown. The fresh green needles are usually in pairs. *P. pinaster* (z8–10), the maritime pine or Bournemouth pine, is cultivated in southwestern France as a source of resin

and turpentine and for stabilizing sand dunes, growing fast even there. It is
an open, medium-sized tree with gray-green paired needles. *P. pinea* (z8–
10), the Italian stone pine or umbrella pine, is as characteristic of the
Mediterranean region as the Italian cypress of the Tuscan plains, forming a
wide, flat or umbrella-shaped crown, shown to best advantage when the
trunk is clean-trimmed to a tall stem. The bright green needles are held in
pairs, and the large cones contain edible nuts.

Pinus nigra

For cooler climates the Corsican pine, *P. nigra* var. *maritima*, is a large
tree with gray-green needles, widely grown as a forestry tree and tolerant of
almost all soils and climates down to z5. *P. heldreichii* var. *leucodermis* (z6–8),
the Bosnian pine, is a medium-sized tree of dense, rounded habit, with
paired needles of very dark green, and small cones that are bright blue in
their first year. It is especially suitable for dry, cool climates. *P. mugo* (z3–7),
the mountain pine, is a very hardy shrub or small tree, densely bushy, with
short, dark green, paired needles. It ranges from very dwarf or prostrate
forms to small tree size. One of the toughest of all is *P. sylvestris* (z2–7), the
Scots pine, which has rust-red bark displayed on a tall trunk; the paired
needles are bluish to gray-green.

Podocarpus PODOCARPACEAE

Some species are drought-resistant enough to thrive with moderate
irrigation even in desert gardens, provided they are grown in the shade.
Podocarpus henkelii (z10–11), the falcate yellowwood, is a South African
species with pendant branches, and long, drooping, often curved needles
after the style of the hardier *P. saligna*. *P. macrophyllus* (z8–10), the
kusamaki or big-leaf podocarp, has large and comparatively broad,
polished, bright green needles packed in spirals along the stems.

Palms & Cycads

OPPOSITE ABOVE The cycads are
a fascinating group of plants
suggestive of both palms and
ferns, but belonging to neither
family. This *Cycas revoluta* is still
comparatively young, for it has
yet to form much of a stem, but
already the radiating fronds
make a bold visual statement.

OPPOSITE BELOW The contrasts of
bright sunshine and near-black
shadow throw the arching
fronds of the Canary Island date
palm, *Phoenix canariensis*, into
sharp relief above this lush green
planting, which suggests the
atmosphere of an oasis enclosed
from the harsh outer world.

Few trees give a garden a tropical or desert aspect in quite the same way as
palms. Their often dramatic silhouette, the trunk topped by spraying
fronds, is associated in our minds with Mediterranean, California, or Gulf
Coast resorts, and also calls to mind the more extreme contrasts of the oasis
with the desert sands.

The true palms fall into two groups: those with feather-like leaves,
composed of leaflets set along a central midrib, and the fan palms with
leaflets radiating from a central point. Cycads often resemble feather
palms. Another group of plants, which I have included among trees and
shrubs, is sometimes given the nickname palm or sword palm; these are the
cordylines, yuccas and allied plants, members of the Agave family. They
have rapier or sword leaves in tufts at the ends of the branches.

Palms can be tricky to move, though with care even quite large
specimens can be transplanted, giving almost instant maturity to a new
planting. They should be moved only when the soil is warm enough to
encourage the growth of new roots, for the old ones die when the palms are
lifted. They should be replanted as much as 3ft/90cm deeper than their
previous planting depth, and must be firmly guyed so that the trunk will
not rock, or the newly forming roots will not take hold. Finally, the leaves
should be tied up around the crown and left this way for a year after
replanting to protect the growing point.

Archontophoenix PALMAE
Archontophoenix cunninghamiana (z10–11), one of the king palms, is also
known as the piccabeen palm. It is an Australian native of stately habit,
very fast-growing to as much as 50ft/15m, and easy from seed but tricky to
transplant. Beneath the long, graceful fronds appear sprays of shell-pink
flowers, in the fall.

Brahea PALMAE
Brahea armata (*Erythea armata*) (z9–11), the Mexican blue palm, blue hesper
palm, gray goddess, blue fan palm, or rock palm from Baja California,
stands greater extremes of heat, cold (to 14F/−10C), and wind than many
palms. It grows slowly to 30ft/9m, with stiff, waxy, blue-gray fronds
forming a crown spreading to 10ft/3m. In summer it bears fragrant,
whitish flower garlands, which develop into hard, russet-red fruits. *Brahea
edulis* is similar, with paler, silvery blue fronds.

Butia PALMAE
Butia capitata (*Cocos australis*, *C. campestris*) (z9–11), the Pindo palm, Yatay
palm, jelly palm, or Brazil butia palm, is especially attractive when young,
with its recurving, gray-green fronds. It grows slowly to an average height

of 10ft/3m, which makes it a good choice for a large tub or planter. It is hardy to 14F/−10C, and even in desert conditions is moderately drought-tolerant; it is said to be resistant to Texas root rot. Female plants produce edible, pineapple-flavored fruits.

Chamaedorea PALMAE
Chamaedorea elegans (z8–11), the parlor palm or goodluck palm, grows to only 6ft/1.8m or so. It has very deep green fronds composed of up to twenty pairs of long, narrow pinnae. The flowers are pale yellow.

Chamaerops PALMAE
Chamaerops humilis (z7–11), the Mediterranean fan palm, is one of the most suitable for colder gardens and for small spaces, or as a container plant. It forms a rounded head of stiff, fanlike, gray-green leaves on thorny, suckering stems to 10–20ft/3–6m, or it can be trained to a single stem. It tolerates spells of drought, but prefers rich soil, and is hardy to 5F/−15C.

Cycas CYCADACEAE
Cycas revoluta (z9–11), the sago palm or Japanese fern, despite its looks, is neither a palm nor a fern. The deeply cut, glossy, herringbone leaves form a whorl or spiral around a cone at the center of the short trunk; offsets develop to create a multistemmed plant which slowly grows to 5–10ft/1.5–3m. Once mature it tolerates long periods of drought and neglect, but at first needs moderate or even ample irrigation in very dry climates. It is said to be hardy to 5F/−15C, but the foliage is badly damaged below 20F/−7C; it also dislikes scorching sun. It is very slow-growing.

Phoenix PALMAE
Phoenix canariensis (z9–11), the Canary Island date palm or pineapple palm, is another good palm for a container or a small garden, for although it will reach 60ft/18m, it may take eighty years to do so. At 13ft/3.5m it will have a crown spread of 20–30ft/6–9m. The fronds are composed of many dark green, polished, narrow filaments. It bears orange dates, which mature to brown, in autumn. Damaged by temperatures below 20F/−7C, it is slow to recover. It tolerates considerable drought, especially in the cool season. *P. dactylifera* (z9–11), the date palm or Arab date, is a more slender, open palm than *P. canariensis*, with a rough gray trunk, and a "feather duster" crown of gray-green fronds. It grows slowly to 60ft/18m, with a crown spread of 25ft/7.5m, and its natural tendency is to form basal offshoots that develop into a multistemmed tree. To enjoy the sweet dates, which ripen in the fall, male and female plants are needed. In desert conditions it needs moderate to deep irrigation on a regular basis, though it can withstand long periods of neglect. It is ideal for coastal gardens.

Syagrus PALMAE
Syagrus romanzoffiana (*Arecastrum romanzoffianum*, *Cocos romanzoffiana*, *C. plumosa*) (z9–11), the South American queen palm, has feathery, polished green fronds forming a crown 10–14ft/3–4m wide, and a smooth, gray, ringed trunk. In desert conditions it grows reasonably fast to 20–23ft/6–7m, but may reach twice that. The small plumes of flowers are followed by miniature coconuts. In the garden it is a civilized palm making little litter, but it needs shelter from searing hot winds and from cold, which turn the fronds yellow and dry. The leaves are scorched by 25F/−4C, while the plant itself is damaged by 20F/−7C and will take a full season to recover.

Chamaerops humilis

Trachycarpus PALMAE

Trachycarpus fortunei (*Chamaerops fortunei*) (z7–11), the windmill palm of China and northern Burma, is a small palm, seldom seen over 15ft/4.5m in height with a crown 7–10ft/2–3m wide, though it can reach 40ft/12m. The upper part of the trunk is clad in the matted fibers remaining from the old leaf bases; the leaves themselves form large, almost circular fans on long stems at the top of the trunk. Though tough, they can be frayed by high winds. In flower and fruit it is handsome, the large arching sprays of many small, yellow flowers maturing to blue-black fruits.

Washingtonia PALMAE

Washingtonia filifera (*W. filamentosa, Pritchardia filifera*) (z9–11), the California fan palm, desert fan palm, or petticoat palm, in contrast to the slender-stemmed phoenix palms, develops a heavy trunk. It can grow to 80ft/24m, though 20–40ft/6–12m is more usual, with a crown spread of 15ft/4.5m, composed of circular, stiff, gray-green fans of deeply pleated leaves fringed with hairy filaments, held on stems set with hooked thorns. There are two strains: the California desert type, which retains the dead leaves down the stem, and the Arizona type which is self-cleaning. Long sprays of abundant, small white flowers spring from the crown in summer, followed by blue-black fruits on female plants. The desert fan palm is one of the most suitable for very dry climates, surviving without attention where the annual rainfall exceeds 10in/250mm.

  W. robusta (*W. gracilis, W. sonorae, Pritchardia robusta*) (z9–11) is the Mexican fan palm, Mexican washingtonia, or thread palm, distinguished from *W. filifera* by its greener leaves and the reddish streak along the underside of the leaf stalk at the trunk end. Rapid-growing to 80–100ft/24–30m, it forms a slender trunk and has a crown spread of 13ft/3.5m. Sprays of tiny white flowers are followed by small dark fruits on female plants. The plants move well with ample watering and feeding. Older plants tolerate periods of neglect. It is damaged by temperatures below 25F/−4C.

Climbers

OPPOSITE ABOVE The best forms of *Jasminum polyanthum* have pink buds opening to propeller-shaped white flowers endowed with a powerful, sweet perfume, evocative of tropical nights. A single small plant in a pot is enough to fill a room with scent; a mature plant will sweeten a whole garden.

OPPOSITE BELOW Often seen trained onto a pergola or house wall, *Wisteria sinensis* can also be allowed to roam free into a tree. Here it has escaped from the original constraints of its supporting arches to soar aloft. The lavender tresses have a wholesome, sweet, beanfield fragrance.

Gardeners in the Mediterranean, in California, and in other areas with warm climates make generous use of climbers to add color to their planting. A stroll through a resort on the Costa del Sol or in Beverly Hills, for example, will take you past vivid blue morning glories (*Ipomoea* spp.) swathing tall trees, pale blue plumbago soothing the stridency of magenta bougainvillea, orange trumpet vines, and yellow bougainvillea striking patterns against a whitewashed wall. Further inland in Spain, a visit to the gardens of the Alhambra in Granada is made magical by the intoxicating perfume of the *Jasminum grandiflorum* that drapes every wall.

Gardeners in cold climates are not quite so well served, but the European honeysuckle (*Lonicera periclymenum*) yields to none in the sweetness of its perfume, wafting far, especially on the evening air, and the Boston ivy (*Parthenocissus tricuspidata*) and Virginia creeper (*P. quinquefolia*) are unrivaled in the brilliance of their autumn colors. Even in areas not usually considered mild, there are surprises; just a few days before I wrote these lines, I came upon a superb specimen of *Rosa banksiae* 'Lutea' trained on an iron fence in the middle of London, its pale green foliage almost hidden beneath clusters of yellow pompons, contrasting with the vivid blue of a ceanothus nearby. Both were obviously quite unaffected by three exceptionally dry years.

Wherever the summer sun is hot, a pergola can provide grateful shade. The classic pergola covering is a grapevine, but wisteria is another excellent choice; both are deciduous, allowing the winter sun to shine through their leafless branches. So long as you avoid its stinging leaves, *Wigandia caracasana* makes a good pergola plant for hotter climates, while a jasmine or passion flower (*Passiflora* spp.), would be other possibilities, as well as the Banksian rose.

Antigonon POLYGONACEAE

Antigonon leptopus (z9–11), the Queen's wreath, coral vine, or Confederate vine, from Mexico, bears its shocking pink flowers in summer. It is a tendril climber with heart-shaped to arrowhead leaves, that becomes dormant in periods of frost or winter drought. It has the ability to regenerate from the roots after the top growth is killed by frost; mulch the roots for protection if temperatures are likely to fall below 20F/− 7C. As it withstands hot sun, it can be planted on a trellis or pillar, or used as shade cover for plants that are sensitive to extreme heat.

Bignonia BIGNONIACEAE

The cross vine of the southeastern United States, *Bignonia capreolata* (z6–9) is a vigorous evergreen tendril climber reaching 25ft/7.5m, enhancing its climbing abilities by hooks or adhesive pads at the tips of the tendrils. The

flowers are typical bignonia trumpets, orange with flared lobes, paler inside, opening in summer. The common name derives from the pattern shown in a cross-section of the cut stem.

Bougainvillea NYCTAGINACEAE

Bougainvillea (z9–11) is one of the most characteristic climbers in hot climates such as the Mediterranean, California, the Indian subcontinent and elsewhere. The showy part of the flower is formed by the papery bracts surrounding the true flowers; few climbers are better at providing massed color in hot, clashing or subtle shades. *B. spectabilis* is considered the hardiest species and the most suitable for areas where the summers are cool; typically, it has bright purple bracts. Other species are *B. peruviana* and *B. glabra*, from Brazil, but it is the hybrids such as those of the group *B.* × *buttiana*, and the cultivars that are most often seen. The original *B.* × *buttiana* 'Mrs. Butt' is bright crimson turning to purple – it is known as 'Crimson Lake' in the United States. All except *B. spectabilis* enjoy hot summers in full sun and are drought-tolerant; indeed, too much moisture or feeding will mean fewer flowers. However, extreme drought results in leaf fall.

There are hundreds of cultivars; the following are a selection from those that do well in hot dry areas in the United States or equivalent climates. 'Barbara Karst' is the hardiest red, able to stand a little frost; the color is red in shade, but nearer to magenta in sun. 'Scarlett O'Hara' ('San Diego Red') is similar, with larger, vivid red bracts, opening later. 'Texan Dawn' is cerise pink and thrives in hot places, but needs high humidity. 'Rainbow Gold' has burnt orange bracts, and 'Mrs. Helen McLean' ('Orange King') orange turning to copper and pink; it is frost tender and does well in long hot summers. 'Golden Glow' ('California Gold') is a *B.* × *buttiana* type which bears its yellow bracts over a long season; it is less hardy than the reds. 'Jamaica White' is tinged with pink in cooler weather. Red 'La Jolla' is shrubby and reasonably frost hardy; other shrubby cultivars are 'Crimson Jewel' and magenta-purple 'Convent' ('Panama Queen'). There are several doubles, including 'Mahara Off White' ('Cherry Blossom') with pink-tipped bracts, 'Mahara Orange' ('Tahitian Gold') which fades to pink, 'Mahara Pink' ('Pink Champagne'), and 'Mahara Red' with massive heads of magenta red. Bougainvilleas climb by the thorns on the leaf axils. Propagation is by ripe heel cuttings or half-ripe cuttings.

Campsis BIGNONIACEAE

The trumpet vines are deciduous, more or less efficient self-clinging climbers with brightly colored flowers of typical bignonia outline, and ash-like leaves. The Chinese trumpet vine, *Campsis grandiflora* (z7–9), is a not very efficient self-sticking climber to 30ft/9m with showy orange trumpets, paler on the flared lobes, in later summer. *C. radicans* (z5–9) is the trumpet creeper, trumpet vine or trumpet honeysuckle of the southeastern United States, a rampant self-sticker to 40ft/12m, bearing its vivid orange-scarlet trumpets from midsummer to the first frosts. There is a beautiful butter-yellow form, *C. r.* f. *flava* (z5–9). The trumpet vine is almost a weed in temperate zones, but is valuable in arid zones for its summer greenery, bright long-lasting color, and tolerance of drought – in desert conditions it needs only a little irrigation in summer. The hybrid *C.* × *tagliabuana* (z6–9) is the most suitable trumpet vine for cool climates as long as it is given full sun, to encourage it to be generous with its salmon-scarlet trumpets borne in showy clusters on growth to 30ft/9m.

Campsis grandiflora

Celastrus CELASTRACEAE

Celastrus scandens (z4–8) is a bittersweet from North America, with vigorously twining stems to 25ft/7.5m, pointed leaves turning yellow in the fall, and showy seed capsules on female plants, the orange lining setting off vivid scarlet seeds.

Clytostoma BIGNONIACEAE

Clytostoma callistegioïdes (*Bignonia callistegioïdes, Bignonia speciosa, B. violacea* of gardens, *Pandorea lindleyana*) (z9–11), the violet trumpet vine or love-charm, is a tendril climber growing rapidly to 13–20ft/3.5–6m, bearing abundant lavender trumpets streaked with violet in spring, amid lush green foliage. In the hottest places it should be given some protection from the full glare of the sun. *C. binatum* (*C. purpurea, Bignonia purpurea*) (z9–11) is an evergreen climber with leaves composed of two leaflets, and wide bignonia trumpets of mauve with white throat.

Fallopia POLYGONACEAE

Fallopia baldschuanica (*Polygonum baldschuanicum*) (z5–9), the Russian vine or mile-a-minute vine, is a rampant climber to 40ft/12m, with pale green, heart-shaped leaves, and large clusters of many tiny whitish, pink-tinged flowers in summer and autumn.

Ficus MORACEAE

The creeping fig or climbing fig, *Ficus pumila* (*F. repens, F. stipulata*) (z8–10), is a self-clinging climber with greedy, invasive roots and small, dark green, heart-shaped leaves neatly two-ranked in the juvenile stage, becoming much larger on adult plants. 'Minima' is even smaller in leaf and remains in the juvenile stage longer; it does well even in quite dense shade. 'Variegata' will lighten a shady place.

Gelsemium LOGANIACEAE

Gelsemium sempervirens (z6–9), the Carolina jasmine or Confederate jasmine (not related to the true jasmines) is a slender, twining climber to 20ft/6m, with glossy, pointed, light green leaves, and fragrant yellow funnel flowers with orange throat in late winter and early spring, or later in cool climates. Once established it is drought-tolerant. The very similar *G. rankinii* (z7–9) lacks scent, but will bloom heavily in late autumn.

Hardenbergia LEGUMINOSAE

The native wisterias of Australia are evergreen climbers bearing sprays of small pea flowers on growth to 10ft/3m. Typically *Hardenbergia comptoniana* (z9–11) has violet-blue flowers, but there is also a pink form, *H. c. rosea* (z10–11). The leaves are composed of three or five leaflets. *H. violacea* (z10–11) has a single leaflet to each leaf, and its violet-blue, yellow-blotched flowers open during winter and spring. 'Happy Wanderer' is paler lavender with primrose blotch, and there are also white and pink forms.

Hedera ARALIACEAE

Hedera algeriensis (z9–11), the Algerian ivy, withstands some drought in desert areas, especially in winter. 'Gloire de Marengo' is a popular variety with leaves marbled with gray and white on green, less frost-resistant than the plain green type. For a hardier variegated ivy with large leaves, turn to

Hardenbergia comptoniana

the Persian ivy, *H. colchica*, (z6–9) which has two fine cultivars in 'Dentata Variegata' with green leaves boldly edged with primrose and cream, and 'Sulphur Heart' ('Paddy's Pride'), where the creamy marbling is at the center of the leaf. The plain green Persian ivy is also a handsome thing in its own right, while all-green 'Dentata' is slightly paler in tone and larger in leaf. The common ivy, *H. helix* (z5–9), is also reasonably drought tolerant, even in desert conditions. There are dozens, if not hundreds, of cultivars with varying leaf size and shape, and with different variegations, to choose from. One of the most valuable for large-scale ground cover is *H. hibernica* z5–9), the Irish ivy.

Ipomoea CONVOLVULACEAE
Gardeners in cold-winter areas cosset the brilliant ultramarine blue morning glories as annuals, but some species grow as perennial climbers in hot dry climates, wreathing fences, walls and trees with their twining stems. In fact care needs to be taken to control their growth in some such climates as they may become very invasive. *Ipomoea purpurea* (z10), the common morning glory, has wide funnels of rich purple-blue on growth to 13ft/ 3.5m, while *I. tricolor* (*I. violacea*) (z10) varies from lilac to blue-purple; the seed strain 'Heavenly Blue' is turquoise. It grows to 14ft/4m. The seeds are hallucinogenic. The blue dawn flower, *I. indica* (*I. learii*) (z10), has blue or violet flowers in clusters, and is very vigorous, capable of reaching 40ft/12m.

Jasminum OLEACEAE
Jasmines are a tropical and subtropical genus, with a few species hardy enough to grow in northern temperate gardens. The name comes from the Arabic *yasmin*; in Arab countries jasmines twine around fences and over shading trellises, filling the air with their perfume, which is most eloquent at dawn and dusk. The tropical jasmines stand little or no frost, but given sufficient warmth, most will flower virtually all year. *Jasminum grandiflorum* (z9–10) is the white-flowered jasmine, native to Arabia, which is widely grown in Spanish, Riviera and Italian gardens (also further east, in Israel and Jordan for example), filling the air with its sweet perfume. It grows to 20ft/6m or more. It is cultivated not only for its garden value, but also for its essential oil, as the name of a popular cultivar, 'De Grasse,' suggests (Grasse is the southern French town where lavender and other fragrant plants are grown for the commercial extraction of oils). Further east, these oils are called *attar* or *ittar*, and sold in the bazaars in tiny bottles for just a few cents. For cooler climates, *J. officinale* (z8–10), the summer jasmine, is a classic climber. A vigorous twiner reaching 20–30ft/6–9m, it bears a succession of delectably fragrant starry white flowers over a long summer season. In cool climates it will benefit from the shelter of a sunny wall. *J. o. f. affine* (z8–10) has larger flowers suffused with pink. There are also two summer jasmines with variegated leaves: the showy, gold-splashed 'Aureum' (z8–10), and more subtle white-marked 'Argenteovariegatum' (z8–10). Unusually, *J. beesianum* (z8–10) has rather small, velvety crimson blooms, only slightly fragrant. They open in early summer on a rather bushy plant. The hybrid *J. × stephanense* (z8–10) is a vigorous twiner to 25ft/7.5m, with pink flowers in summer, and leaves that tend to become white-mottled.

There are several less familiar jasmines for warmer zones, most deliciously fragrant. *J. angulare* (z9–10), from South Africa, bears its very sweet-scented white flowers chiefly in late summer amid dark, evergreen foliage. The semi-twining stems need support and reach 10ft/3m. The Madeiran *J. azoricum* (z9–10) is more twining to 14ft/4m, with slightly smaller, fragrant white flowers opening from purple-tinted buds from summer into fall. *J. nitidum*, from the Admiralty Islands in the Pacific, is slow-growing, but ultimately quite tall. It has large, pure white flowers faintly pink-tinted at first, powerfully scented and shaped like a propellor or the sails of a windmill. The Australian *J. simplicifolium* ssp. *sauvissimum* (z9–10) has very narrow leaves, and fragrant, white, pink-flushed flowers in late summer. Returning to species from the northern hemisphere, *J. dispermum* (z8–10), from the Himalayas, has twining stems set with clusters of scented white, pink-flushed flowers in summer.

Much more familiar is *J. polyanthum* (z9–10), which bears large clusters of white flowers, often touched with pink or crimson in long-pointed bud, in winter in frost-free areas and from spring to summer in cooler climates. It is also popular as a pot plant to flower indoors in winter. The flowers are powerfully and deliciously fragrant; even a small plant will fill a room with its perfume. Unchecked by frost or pruning, it can reach 25ft/7.5m. The queen of tender jasmines, though, is *J. sambac* (z9–10), a native of Arabia and India. It must have a winter temperature of at least 50F/10C to flower well; given this, it is seldom without its large, white, fragrant flowers amid evergreen foliage. It was introduced to Europe by the Arabs many centuries ago, when they ruled Spain (the last Muslim kingdom, Granada, fell in 1492). 'Maid of Orléans' has the largest flowers of all, with extra, overlapping petals, and the usual wonderful perfume. 'Grand Duke of Tuscany' is a fully double form with smaller flowers packed with petals.

In addition to the winter jasmine, which has been described in the section on trees and shrubs, there are some yellow-flowered climbing

Jasminum sambac

jasmines well worth yard space. Almost as familiar in Mediterranean gardens as *J. grandiflorum* (z9–10) is the primrose jasmine, *J. mesnyi* (*J. primulinum*) (z8–9), which bears bright clear yellow, semi-double flowers in spring on 15ft/4.5m stems. The large, three-leafletted leaves are almost evergreen. Its only fault is to lack fragrance. *J. floridum* (z8–11) is an evergreen species with clusters of small but very abundant yellow flowers in late summer and early fall. It is a scrambler growing to 8ft/2.5m. Unusually among yellow jasmines, *J. odoratissimum* (z9–10) has small but very abundant flowers with a rich carnation-like perfume, borne from late summer to late fall. It will reach 6ft/1.8m or more.

Lonicera CAPRIFOLIACEAE

The brightest honeysuckles have no perfume, but several of the most poignantly scented are also drought-tolerant, as if to compensate for their comparative lack of color. *Lonicera etrusca* (z8–9) is a Mediterranean species with cream flowers aging to soft yellow; 'Michael Rosse' is a very fine form with large heads of flower, while 'Superba' has smaller, brighter yellow flowers. Its hybrid offspring *L. × italica* (the other parent probably *L. caprifolium* (z6–8), the early cream honeysuckle), is commonly offered as *L. × americana* (which it is not); it has pink-tubed cream flowers opening from pink-red buds.

Though it can become overbearing in congenial conditions, *L. japonica* 'Halliana' (z5–9), Hall's honeysuckle, is valued by gardeners in drought areas for its vigor and willingness to adapt to difficult conditions, including poor soil, hot winds, and sun. It grows rampantly to 30ft/9m or more, once established, and is ideal for quick shade on a fence or pergola, but it can be a danger to a tree, choking the host branches with its twining stems. In hot

BELOW LEFT *Lonicera japonica* 'Halliana'

BELOW RIGHT *Lonicera periclymenum* 'Serotina'

climates it flowers with abandon from spring, but elsewhere its first blooms do not appear until midsummer. It will continue bearing a few sprays of creamy flowers, aging to buff-yellow, throughout the summer and fall. It is evergreen, or semi-evergreen in cold areas. *L. j.* var. *repens* (z5–9) has sultry dark green foliage, glaucous-backed, and smaller flowers, dusky crimson in bud, opening to show white lobes contrasting with the red tube, and aging to buff-yellow. *L. periclymenum* (z5–9), the woodbine or common honeysuckle of woodland margins in Europe and North Africa, appreciates shade at the roots, but is tolerant of dry soils. The flowers are larger than those of *L. japonica*, their fragrance filling the air with sweetness, powerfully at dawn and dusk. 'Belgica,' the early Dutch honeysuckle, has straw-yellow flowers stained with red-purple outside fading to pink, on bushy growth; 'Serotina,' the late Dutch honeysuckle, flowers later and longer, its petals pinkish within and richly colored with rose madder where touched by the sun. 'Graham Thomas' is a fine new selection with large creamy flowers, reaching 20ft/6m or so.

Macfadyena BIGNONIACEAE

Macfadyena unguis-cati (*Bignonia unguis-cati*, *B. tweediana*, *Doxantha unguis-cati*) (z9–10), the cat's claw vine or yellow trumpet, is an evergreen or partly deciduous vine from Central America that forms underground tubers, enabling it to resist long spells of drought once established. It is also very tolerant of heat. Its fierce little triple tendrils cling to almost any surface. The large yellow trumpets of typical bignonia outline are borne in spring on the old growths. It will resist cold down to about 10F/−12C if the growths are well ripened by summer sun, and grows to 30ft/9m or more.

Parthenocissus VITACEAE

The Boston ivy and Virginia creeper have small adhesive pads at the tips of the leaf tendrils, so that they can cling unaided to walls, fences, poles and trees. They are ideal for covering a large wall or masking a stretch of utilitarian fencing. If you decide to fling them into a tree, be sure it can cope with their vigorous growth; a mature silver birch would be ideal to contrast with their vivid fall colors. If you can, plant them where the autumn sun will gleam through the translucent, glowing leaves. The Virginia creeper, *Parthenocissus quinquefolia* (*Vitis quinquefolia*) (z4–9), is a vigorous climber to 40ft/12m or more, native of eastern North America. The thin-textured leaves formed of fine leaflets color brilliantly in the fall. *P. tricuspidata* (*Ampelopsis tricuspidata*) (z5–8), the Boston ivy, is even more vigorous than the Virginia creeper, and coarser, with thick, glossy, three-lobed leaves that also color vividly in the fall. 'Veitchii,' the form originally introduced from the Far East, has purplish young growths. Its vigor makes it ideal for masking high walls, where it can grow to 60ft/18m or more. If a newly planted Boston ivy is unwilling to cling to its intended support, the suckers tipping the tendrils may have dried up: cut it back hard to encourage soft new growth.

Passiflora PASSIFLORACEAE

The passion flowers were so named by Spanish priests who, finding *Passiflora caerulea* growing wild in South America, fancied that the intricate blooms represented the instruments of Christ's passion. The ten tepals are ten apostles, the corona or ring of filaments within the tepals is the crown of thorns, the five stamens stand for the five wounds, and the three stigmas the three nails. The blue passion flower, *Passiflora caerulea* (z7–10), retains its deep green, divided leaves in mild winter areas, and like many passion flowers will grow from below ground if frost kills the top growths. Undamaged by cold, it will grow to 30ft/9m or more; even after a severe winter, one season's growth may be as much as 15ft/4.5m. The striking flowers, with corona zoned in rich purple, white and blue, surrounded by white tepals, are borne over a long summer season; in hot climates, or following exceptional summers in cooler areas, orange ovoid fruits may form. There is an exquisite white form, 'Constance Elliott' (z8–10). *P. × belotii* (*P. × alatocaerulea*, *P. pfordtii*) (z8–10) grows rapidly to 20–30ft/6–9m, attaching itself by both tendrils and aerial rootlets to make a dense cover with its three-lobed leaves. The fragrant flowers, similar to those of *P. caerulea*, vary from ice-white or lavender to deep purple, and are borne sporadically from spring into summer. This passion flower needs a reasonable soil, but will even survive in desert conditions with moderate irrigation; a climate that suits citrus is ideal for it. With only mild frost it loses its leaves; at 20F/−7C, it will lose its top growth, but should quickly recover from below ground; at 10F/−12C it may be killed outright.

Passiflora quadrangularis

The granadilla or passion fruit, *P. edulis* (z8–10), thrives in a frost-free climate, though if the roots are well protected it will stand a mild frost. Three-lobed leaves are borne on strong growth to 20ft/6m or so. The corona of the large white flowers is formed of curly white, violet-zoned filaments; the fruits that follow are the purplish, egg-shaped passion fruits widely available in shops. The giant granadilla, *P. quadrangularis* (z9–10), has striking large, cupped flowers, in white, pink or mauve with a corona composed of very long, rippling filaments banded with purple. The large yellow fruits look somewhat like melons and are used to make a cooling drink. It grows to 20ft/6m and needs a frost-free climate.

Podranea BIGNONIACEAE
Podranea ricasoliana (*Tecoma ricasoliana*) (z9–11), the pink trumpet vine, is a deciduous climber with large clusters of fragrant pink trumpets, striated with deeper pink, in the fall. It can grow to 33ft/10m.

Passiflora × belotii

Rosa ROSACEAE
Rosa banksiae (z7–9), Lady Banks's rose or Banksian rose, is a vigorous rose with green, thornless, scandent stems, light green leaves, and clusters of many small flowers in spring. The first form to be introduced to cultivation in the west from China was the double white, the flowers like little rosettes endowed with a delicate violet perfume. *R. b.* var. *normalis* (z7–9) is the wild, single white form, and 'Lutescens' (z7–9) has fragrant, single, soft yellow flowers. 'Lutea' (z7–9) is the double yellow form, exceptionally pretty but only lightly scented.

Senecio COMPOSITAE
Senecio mikanioïdes (*Delairea odorata*) (z10–11), the German ivy, has yellow rayless flower heads in winter, and semi-succulent evergreen leaves. It can grow to 20ft/6m.

Solanum SOLANACEAE
Solanum crispum (z8–9) is a scrambling or semi-climbing potato with evergreen or semi-evergreen foliage on stems growing to 20ft/6m. The showy violet-purple flowers, enhanced with the usual yellow "beak" of stamens, are borne in loose clusters over a long summer-to-fall season, especially in the cultivar 'Glasnevin' (z7–9). The twining *S. jasminoïdes*

Passiflora caerulea

(z8–9) has slender stems growing to 30ft/9m, thin-textured leaves, and open sprays of pale slate-blue flowers in summer and fall. The white form 'Album' is especially pretty with its yellow-beaked flowers. *S. pensile* (z9–10) has darker green leaves than *S. jasminoïdes*, and amethyst-blue flowers with a white central star, followed by pale violet fruits.

Tecoma BIGNONIACEAE
Tecoma stans (z9–11) is a bushy climber with pale green pinnate leaves and clusters of fragrant yellow trumpets over a long summer to fall season. It grows to 13ft/4m or so.

Tecomaria BIGNONIACEAE
The trumpet vine family turns up yet again in *Tecomaria capensis* (z9–11), a South African species with self-clinging twining stems and brilliant scarlet trumpets in the fall and winter. Selected forms have been named: they include 'Apricot,' bright red 'Coccinea,' yolk-yellow 'Lutea' and pale coral 'Salmonea.'

Thunbergia ACANTHACEAE
Thunbergia alata (z10–11), the black-eyed Susan, is an annual climber raised from seed to reach 10ft/3m, with black-centered bright orange flowers; it also comes in softer yellow. The beautiful *T. grandiflora* (z10–11) is a climber from India, with large violet-blue flowers and evergreen foliage. It grows to 20ft/6m and is best propagated from cuttings.

Trachelospermum APOCYNACEAE
Trachelospermum asiaticum (z8–9), the asiatic jasmine, ground jasmine, or dwarf star jasmine, will stand some drought in winter in desert conditions, where it will need moderate irrigation in summer. In less extreme conditions, it is reasonably drought tolerant. It is a twining climber with neat, polished, evergreen foliage as the background to the sweetly fragrant, starry, cream flowers that age to soft buff-yellow, appearing in summer and fall. The star jasmine, *T. jasminoïdes* (z8–9), is not quite so drought-resistant. It has bolder foliage and larger, purer white flowers with the same delicious perfume, in summer and fall. 'Variegatum' is a handsome foliage plant with leaves marbled cream, flushed with pink and crimson in cold weather.

Wigandia HYDROPHYLLACEAE
Wigandia caracasana (z10–11), the Caracas creeper or Caracas big-leaf, is a semi-evergreen climber with very large leaves, as much as 18in/45cm long and almost as wide, covered with stinging hairs. The rich mauve flowers, held in clusters, open in summer. The Caracas creeper can be increased by seed and grows to 14ft/4m or so.

Wisteria LEGUMINOSAE
Drought-tolerant once established in cool climates or those where winter rainfall is plentiful, wisterias need moderate to ample irrigation in desert conditions. The Japanese *Wisteria floribunda* (z5–9) has clockwise-twining stems up to 30ft/9m, and slender tresses of lavender-mauve flowers in early summer. In parts of the southeastern United States it is very vigorous and may become an invasive weed. 'Multijuga' has exceptionally long racemes, occasionally as much as 6ft/1.8m and commonly 36in/90cm long. There are also several color forms: 'Alba' and the newer 'Snowstorm' in white,

lilac-pink 'Rosea' ('Honko'), clear pink 'Pink Ice' and pink-budded 'Peaches and Cream,' which opens to white. 'Violacea Plena' has double lilac-blue flowers. In Europe, the Chinese wisteria, *W. sinensis* (z5–8), is even more vigorous than the Japanese, reaching as much as 100ft/30m and further distinguished by its counterclockwise twining stems. The lilac-mauve flowers are more fragrant than those of the Japanese wisteria and normally open all at once the length of the raceme, whereas the Japanese opens in succession from base to tip. The white Chinese wisteria, 'Alba,' is especially fragrant, and the more recent 'Caroline,' with deep blue-violet flowers, is also sweetly scented. One of the Chinese wisteria's failings is a tendency not to flower in youth. Sometimes this is due to over-rich soil, leading to leafy growth at the expense of bloom. Varieties such as 'Prematura' and 'Prematura Alba' are said to be more reliable in flowering from an early age. *W. × formosa* (z5–9) is the name given to crosses between the Japanese and Chinese wisterias. 'Issai' is a lilac-flowered cultivar with shorter tresses than the Japanese wisteria, and 'Kokkuryu' ('Black Dragon') has double, deep purple flowers.

Wisterias are ideal for training on pergolas or arches, where they provide welcome shade. On a wall, they need careful training to allow each of the tresses of flower to hang free. Wisterias can also be allowed to grow naturally into supporting trees, though their vigor calls for a host of matching size. The lilac-mauve varieties combine delightfully with the yellow Banksian rose, which flowers at much the same season, and in mild climates can be grown free-standing or in a host tree.

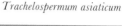

Trachelospermum asiaticum

Perennials & Ephemerals

OPPOSITE ABOVE The pink
Mexican primrose or pajarito,
Oenothera speciosa 'Rosea,' bears
its pink cups on slender stems set
with narrow leaves, blooming in
spring in desert regions.
Spreading far and wide by
underground roots, it is ideally
suited to naturalistic desert or
wild plantings.

OPPOSITE BELOW The Afghan
sage, *Perovskia atriplicifolia*, grows
in dry mountainous regions from
Afghanistan to Tibet. 'Blue
Spire' is a fine hybrid with a
long succession of airy spires, the
bright violet-blue flowers
enhanced by white stems and
gray foliage.

Although "perennial" and "ephemeral" might seem wholly opposite concepts, the plants that they exemplify do have similarities from the gardener's point of view; and in any case, the dividing line is not clearly drawn: a plant that is treated as an annual by someone gardening in cool zones may in fact be a perfectly good perennial in warmer climates. That is why I have decided to group all these non-woody plants together under one heading.

There are, of course, true annuals, that grow, flower, seed and die in the year; but many of the plants so described in seed catalogues are in fact perennials obliging enough to reach flowering size in one season, so that their death (from whatever cause) after blooming is of little consequence. Then again, a good many true annuals perpetuate themselves by self-seeding, once in the garden; so as far as keeping them is concerned, they are as good as perennial.

Nor do plants submit willingly to the human passion for categorization in the distinction between woody and non-woody. In the list that follows are several plants – *Ballota* is one – that are sub-shrubby or, to put it another way, they are woody-based perennials. My excuses for including them here, if excuse is needed, are that the distinction between a shrub and a non-woody plant is often pretty subjective and that *Ballota* and other soft-wooded shrubs assort well with border plants.

And that brings me to the value of these plants in the garden. Most of them are grown for their flowers or their foliage, for their contribution to the color or the texture of a planting, rather than for their structure or outline (but you will not need to read far before finding exceptions: no further than *Acanthus*). Using either shrubs or non-woody plants, or the two in combination, it is possible to make a very satisfying composition with foliage alone, blending the limited variety of colors – shades of green, gray and glaucous-blue predominantly – and the many textures of leaves in an enduring and soothing picture. A completely different picture would result from using flowering plants, massed as in nature: broad sweeps of Texas bluebonnet (*Lupinus texensis*) or Californian poppy (*Eschscholzia californica*), of star of the veldt (*Osteospermum*) or blue flax (*Linum narbonense*) – the gardener's equivalent of the paintbrush filled with color and washed across the taut-stretched paper. Most of us, no doubt, prefer to use both color and form: to create a framework of plants with bold or finely drawn foliage and to add sparkle with flowers.

Abronia NYCTAGINACEAE

The sand verbenas, natives of western North American coasts, make prostrate mats spangled with flowers. In *Abronia latifolia* (z7–9), they are yellow, with a honeysuckle-like fragrance, and in the more southerly *A.*

umbellata (z8–9) or beach sand verbena, rose or white. *A. umbellata* 'Grandiflora' (z7–9) has large flowers, and 'Rosea' is a good pink. They are honey-scented, especially at night.

Acanthus ACANTHACEAE

These are bold plants with striking leaves and stiff flower spikes, handsome rather than colorful with their hooded flowers in spiky calyces that can be dried for indoor decoration. They have invasive roots, and are increased by division or seed. They will grow in the most difficult conditions, under trees or in dust-dry places; in Granada in Spain, the woods leading up the hill to the Alhambra are full of them; on the summit they sprout from the sizzling stones against sun-drenched walls. During summer drought the leaves wilt (and are best removed), but regenerate in autumn with the rains. The bear's breeches, *Acanthus mollis*, has long, deeply dissected leaves, large and glossy green in the Latifolius Group (z7–10), and mauve flowers in 4ft/1.2m spikes. This Italian species, long naturalized in Greece, may have inspired the stylized leaves of Corinthian capitals; another convincing contender for that role is *A. spinosus* (z7–10), which has long, dark green, deeply cut, spiny leaves of erect, arching poise. It is very free with its handsome mauve flowers. The Spinosissimus Group is even more elegant in leaf, the spines silvery in contrast to the dark blades; it is less free-flowering unless well baked. The native Greek species, *A. caroli-alexandri* (z7–9), has narrow, prickly leaves and short (12in/30cm) spikes of pink and white flowers in summer. *A. balcanicus* (z6–10) is very free with its 36in/90cm spikes of pinkish-mauve flowers, but in leaf it cannot compare with *A. mollis*. The Middle Eastern *A. dioscoridis* var. *perringii* (z7–9) is a strikingly handsome plant with deeply cut, gray-green leaves, and pink flowers on 18in/45cm spikes in late summer.

Achillea COMPOSITAE

Varying from small mat-formers to tall border plants, most achilleas bear flat heads of tiny, close-packed, rayless daisies, yellow, white or occasionally pink to crimson, that can be picked to dry for winter arrangements. Among the miniatures, suited for dry rocky places or small-scale ground-cover, *Achillea ageratifolia* (z5–7), from Greece, has deeply toothed, silvery leaves, and white flowers on 4–6in/10–15cm stems in summer, while *A. clavennae* (*A. argentea* of gardens) (z5–7) has dazzlingly silver, irregularly toothed leaves, and white flowers on 6in/15cm stems. *A.* × *huteri* (z5–7), from the European Alps, makes mats of aromatic gray foliage topped by pure white flowers on 4in/10cm stems. Of looser growth, *A.* × *wilczekii* (z5–7) has toothed leaves and bears nodding heads of white flowers on 6–8in/15–20cm stems in summer. Other small achilleas have yellow flowers: *A. chrysocoma* (z4–7), with very aromatic, ferny, silvery-hairy foliage and flowers on 6in/15cm stems; *A. tomentosa* (z4–7), whose dense mats of soft, ferny leaves are topped by flat heads of flower on 6in/15cm stems in summer; and its child, *A.* × *lewisii* 'King Edward' (z4–7), which makes low carpets of gray-green leaves, topped by clusters of lemon-yellow flowers on 4in/10cm stems. A size or two up from these is *A.* 'Taygetea' (z5–8), an appealing hybrid with feathery, silvery green leaves and flat heads of soft primrose-lemon on 24in/60cm stems in summer. The common European yarrow or milfoil, *A. millefolium* (z3–8), is an invasive weed, but selected garden forms are worth growing for their ferny, dark green leaves and colorful flowers: to name but two, 'Cerise Queen' is bright crimson-pink, 'Lilac Beauty' cool mauve. They reach 24in/60cm in flower. The giant

Acanthus spinosus

among achilleas is *A. filipendulina* (z4–8), a bold border perennial with ferny green leaves and strong 4ft/1.2m stems topped by flat plate-like heads of bright yellow flowers in summer. They dry to a mustard shade. The combination of this strong yellow with the rich purple of *Salvia × superba* 'Superba,' complementary colors and contrasting shapes, is by now rather a cliché; the paler *A.* 'Taygetea' (z5–8) makes the point less stridently. All the achilleas can be propagated by division.

Aethionema CRUCIFERAE

These dwarf subshrubs and perennials revel in sun, appreciating a rocky cleft or wall crevice. They flower from early summer on, and are increased by cuttings or seed. The prettiest is *Aethionema grandiflorum* (z6–7), a bushlet of 12in/30cm, very free with its pink flowers over a long season. The plant is especially appealing in the Pulchellum Group (*A. pulchellum*) (z6–7), with blue-gray foliage and masses of pale candy pink flowers. *A. schistosum* (z5–7) varies in height up to 12in/30cm and has large flowers of rich, bright pink. *A. armenum* (z5–7) has small, narrow, blue-gray leaves and terminal racemes of pink flowers, and the non-woody *A. iberideum* (z6–7) is mat-forming, its gray-green leaves hidden beneath white flowers in summer. The deep pink *A.* 'Warley Rose' (z4–7), a compact and free-flowering bushlet, is slightly less drought-tolerant than the others.

Agapanthus LILIACEAE/ALLIACEAE

The African lilies are grand plants, most of them carrying spherical heads of many small, lily-like flowers, in shades of blue or white, in summer. Species with narrow, deciduous leaves, and the hybrids that inherit this characteristic, are more frost-resistant than those with broad, evergreen blades. Agapanthus can be increased by seed, but anything may result; they can also be divided. They must be kept well watered until established. They assort well with other monocots such as *Kniphofia*, *Crocosmia* and *Galtonia*, and with the Cape figworts (*Phygelius*).

Agapanthus campanulatus

Of those which die down in winter, *Agapanthus campanulatus* (z8–11) has narrow, gray-green leaves and flattish heads of soft blue, trumpet-shaped flowers on 24–48in/60–120cm stems: *A. campanulatus* ssp. *patens* (z8–11) differs in its wider-open flowers borne in dense round heads. The first species to be introduced to cultivation from South Africa was *A. africanus* (z9–10), which has evergreen leaves and large heads of deep blue flowers; the naming of these old garden plants is very confused, and another name that is bandied about is *A. umbellatus*, which may refer to forms of *A. campanulatus* or of *A. caulescens* or to *A. praecox*; old clones of *A. praecox* are also sometimes confused with *A. africanus*. The real *A. praecox* (z9–10) is a bold plant with dark evergreen leaves and large heads of rich blue trumpet flowers on 4ft/1.2m stems. The splendid white 'Albatross' may belong here.

Alstroemeria LILIACEAE/ALSTROMERIACEAE

Alstroemeria aurea (*A. aurantiaca*) (z7–10), the Peruvian lily, is a perfect plant for cutting, with its orange, tiger-striped, lily-like flowers on 36in/90cm stems; but it has running roots and easily becomes invasive. It can be easily increased by lifting a spadeful of roots with the minimum of disturbance and replanting them elsewhere. The taller *A. ligtu* (z6–10), which has pink to blush flowers, is usually encountered through the Ligtu hybrids, a delightful strain with coral, salmon or soft pink flowers, striped and freckled; they are easily increased by seed, sown individually in small pots or scattered where the plants are to grow. If you have a spare plot wherein to throw the seed heads each year, you will soon have a mass of dainty blooms to cut for the house.

Alyssum CRUCIFERAE

Alyssum saxatile (*Aurinia saxatilis*) (z3–7), gold dust, forms loose 8–12in/20–30cm hummocks of gray-green leaves, smothered in spring beneath masses of tiny bright yellow flowers. There is a pretty pale form, *A. s.* var. *citrinum*, which comes true from seed; a miniature, 'Compactum,' and one with unusual buff-orange flowers, 'Dudley Neville'; these last must be propagated by cuttings. All are well suited to growing in dry, rocky places or wall crevices, which they fill with bright swags in spring.

Antennaria COMPOSITAE

Antennaria dioica (z3–7) is an easy-going, mat-forming plant with gray leaves and 3in/7.5cm stems carrying small heads of blush-white flowers, readily increased by division. It is a pretty companion for other small, undemanding rock plants such as the little achilleas, creeping thymes, rock roses (*Helianthemum*), and the blue grass *Festuca glauca*.

Anthemis COMPOSITAE

Anthemis punctata ssp. *cupaniana* (z5–8) makes wide masses of finely dissected, silver-gray leaves, topped in spring by large, white, yellow-eyed daisies on 12in/30cm stems. Take out the flowered stems as the heads fade to keep the plant neat and encourage more flowers; propagate by cuttings. The neat little *A. tuberculata* (z5–8) has gray leaves and white daisies in summer.

Antirrhinum SCROPHULARIACEAE

The common snapdragon, *Antirrhinum majus*, is often grown as an annual or biennial in a wide range of colors, sizes and flower shapes. The tall strains with flowers of the original shape are handsome border plants and valuable for cutting, as well as fun to "pop" to see the dragon mouths open. There are several miniatures for dry, sunny places, such as the wonderfully named *A. braun-blanquetii*. with cream and yellow flowers over a long summer season, or velvet-soft *A. molle* (z8–9), a dwarf bushlet with downy leaves and yellow and white or pink flowers. *A. hispanicum* (z8–9) makes 12in/30cm mounds with cream, pink or purple snapdragon flowers.

Aphyllanthes LILIACEAE/APHYLLANTHACEAE

Aphyllanthes monspeliensis (z9–10) is a native of hot hillsides in the Mediterranean region. It has rush-like stems and bears clear blue flowers in papery bracts during the summer.

Arctotis COMPOSITAE

One of the South African daisy tribe that brings so much color to dry, sunny gardens, *Arctotis acaulis* (z9) is a low, spreading perennial with yellow to orange, dark-eyed flowers in early spring. It needs moisture during its winter growing season, but should be kept dry thereafter; as this suggests, it is not suitable for cold winter areas. It can be increased by seed and flowers in its first year. *Arctotis* hybrids (*Venidioarctotis* hybrids) are named for their colors: the bold daisy flowers, opening over a long summer season on 18in/45cm stems, are 'Apricot,' 'Flame,' or 'Wine,' over crinkly gray foliage. They are propagated by cuttings.

Argemone platyceras

Argemone PAPAVERACEAE

The prickly poppies of California and Mexico have glaucous, thistle-like leaves, and are increased by seed. The devil's fig, *Argemone mexicana* (z8–10), is an annual with satiny lemon or tangerine poppies and glaucous leaves and milky blotches over the veins; the larger *A. grandiflora* (z9–10) is an annual or short-lived perennial with white or clear yellow, silken-petaled poppy flowers on 24–36in/60–90cm stems over white-veined, bluish, deeply lobed leaves. The splendid *A. platyceras* (z9–10), the thistle poppy or chicalote, is a short-lived perennial with spiny, lobed, gray-green leaves, and large, silky, white poppies with a central boss of golden stamens.

Argyranthemum COMPOSITAE

The Paris daisies or marguerites are woody perennials flowering over a long summer to fall season; they are increased by cuttings. The typical marguerite, with green, deeply cut leaves and white daisies, is *Argyranthemum frutescens* (z9–10), which may grow to 36in/90cm or more if not cut by frost. More beautiful, on account of its very finely dissected, blue-gray foliage, is *A. f.* ssp. *foeniculaceum* (*A. foeniculaceum*). There are many cultivars available, such as anemone-centered 'Edelweiss,' and double 'Mrs. F. Sanders' and 'Snowflake' ('Blizzard'); 'Levada Cream'; yellows ranging from 'Jamaica Primrose' and the slightly deeper 'Brontes' to a cheery double yellow; pale pink, anemone-centered 'Mary Wootton' and deeper pink 'Vancouver'; and the crushed-strawberry 'Rollason's Red.' *A. maderense* (z9–10) is particularly appealing, making compact 18in/45cm mounds of blue-gray foliage with soft yellow daisies.

Armeria PLUMBAGINACEAE

Armeria maritima (z4–8), the sea pink or sea thrift, makes wide cushiony mats of grass-fine green leaves on 6in/15cm stems topped by pink flower heads. Several selections have been made with brighter or deeper-colored flowers, increased by division to keep them true to type. Dwarf *A. girardii* (*A. setacea*) (z4–8) has bright pink flower heads on 4in/10cm stems.

Artemisia COMPOSITAE

The drought-tolerant wormwoods are foliage plants above all, with their silver or pewter-gray, dissected or thread-fine leaves. They are increased by cuttings or division. The absinth, *Artemisia absinthium* (z4–9), has grayish, finely cut foliage; the selection 'Lambrook Silver,' the color of polished pewter, grows to 30in/75cm. The tiny flowers, in branching spires, are gray. The prairie-dwelling *A. ludoviciana* (z4–9) is a splendid border plant, except that its roots can be rather invasive. The 4ft/1.2m stems are topped in summer by tiny gray flowers; the silver-gray leaves may be entire and willow-like, or jaggedly lobed, as in the very white-silvery *A. l.* var. *latiloba*, which is shorter in growth. The dusty miller, *A. stelleriana* (z4–8), is a good substitute for *Senecio bicolor* ssp. *cineraria* in coldish climates, spreading to form carpets of broad, deeply lobed, silvery white leaves, evergreen in mild districts. The tiny yellow flowers do nothing for it and can be removed. In contrast, *A. canescens* (z5–9) has silvery, filigree-fine leaves on a forest of branching, 18in/45cm stems; *A. splendens* (z5–9) is similar, with thready, silver-gray leaves. The very feathery, aromatic *A. vallesiaca* (z5–8) grows to about 12in/30cm as a silver-white companion for blue flax and the steel-blue grass *Helictotrichon sempervirens*. There are diminutive artemisias, for rock gardens or the front of small borders. *A. caucasica* (*A. lanata*) (z5–7) makes a prostrate mat of silvery leaves; *A. frigida* (z5–7) is a miniature shrublet with woody stems and silky silver leaves; and the adorable *A. schmidtiana* (z3–7) is a foamy mass of silky, platinum-pale, finely dissected leaves. *A. s.* 'Nana' is a choice miniature.

Asarina SCROPHULARIACEAE

Asarina procumbens (*Antirrhinum asarina*) (z6–8) is a trailing, sticky-stemmed plant with softly furred, gray-green leaves, and white snapdragon flowers tinged with yellow. It prefers to be out of the hottest sun, but is content in a dry wall in light shade, where it is likely to sow itself in small crevices.

Asparagus LILIACEAE/ASPARAGACEAE

Asparagus is not just a delicious vegetable, thick and white-stemmed *à la française* with hollandaise sauce, or slender and green in its pool of melted butter; the genus also offers a number of beautiful foliage plants. *Asparagus densiflorus* (z9–11) is a tuberous, sprawling, or weakly climbing perennial with fine, plumy foliage. There are selected cultivars: 'Meyeri' is densely branched, with erect or stiffly spreading stems to 24in/60cm, and tapering, narrow plumes of very dark green foliage; while 'Sprengeri,' the emerald fern or emerald feather, grows taller and more lax, with gracefully drooping stems, loosely branched and airy in texture.

Aspidistra LILIACEAE/CONVALLARIACEAE

Aspidistra elatior (z7–11), often grown as a house plant in cold climates and renowned for its ability to survive extreme neglect in dark, chilly corners, is a handsome foliage plant with broad, shining, dark evergreen leaves. It can be increased by division.

Ballota LABIATAE

Ballota pseudodictamnus (z7–9), already briefly discussed in the introduction to this section, is a white-wooly evergreen subshrub, its pipecleaner stems strung with whorls of pale jade bracts. The lesser-known *B. acetabulosa* (z7–9) is similar, with greener foliage and bold upright flowering stems. Both are increased by soft or half-ripe cuttings.

Argyranthemum maderense

Baptisia LEGUMINOSAE

These lupine-like plants have a deep taproot and should be planted when small; they are raised from seed. *Baptisia australis* (z3–9) has glaucous leaves and stems as a plinth for the muted blue flowers on 4ft/1.2m stems, opening in early summer. Other species have yellow or white flowers, and are mostly suitable for zones 5–9.

Bergenia SAXIFRAGACEAE

Bergenia (z3–8) species and hybrids are long-suffering, mainly evergreen perennials with bold, leathery leaves, suited to cooler areas too dry for hostas. The foliage is of many colors in winter where touched by the sun. The flowers appear in early to late spring and range from white through pink to rich magenta. They are increased by division of the stout rhizomes, which can be cut into small sections, each with a growth bud.

Bidens COMPOSITAE

Bidens ferulifolia (z8–10) is a perennial with finely dissected leaves and a seemingly unending succession of bright citron "lazy daisy" flowers, perfect in a tub on account of its flowing growth. It is very drought-resistant, and though it may look limp after a long dry spell it quickly perks up again when watered. It is easily increased by cuttings.

Billbergia BROMELIACEAE

Many bromeliads are drought-resistant; I list some, arbitrarily, among succulents and xerophytes. *Billbergia nutans* (z9–10) has long, narrow, dark green, finely toothed leaves, forming an open rosette. The flowering stems grow to 12in/30cm or so, bearing an unbranched inflorescence of blue, green and rose-colored flowers, dropping from bright pink bracts. It is increased by division.

Calamintha LABIATAE

These bushy little plants from southern Europe are aromatic sun-lovers, assorting well with pinks and sedums. *Calamintha grandiflora* (z5–9) has lilac-pink flowers, while *C. nepeta* (z5–9), an indispensable bee plant, has tiny, pale lilac, thyme-like flowers in great profusion over a long season. It has something of the minty aroma suggested by the generic name. Both can be increased by division or seed.

Callirhoë MALVACEAE

The poppy mallow or wine cups, *Callirhoë involucrata* (z4–8), is a low-growing plant with a carrot-like root and deeply lobed leaves, amid which nestle the bright vivid cerise, cupped flowers. It makes a bright carpet around yuccas or mingling with dwarf spurges and sedums.

Carduncellus COMPOSITAE

These are little thistly plants from Mediterranean regions. *Carduncellus mitissimus* (z8–9) has deeply cut leaves forming cupped rosettes, and pale lilac thistle heads, while *C. rhaponticoïdes* (z8–9), from the Atlas Mountains, has rosettes of long, spine-edged leaves around a stemless central boss of bright blue cornflowers. Increase by root cuttings or division.

Carlina COMPOSITAE

Carlina acaulis (z5–7), the alpine thistle of Europe, is at its most attractive when the large, whitish-silver flower head nestles stemless in the rosette of leaves, as its name suggests it should; sometimes, though, it is stemmy. It looks right among stones, or in a carpet of antennaria. It is monocarpic and raised from seed; plant it out when still small, before the taproot becomes too large.

Catananche COMPOSITAE

Catananche caerulea (z4–8), the blue cupidone, has lavender-blue, corn-flower-like heads in a papery calyx, borne on thin 24in/60cm stems over grassy, grayish foliage. There are also white and 'Bicolor' selections, needing to be propagated by root cuttings, for seed gives mixed results.

Centaurea COMPOSITAE

Many centaureas are hardy perennials; two are silver foliage plants of quality, commonly raised from seed. However, seed strains are apt to run to flower, which spoils the foliage effect. It is worth ruthlessly cutting back any shoots with buds, in the hope of encouraging the plant to settle down to a celibate, and perennial, existence. Try this with *Centaurea cineraria* ssp. *cineraria* (*C. gymnocarpa*) (z8–9), which has finely cut foliage of silver-gray, and grows to 18–24in/45–60cm; and with *C. rutifolia* (*C. candidissima*) (z8–9), a lesser plant growing to 12in/30cm, with broad-lobed, white-felted leaves, and grown annually from cuttings and seed. *C. macrocephala* (z3–8), the great golden knapweed, as its name suggests, is of a very different stamp: a coarse plant with 36in/90cm stems bearing big yellow flower heads in papery brown bracts, good for drying. *C. ruthenica* (z5–8) has more quality, with its finely dissected, dark green leaves making a plinth for heads of pale lemon flowers on 36in/90cm stems.

Centranthus VALERIANACEAE

Centranthus ruber (z5–8), the red valerian, is a tough and easy plant which flowers over a long season. It does very well in walls and survives summer drought without assistance, sowing itself freely. The fleshy leaves are glaucous green, the flowers muted dusty pink; there is a deep red form, *atrococcineus*, and a charming white, *albus*. They grow to 36in/90cm.

Cerastium CARYOPHYLLACEAE

Cerastium tomentosum (z2–7), or snow in summer, is sometimes planted in rock gardens – a mistake, as it is a real thug, invading and smothering lesser plants. On a dry wall or bank, its territorial ambitions may be welcome, for it is a pretty plant with silver-gray leaves and abundant white flowers. The least scrap seems to grow; control, rather than propagation, is usually the problem. *C. t.* var. *columnae* has brighter, white foliage and is less rampant.

Commelina COMMELINACEAE

Commelina tuberosa (z8–10) is valued for the almost turquoise-blue, three-petaled flowers dropping from green bracts on 24in/60cm stems of the Coelestis Group, in summer and autumn. There is also a white form. It has running roots and can be propagated by division or seed.

Convolvulus CONVOLVULACEAE

The twining, sprawling, pink-flowered *Convolvulus althaeoïdes* (z6–8) is a charmer, with finely cut silver foliage setting off chalkpink funnels all summer. It can be invasive, smothering neighboring plants. *C. elegantissimus* (z6–8) is similar, with even more finely dissected foliage. Though its foliage cannot compare, *C. sabatius* (*C. mauritanicus*) (z8–9) is no less appeal-

Convolvulus sabatius

ing: a low mound of grayish leaves topped by a succession of lilac-blue funnels. It is not invasive and can be propagated by soft cuttings.

Coreopsis COMPOSITAE

The unglamorously nicknamed tickseeds are cheery yellow daisies, of which at least one, *Coreopsis verticillata* (z4–9), is an attractive thing, with thread-fine leaves and vivid flowers over a long season. It reaches its apogee in the cultivar 'Moonbeam,' which has primrose-yellow, sheeny petals. It grows to about 24in/60cm and is increased by division. Other species, prairie-dwellers all, are shorter-lived and best raised from seed.

Crambe CRUCIFERAE

The Caucasian *Crambe cordifolia* (z6–8) is a massive plant with huge, dark green leaves, topped by strong, branching, 6ft/1.8m stems developing into a cumulus of tiny, white, starry flowers. The seakale, *C. maritima* (z6–9), is a connoisseur's vegetable (blanched and eaten like asparagus), but also a superb foliage plant, with large, blue-gray, undulating, lobed leaves. The flowers are white, on 24in/60cm stems. Both are increased by division, or by root cuttings, and can be paired with other dune plants such as sea holly or lyme grass.

Crepis COMPOSITAE

Crepis incana (z5–7) is in effect a pink dandelion, with narrow, gray, toothed leaves and branching heads of flowers on 12in/30cm stems in summer.

Cynara COMPOSITAE

The quirks of the botanical alphabet bring yet another genus in which an aristocrat of the table is to be found: the globe artichoke, *Cynara cardunculus*, of the Scolymus Group (z7–9). Edible, but above all ornamental, *C.*

Dianthus hybrid

cardunculus (z7–9), the cardoon, has very large, silvery leaves like some gigantic thistle. The purple, thistle-like flower heads, on 6ft/1.8m edible stems, can be removed if you want to enjoy the foliage at its best. If you need more plants, you can summon your strength to divide the rootstock, or take root cuttings. It would be a crime to behead the Moroccan *C. baetica* ssp. *maroccana* (*C. hystrix*) (z8–9), which quickly loses its foliage to the summer heat, but bears wonderful thistle flowers, blue with spiky, lilac-pink calyces. It is propagated by seed.

Datura SOLANACEAE

Datura inoxia (*D. meteloides*) (z9–11) has palest ice-lilac trumpets with a powerful sweet perfume, set off by gray foliage. Unlike the flowers of the shrubby brugmansias, these are held upright. Propagation is by seed.

Dianthus CARYOPHYLLACEAE

The carnations and pinks form clumps of often blue-gray foliage, attractive in itself, especially if the plants are frequently renewed from cuttings. The flowers are single or double, and come in a variety of colors from white through pink to red; some have a rich clove perfume. There is a huge variety available, from tiny rock pinks to border plants. The smaller species and hybrids are enchanting with silky soft *Artemisia schmidtiana* 'Nana' and small sedums such as *S. cauticola*. The sweet William, *Dianthus barbatus* (z4–8), is a biennial with brightly colored flowers, raised from seed, as are some carnation strains. Exceptionally, *D. knappii* (z3–8) has lemon-yellow flowers on 12in/30cm stems over gray foliage; it is short-lived and needs to be raised from seed.

Dicentra FUMARIACEAE

Dicentra chrysantha (z6–8) is an exception in a genus that tends to prefer cool soil and shelter from sun and wind. This Californian tendril climber has pale glaucous, much-divided leaves and holds its bright yellow flowers in upright clusters.

Dictamnus RUTACEAE

Dictamnus albus (z3–8), the dittany, is a bushy perennial with aromatic, divided leaves, and spikes of white, long-stamened flowers in early summer. *D. a.* var. *purpureus* (*D. fraxinella*) (z3–8) has lilac-pink flowers. *Dictamnus* is also known as burning bush, for on hot, still days after the flowers have faded, the plant gives off a volatile oil which will ignite. Like the Biblical burning bush, the plant is unharmed by this "party trick." Seed is the best method of increase.

Digitalis SCROPHULARIACEAE

Digitalis grandiflora (z4–8) is a Greek foxglove with narrow, evergreen basal leaves and 24in/60cm stems bearing quite large, soft yellow flowers, brown-freckled within. The Mediterranean *D. lutea* (z4–8) has much smaller, clear primrose flowers. Both are increased by seed. They are not remotely woody, but the Spanish *D. obscura* (z7–8) is a shrubby foxglove with very narrow, blue-gray leaves to set off its slim spires of tawny orange "gloves." Propagate by cuttings.

Diplarrhena IRIDACEAE

In the southern hemisphere, the genus *Iris* is replaced by close relatives, of which *Diplarrhena moraea* (z9–10) is one. It has long, narrow leaves and

Spires of *Echium pininana* tower over the smaller *E. candicans*.

heads of several small flowers composed of three spreading, white segments and three tiny, erect central segments, two mauve, one yellow, on 24in/ 60cm stems. It has the butterfly charm of the family and can be increased easily by seed or division.

Echinops COMPOSITAE

The globe thistles have prickly, dissected foliage, and spherical flower heads on strong stems. The most familiar in gardens are the 4ft/1.2m *Echinops ritro* (z3–8) and its cultivars, such as 'Veitch's Blue,' which show their steel-blue coloring over a long season; the foliage is green backed with gray. The taller *E. bannaticus* 'Taplow Blue' (z3–8) has similar gray-blue coloring. For a bigger plant still, choose *E. sphaerocephalus* (z3–8), which has gray-white flower heads on 6ft/1.8m stems.

Though not in the first rank as ornamentals, the globe thistles are useful for their willingness to thrive in poor chalky or sandy soils. They look good with the taller achilleas and verbascums, and are increased by division or root cuttings.

Echium BORAGINACEAE

The Atlantic island echiums are handsome, bold perennials, subshrubs or biennials, most easy from seed, which is set in abundance, for the flower spikes are composed of myriad small flowers, usually blue. The pride of Madeira, *Echium candicans* (z9–10), is a branching, shrubby perennial reaching 6ft/1.8m, with narrow, hairy gray or white leaves. The foliage forms a plinth for dense, long, cylindrical spikes of many small flowers, in colors from dark blue to white, appearing from spring to summer. Those with deep blue or purple, red-stamened flowers are often known as *E. fastuosum* (z9–10). *E. coeleste* (z9–10) is similar, with paler blue flowers. *E. nervosum* (z9–10) is another Madeiran species, a spreading subshrub of 5ft/1.5m or so, with grayish foliage and pale blue-mauve flowers from spring on. *E. × scilloniense* (z9–10) originated in the gardens of Tresco Abbey on Tresco in the British Isles of Scilly. A perennial hybrid that must be increased by cuttings, it has erect, deep blue spikes. The giant of the family is *E. pininana* (z9–10), a Canary Island echium with immense, tapering spires, 10ft/3m tall or more, of close-packed lavender-blue flowers over green basal rosettes. A biennial, it seeds itself abundantly where suited. One of the most distinct is *E. wildpretii* (z5–10), another Canary Island species forming a multibranched, shrubby perennial with soft, hairy, narrow leaves. The flowers, in thick pyramidal spikes up to 10ft/3m tall, depart from the family tradition, for they are rich red in color. None bears much resemblance to *E. plantagineum* (z9–10), the viper's bugloss, a low, spreading annual with violet-blue flowers – seed strains also come in shades of purer blue, mauve, purple, rose-pink and white, and have been developed to form more compact, bushy plants with larger flowers. However, in Australia it is known as Paterson's curse and is a noxious weed.

Echium candicans

Erigeron COMPOSITAE

Erigeron karvinskianus (*E. mucronatus*, *Vittadinia triloba*) (z8–9), the Mexican daisy, is – with the red valerian – one of the most accommodating plants in our very dry, rather wild garden in Switzerland, seeding itself into cracks in the hottest, sun-baked walls or swarming about the boles of the cherry and peach trees. It has unobtrusive foliage and abundant starry daisies, which open white and age through pink to crimson.

Eriophyllum COMPOSITAE

Eriophyllum lanatum (*Bahia lanata*) (z5–8) bears yellow daisies on 12in/30cm stems over silvery, finely cut leaves. Easy in dry or rocky places, it looks good with *Artemisia stelleriana* and nepeta as companions. It can be increased by division of the running roots, or from seed.

Erodium GERANIACEAE

The heron's bills are natives of the Mediterranean region and Asia Minor; most are easy in dry soil in sun. Some have pale flowers with a dark spot on the two upper petals: *Erodium guttatum* (z7–8), its 8in/20cm stems carrying white flowers with a purple blotch over finely cut light green foliage; *E. pelargoniiflorum* (z7–8), a slightly larger plant with white, maroon-spotted flowers over velvet-soft apple-green leaves. The carrot-leaved *E. manescaui* (z5–8) has assertive magenta flowers on 18in/45cm stems. There are some miniatures for rock gardens and raised beds, and one beautiful oddity that forsakes the family tendency to white, pink or magenta: *E. chrysanthum* (z7–8) has mounds of feathery fine, silver-green foliage, forming a quiet harmony with the pale sulfur-yellow flowers on 8in/20cm stems.

Eryngium maritimum

Euphorbia rigida

Eryngium UMBELLIFERAE

Although many of the European species look superficially like thistles, these are cow parsley relatives. They fall into two groups: the sea holly or eryngo types from Europe, which work well with blue grasses (*Festuca glauca*, *Helictotrichon* and others), gypsophila, lychnis and pale yellow achilleas, and the American species, which have long, evergreen, sword-like leaves. The species can be increased by seed; all by division; and the Europeans grow successfully from root cuttings. The Europeans are more colorful; most have blue flower heads in a prickly calyx ruff. Exceptionally, the wide inflorescence of *Eryngium alpinum* (z5–8) is soft to the touch; this is the largest in flower, and the blue of the central cone and the surrounding collar extends to the 30in/75cm flowering stem. Taller, at 36in/90cm, is *E. planum* (z5–9), which has heads of small blue flowers in spiky blue bracts, lovely for cutting. With its greenish flowers, *E. spinalba* (z5–8) is valued more for its structure than its color, and the same goes for Miss Willmott's ghost, the biennial *E. giganteum* (z4–7), a stout 36in/90cm plant with wide, jade-white bracts fading to parchment, and blue-white leaves. The perennial sea holly, *E. maritimum* (z5–8), demands a very free-draining soil to recall its native coastal sands; it is intensely glaucous-blue in leaf and blue of flower. It grows to only 12in/30cm or so; another for small spaces is *E. variifolium* (z5–9), which has prettily white-veined, evergreen, spiny leaves. The flowers are blue-gray in white, prickly frills.

The South American species mostly run to tall stems of small flowers lacking the showy ruff of bracts, although the Mexican *E. proteiflorum* (z9–10), which has long, narrow, evergreen leaves like these, also has boldly bracted flowers of metallic white, on 36in/90cm stems. Both *E. agavifolium* (z9–10) and *E. yuccifolium* (z4–8), the rattlesnake master, suggest the appearance of their leaves in their specific names, the first with a rosette of green, sword-like, sharply armed leaves, the second blue-gray, with prickly margins. The agave eryngium has green, thimble-like flowers on 4–5ft/1.2–1.5m stems; the yucca-leaved eryngium, white golfball-sized clusters on 5ft/1.5m stems. The massive *E. decaisneanum* (z9–10) has been known as *E. pandanifolium*, again a name suggesting the narrow, sword-like leaves, which form a great tuft, topped by 8ft/2.4m flowering stems bearing a wide head of tiny maroon flowers. *E. eburneum* (*E. paniculatum*) (z9–10) is a lesser plant with arching, narrow, spiny leaves, and arching 5ft/1.5m stems, branching to carry green flowers with white stamens.

Erysimum CRUCIFERAE

Erysimum capitatum (z8–10) is a subshrubby wallflower from coastal regions of California and Oregon, with pale creamy primrose flowers, endowed with a warm fragrance of cloves. It can be grown from seed or cuttings. *E. linifolium* (z6–8), the flax-leaved wallflower, has narrow, grayish leaves and clouds of lilac flowers on 12in/30cm stems. Its variegated form must be propagated by cuttings, as must *E.* 'Bowles' Mauve' (z7), a shrubby wallflower with blue-gray leaves and purple flowers.

Eschscholzia PAPAVERACEAE

Its name may be a tongue-twister and difficult to spell, but *Eschscholzia californica*, the California poppy, is an easy annual, adapted to growing in dry, sunny places. Its silky poppy flowers, which vary from yellow through orange to scarlet, dance over dissected foliage. *E. caespitosa* is smaller, a real charmer for small spaces, with finely dissected, gray-blue leaves and primrose poppy flowers.

Eschscholzia californica

Euphorbia EUPHORBIACEAE

In addition to the shrubby spurges, some lesser species are of value in gardens. One of the most undemanding plants imaginable is Mrs. Robb's bonnet, *Euphorbia amygdaloides* var. *robbiae* (z7–9); it will grow in the driest soil and darkest shade beneath trees, lighting the gloom in spring with its 24in/60cm spires of sharp green flowers over dark evergreen leaves. Cut out the flowered stems as they fade to keep the plant neat: it spreads easily, but a build-up of fungal disease over the years may cause the center of the group to die out though the outer margins will remain healthy. For sunny, rocky places, the Greek *E. rigida* (*E. biglandulosa*) (z7–10) is fine, with narrow, pointed, blue-gray leaves and chartreuse bracts, resembling the better-known *E. myrsinites* (z5–8). This has been described as looking like a spray of monkey-puzzle tree dipped in aluminum paint, though it gives the game away with its lime-yellow flower heads. It is a sprawler, reaching no more than 6in/15cm in height, unlike the upright *E. rigida* which grows to 18in/45cm. Both are increased from seed. A much smaller blue-gray spurge suited to rocky pockets is *E. capitulata* (z7–9), a flat carpet of rooting stems topped with sharp yellow bracts. *E. nicaeensis* (z6–9) has blue-gray foliage and flowers in summer.

Evolvulus CONVOLVULACEAE

Evolvulus glomeratus 'Blue Daze' (z8–10) is a small, trailing plant, with gray-green foliage complementing deep blue saucer flowers, which open over a long season. It needs hot summers to do well.

Gazania rigens

Ferula UMBELLIFERAE

Ferula communis (z6–9), the giant fennel, makes a great pile of fine, plumy foliage, topped after some years of growth by a 7ft/2m flowering stem bearing a wide umbel of yellow flowers. *F. tingitana* (z7–9) is similar; both make long taproots and must therefore be grown from seed in pots and planted out while still small.

Foeniculum UMBELLIFERAE

The common fennel, *Foeniculum vulgare* (z4–9), has feathery, aromatic leaves that are a classic flavoring for fish dishes, and lime-green flower heads on 6ft/1.8m stems. *F. v. purpureum* has tawny purple foliage, like a fox's brush in youth, expanding to smoky bronze as the flowers open. It seeds virtually true, but both forms can be overenthusiastically dynastic, so it is worth removing the faded flower heads before the seeds – themselves a delicious seasoning – fall to the ground.

Gaura ONAGRACEAE

Gaura lindheimeri (z5–9) is a perennial of discreet charm, with a long season of small, blush-white flowers on 4ft/1.2m stems; it is easily grown from seed. The brighter *G. coccinea* (z4–8), the scarlet gaura, is a prairie plant growing to 18in/45cm, with spikes of rosy red, honeysuckle-like flowers.

Gazania COMPOSITAE

The gazanias are southern African daisies, well known as low-growing bedding plants, raised from seed or cuttings. The flowers do not open on dull days, and even on sunny days they close well before sundown. They need some watering in very hot climates, and even in cooler regions are surprisingly tolerant of heavy soils. Hybrids range in color from cream through all the shades of yellow and orange as well as soft or plummy pinks, often with central zones of black or green; some, such as 'Silver Beauty,' have striking silver foliage to set off their bright flowers. Any batch of seedlings is likely to include a few sufficiently attractive to perpetuate by cuttings. *Gazania rigens* (*G. splendens*) (z8–10) is a prostrate species with orange flowers; a variegated form has cream and green leaves; while *G. rigens* var. *leucolaena* (z8–10) has vivid yellow flowers on trailing stems over a long summer to fall season.

Geranium GERANIACEAE

The crane's bills are invaluable plants in cool, temperate zones, both as flower-border components and among shrubs; several are efficient weed-excluders and can be quickly increased by division. Among these, one of the best is the vigorous, evergreen *Geranium* × *oxonianum* 'Claridge Druce' (z4–8), which even in the dry shade beneath trees will spread its carpet of gray-green leaves and shocking pink flowers on 24in/60cm stems, opening over a long season. Another, more manageable ground cover is the strongly aromatic *G. macrorrhizum* (z4–8), which has light green leaves coloring brightly in autumn, and 12in/30cm stems bearing flowers typically dull magenta, but varying to bright purple-red in 'Bevan's Variety,' pale pink in 'Ingwersen's Variety,' and white with pink calyces in 'Album.' Uncompromising magenta is the color of *G. cinereum* var. *subcaulescens* (z5–8), a low, mound-forming plant with gray foliage. 'Russell Prichard' (z5–8), barely taller at 10in/25cm, but much more a sprawling carpet, has foliage of similar tone to set off paler, chalky pink flowers appearing over an exceptionally long season. 'Mavis Simpson' (z7–8) is lovely and has rose-pink flowers with a satin sheen and gray leaves. The long stems die back to a central rootstock in the fall, whereas *G. malviflorum* (z6–8) does its growing in autumn and winter, when its dissected leaves are spring-fresh, dying away to the tuberous roots in summer after the deep lilac, veined flowers have faded. One of the most beautiful in foliage is *G. renardii* (z6–8), its gray leaves feeling to the touch like fine figured velvet. The flowers are cool gray-white, on 12in/30cm stems. *G. argenteum* (z6–8) is smaller with dissected, silvery leaves and pale pink flowers on 4in/10cm stems.

Gillenia ROSACEAE
Gillenia trifoliata (z4–8), bowman's root, does equally well in hot, dry, sunny places or moist shade. The sprays of starry, white or blush flowers are held in long-lasting red calyces on 30in/75cm stems. In the fall the plant turns to gold and orange. It is increased by division or seed.

Glaucium PAPAVERACEAE
The foliage of the biennial horned poppies is beautiful, intensely blue-gray, crimpled and divided, forming striking rosettes in their first season. Plants of the shore and of dry, stony places, they are remarkably tolerant of drought, though the finest leaf rosettes develop in well-nourished soil. *Glaucium flavum* (z5–8) has clear yellow flowers, and *G. corniculatum* (z5–8) deep orange-red; long blue-gray seed pods follow, from which the name horned poppy derives, and from the contents of which new plants are raised.

Gypsophila CARYOPHYLLACEAE
Gypsophila paniculata (z4–9) needs a deep, open soil and does very well on chalk, as long as the soil is well broken up to allow the roots to penetrate. Formerly a classic cut flower, it makes a cloudy mound of white up to 4ft/1.2m high and wide in summer. It is grown from seed, but named selections must be increased by cuttings or grafts, as must the much more compact, pink-flowered hybrid 'Rosenschleier' ('Rosy Veil') (z4–9).

Hedysarum LEGUMINOSAE
The French honeysuckle or sulla sweet vetch, *Hedysarum coronarium* (z6–9), has bright red pea flowers in long racemes, deliciously scented of cloves, on 36in/90cm stems. It is variable in its hardiness. *H. multijugum* var. *apiculatum* (z3–8), the Mongolian sweet vetch, is a taller plant, somewhat woody, with glaucous foliage and violet or brilliant purple, fragrant flowers.

Helichrysum COMPOSITAE
Helichrysum bracteatum (*Bracteantha bracteata*) (z9), an Australian annual or perennial, has given rise to some perennial cultivars (increased by cuttings) such as 'Dargan Hill Monarch,' striking with its large orange-gold everlasting flowers on 36in/90cm stems, over gray, cobwebby leaves.

Helleborus RANUNCULACEAE
The Corsican hellebore, *Helleborus argutifolius* (*H. corsicus*) (z7–9), is a handsome, evergreen foliage plant, with strong 24in/60cm stems that bear only leaves in their first year, the flowers appearing in their second season, after which they die away to make room for the next generation of stems. The tripartite leaves are gray-green and subprickly along their margins; the flowers, held in sheaves, are nodding jade-green cups opening early in the year. Seedlings often appear around the parent plant.

Helleborus argutifolius

Hemerocallis 'Stafford'

Hemerocallis LILIACEAE/HEMEROCALLIDACEAE

Even among the most extreme manifestations of the breeders' art, there is hardly an unattractive daylily, though it is a matter of taste whether you prefer the grace of the species or the flamboyance of the larger-flowered hybrids, some of which have crimpled or ruffled segments or brazenly staring blooms in contrast to the clean, pure lines of the species and early garden hybrids. Some, especially those with yellow flowers, have a delicious lily fragrance; most bring a note of freshness to the spring garden as their grassy blades spear through the soil in shades of chartreuse and peridot green.

The old lemon lily, *Hemerocallis lilioasphodelus* (*H. flava*) (z3–9), is one of the first to flower, and one of the most fragrant; its clear yellow blooms on 30in/75cm stems are beautifully shaped and freely borne. Earlier in the season are two smaller species, *H. dumortieri* (z3–9) and *H. middendorfii* (z3–9), both with scented, warm yellow flowers touched with mahogany on the reverse, borne on 24in/60cm stems. *H. multiflora* (z5–9) brings similar coloring to the later season; the small, fragrant flowers are borne on branching 4ft/1.2m stems. The brick-pink to soft orange *H. fulva* (z3–9) increases fast at the root; it has double forms, 'Flore Pleno' and 'Green Kwanso,' less elegant but longer-lasting in flower.

Being both popular and, on the whole, long-lived, daylilies have been much hybridized until there are thousands of named cultivars still extant (the registered names exceed 30,000), and certainly some hundreds in commerce at any one time. Selecting them must therefore be highly subjective; my own choice is from among those which are fragrant, beautifully poised, and not too far distant in grace from the species. Clear yellows with these qualities include 'Marion Vaughn,' the older 'Hyperion,' 'Lark Song' and 'Whichford.' Rich dark reds, though they lack fragrance, are valued for their unusual coloring: old 'Stafford' remains a good garden plant, much more weatherproof than newer cultivars of this shade, and 'Black Magic' has starry flowers of very deep maroon-red. The pinks, which lean to warm brick tones, have their own allure: 'Pink Damask,' 'Pink Charm.' The "miniatures" have small flowers after the style of *H. multiflora*, but are not necessarily short in growth: well-established cultivars with the butterfly grace of this group include the warm-toned 'Isis' and 'Golden Chimes,' and lemon-yellow 'Corky.'

One of the great gains in modern hybrids, to balance the loss of purity of line, is the length of the flowering season, in some cases even with a repeat season. 'Stella de Oro' is proving very popular on this account, with its continuous flowering of rich yellow flowers on 18in/45cm stems, one of many in the "dwarf" class. Another gain has been in the choice of colors, which now includes lavender and purple.

Hesperis CRUCIFERAE

The sweet rocket or dame's violet, *Hesperis matronalis* (z4–8), is a free-seeding perennial valued for its exquisite clove perfume, carrying far on the summer air, especially at dusk. The flowers, like single stocks, are white or lilac, and are borne on 4ft/1.2m stems. The double-flowered cultivars are tricky beasts to grow, not to be risked in the stressful conditions of a droughty garden.

Hieracium COMPOSITAE

Many of the hawkweeds are indeed weeds, and *Hieracium aurantiacum* (*Pilosella aurantiaca*) (z4–8), or Grim the collier, is borderline, but handsome with its black-budded, bright orange flowers. Others are above all foliage plants, with silver-felted or wooly leaves. *H. lanatum* and *H. waldsteinii* (z5–8) are similar, with broad, silvery leaves forming striking rosettes; the bright yellow flowers are best removed, though if you leave them you should get a family of silver seedlings. *H. villosum* (z4–8) is woolier in leaf and produces a long succession of large yellow flowers.

Hippocrepis LEGUMINOSAE

Hippocrepis comosa (z6–8) is a spreading, prostrate perennial, tolerant of the driest soils, with bright yellow pea flowers; more appealing is the cultivar 'E. R. Janes,' with pale lemon flowers. Like the larger helianthemums, this will quickly make a complete cover on dry banks.

Iris IRIDACEAE

No dry garden is complete without some irises, be it the tough and resilient gladwin, bulbous, crested or bearded irises. These are for the most part easy to grow in drained soil, enjoying a summer baking. (Moisture-loving irises, naturally, receive no mention here.) The most challenging are the Oncocyclus and Regelias and their hybrids (z6–8). These are without exception intricately beautiful, with their large, perfectly formed flowers in subtle shades of gray, silver, bronze or mourning purple, net-veined or blotched with deeper tones. Try them in a stony, free-draining, but rich mixture in a dry, lightly shaded raised bed, with protection from winter wet. The Regeliocyclus Group of hybrids (z6–8) are marginally less obdurate than the pure species which are their parents.

Iris unguicularis

Nothing could be easier than *Iris foetidissima* (z5–9), the gladwin or stinking gladdon, also sometimes called roast beef plant, because of the odor of the leaves when bruised. Its glossy, evergreen sword leaves form bold clumps; the flowers are so discreet as to be hardly noticeable, but they are followed by fat pods of bright orange seeds on 18in/45cm stems, that can be picked and dried for winter arrangements. The gladwin will grow in any soil and copes well with dark, dry shade; it has a first-rate variegated form with cream-striped leaves. Another much smaller iris which is coy with its flowers is the plum tart iris, *I. graminea* (z5–9); it is modesty, not inferiority, in this case, for the little blooms, hidden among the narrow polished leaves, are not only very pretty, in shades of purple and violet, but also deliciously and unmistakably scented of stewed plums, reminding me of the aromatic and juicy open tarts of Fellemberg plums we used to eat as children in Switzerland on the annual day of the fast.

The easier crested irises do well in dry conditions; indeed, *I. tectorum* (z5–9) is called the roof iris, because in Japan it is apparently planted on roofs. It has polished, dark green leaves and crimpled lilac flowers, crested with white. There is a pure white form, *I. t. alba*, and one with cream-striated leaves, 'Variegata.' *I. japonica* (z7–9) has orchid-like flowers, white marked with lilac and crested with gold. They open in spring and summer on branching, 18in/45cm stems among the broad, dark green leaf blades. 'Ledger's Variety' is the form usually grown; 'Variegata' has cream-striped leaves. Also for well-drained soils is the winter iris or Algerian iris, *I. unguicularis* (*I. stylosa*) (z7–8), which flowers for three or four months during winter. The scrolled buds are hard to discern among the narrow leaves, for the reverse of the petals is pale beige, but as they unfurl, they reveal their clear lavender coloring and perfection of outline. Sweetly scented, they can be picked in bud (pull the stems from as near the base as possible) and taken indoors to open. The winter iris is at its best in dry, rocky soils and flowers most freely after a summer baking. The leaves become untidy in summer and can be cut back. There is a beautiful white form, *I. u. alba*, and selections with deeper violet flowers such as 'Mary Barnard.' 'Walter Butt' has wide, pale lilac blooms.

Bearded irises have been extensively hybridized; they are of complex parentage. Even the old *I. germanica* (z4–9), with its purple-violet, fragrant flowers of classic *fleur de lis* shape on 36in/90cm stems, is a sterile hybrid. Another sterile bearded iris of great antiquity is *I.* 'Florentina' (z4–9), the dried roots of which are fragrant, and sold as orris root (for use in potpourri, among other things). A shorter plant, with fragrant gray-white flowers over grayish leaves, it is seen in the fields and among the olive groves and Judas trees of northern Italy, as well as over a vast area of the Muslim world in cemeteries. The noble *I. pallida* ssp. *pallida* (*I. p.* var. *dalmatica*) (z4–8) has beautiful lavender-blue, scented *fleur de lis* blooms on 36in/90cm stems, amid broad, very gray leaves. From southern France and northern Italy comes the diminutive *I. lutescens* (*I. chamaeiris*) (z7–8), variable in color, but seldom over 4–6in/10–15cm in height. *I. pumila*, (z5–8), which extends into Asia Minor, is another dwarf iris with flowers of varying colors. Both make good little mats of growth.

It remains for me to refer to the Junos, small irises with tuberous roots and leaves folded in one plane into a fan-like sheaf. *I. bucharica* (z4–8) is typical of the group in white and yellow, growing to 18in/45cm; *I. magnifica* (z5–8) is lilac and yellow, *I. aucheri* (*I. sindjarensis*) (z7) lilac. There are others; all are extremely desirable. All irises can be increased by division of the roots, and many by seed.

Kniphofia LILIACEAE/ASPHODELACEAE

The red hot pokers have been done a disservice by this vernacular name, which should really belong only to the coarse old garden plant called *kniphofia uvaria* (z5–9), with red and yellow torches on 5ft/1.5m stems. It does make a brave splash of color, but others are superior in many ways, and their range of colors is wide, from creamy white to deep red via all the yellows and oranges, as well as shades of pink and of green. It is tempting, especially as I used to collect them, to describe dozens; as it is, I shall restrict myself to just two groups: those with bold, leek-like, evergreen foliage, and the grassy-leaved, slender-spired, late-flowering dwarf pokers. Of the former, the better-known is *K. caulescens* (z6–9), which forms stout procumbent stems like elephants' trunks lying on the ground; the lovely gray leaves are topped by 4ft/1.2m stems bearing pale coral and greenish-ivory flower heads. It is distinguished from *K. northiae* (z6–9) by having keeled leaves, whereas those of Miss North's plant are U-shaped in cross-section. It makes terrific rosettes of gray foliage and has flowers rather similar to those of *K. caulescens*. The slender *K. galpinii* (of gardens) belongs with *K. triangularis* (z6–9), a dainty, slim-spiked poker of 18-24in/45–60cm, in shades of orange and vermilion, opening late in the poker season, lovely with silvers, caryopteris and *Ceratostigma willmottianum*.

Lathyrus LEGUMINOSAE

The perennial peas are cousins of the annual sweet pea, though few have any fragrance. For all that, they are splendid garden plants; those that follow are all tendril climbers and can be grown like woody climbers on a permanent support – living or artificial – or allowed to flop down a bank or sprawl over gravel. They can also be encouraged to spread into the space in a border vacated by an early-flowering plant. *Lathyrus grandiflorus* (z6–9), the everlasting pea of southern Europe, is a rapid spreader, its large flowers a deep shocking pink with a maroon keel. The perennial pea, *L. latifolius* (z5–9), has slightly smaller flowers of elegant shape; 'White Pearl,' especially, is almost like a small phalaenopsis orchid. There is also a pretty pale pink, but the standard color is an assertive magenta-pink. The clear pink *L. tuberosus* (z5–9) is like a smaller version of less potent coloring. If this is not your color, there is the Persian everlasting pea, *L. rotundifolius* (z5–9), which has brick-pink flowers. The peas can be increased by seed (color variants coming reasonably true) or by division.

Lavatera MALVACEAE

Lavatera trimestris is a branching annual with white, pink or rose-red flowers. Popular seed strains include 'Mont Blanc,' which is a startling white with dark green foliage but of rather dumpy growth, and the taller, satiny pink 'Silver Cup.'

Leptinella COMPOSITAE

Leptinella squalida (*Cotula squalida*) (z5–7) is an easy-going mat-former, looking for all the world like some tiny, bronzed fern, but, unlike ferns, it tolerates dry conditions. It is propagated by division of the creeping roots.

Leucophyta COMPOSITAE

Leucophyta brownii (*Calocephalus brownii*) (z10) is one of the most appealing of "silvers," with slender, twisted stems, and tiny adpressed leaves giving it the appearance of a tangle of platinum wire. It can be propagated from cuttings and reaches 24in/60cm in a season.

Iris 'Florentina'

Linum narbonense

Liatris COMPOSITAE

The Kansas gay feather, *Liatris pycnostachya* (z4–9), opens its bottlebrush flowers from the top down; they are bright lilac-pink, on 4ft/1.2m stems. At half the height, *L. spicata* (z4–9) shares the upside-down nature of its taller cousin; it is even more vivid in color and has a delicious white form. They combine well with other prairie plants such as *Penstemon hirsutus* and the pale tickseed (*Coreopsis verticillata* 'Moonbeam'). All can be propagated by seed, or by division of named cultivars.

Libertia IRIDACEAE

The libertias are antipodean iris relatives with, for the most part, vividly white, three-petaled flowers on iris-like stems. Bright orange-brown seed heads follow, from which more plants can be raised. They can also be divided. Both *Libertia formosa* (z8–10) and *L. grandiflora* (z9–10) form weed-excluding clumps of narrow, dark green leaves. They will grow even in the dry shade beneath high-limbed pines, where their stark white flowers on 36in/90cm stems stand out against the dark trunks of the trees. *L. ixioides* (z8–10) is a slighter plant reaching 24in/60cm, with narrow leaves that often change color to orange-brown in winter. *L. peregrinans* (z8–10) is similar again, but with creeping roots.

Limonium PLUMBAGINACEAE

The statices or sea lavenders, as their name suggests, are valuable in dry, seashore gardens. The European *Limonium bellidifolium* (z3–9) has leathery, blunt leaves and sprays of tiny pinkish flowers on short stems. The more substantial *L. latifolium* (z3–9) has tough, coarse, dark green foliage and branching 12in/30cm stems of many minute lavender-blue flowers, long lasting and good for drying; named cultivars, which must be propagated by division or root cuttings, have brighter flowers or taller stems. One of the most handsome of the genus is *L. perezii* (z3–9), in which the dark gray-green leaves form tufts above which deep indigo, white-flecked flowers are borne on wiry 36in/90cm stems over a long season. It makes an attractive companion for pale achilleas, sea hollies (*Eryngium maritimum*), the Missouri primrose (*Oenothera missouriensis*), and blue grasses (*Festuca glauca* and others).

Linaria SCROPHULARIACEAE

Linaria dalmatica (z5–8) is like a glorified version of the wild European toadflax, with glaucous-blue leaves and branching 36in/90cm stems bearing bright yellow miniature snapdragons over a long summer season. If you are seeking a plant of this character for a purple or pink color scheme, there is *L. triornithophora* (z7–10), nicknamed three birds flying, because the clusters of larger purple or pale pink flowers at intervals up the stem look almost like parakeets, caught in repose not flight; it has the same months-long season and somewhat fleshy, blue-green leaves. Both species have running roots which can be divided for increase.

Linum LINACEAE

Fields of blue flax color the landscape in Europe like fallen sky as the fierce yellow of rape fades to green. In the garden, the perennial blue flaxes such as *Linum narbonense* (z5–8) are equally charming at close quarters, with their silky, azure funnels on 18in/45cm stems. It can be grown from seed, as can the short-lived perennial *L. perenne* (z4–8) (also blue); and this is the way to raise *L. grandiflorum rubrum*, an annual flax which self-seeds and bears its crimson flowers on 18in/45cm stems. Quite different is the small, shrubby *L. arboreum* (z6–9), which makes a low mound of blue-glaucous leaves contrasting with satiny, bright yellow cups.

Liriope LILIACEAE/CONVALLARIACEAE

Liriope muscari (z6–10) is a spreading, weed-excluding plant forming dense tufts of dark grassy leaves, decorated with 12in/30cm grape hyacinth-like spikes of bright purple flowers in the fall. The fast-spreading *L. spicata* (z4–10) is a lesser plant with lilac or white flowers, but just as efficient at covering its patch. Both are known as lily turf for this reason.

Lunaria CRUCIFERAE

Lunaria annua, the biennial honesty, is a well-loved old garden plant, on account of its cheerful violet-purple flowers in spring as much as its papery "honest money" seed heads in autumn. There are richer and paler purple forms as well as white, and others with variegated foliage, coming true from seed. The perennial *L. rediviva* (z4–8) is a charming early-flowering honesty with lilac-white flowers on 24in/60cm stems, followed by elliptical white "money." It can be grown from seed or divisions.

Lupinus LEGUMINOSAE

The shrubby and subshrubby lupines of California have already been described. The annual species of *Lupinus* are also valuable for dry gardens, and the new true-to-color seed strains derived mainly from *L. polyphyllus* (z3–6) could be worth trying too. The true annuals include blue-and-white *L. hartwegii* and fragrant yellow *L. luteus*, both flowering at a height of

Lupinus polyphyllus

Lychnis coronaria Alba group

Nepeta × faasenii amid pale
Osteospermum ecklonis

18-30in/45-75cm, and the adorable Texas bluebonnet, *L. texensis*, with vivid blue flowers in white-tipped spikes on 8in/20cm stems in spring. It occurs naturally in white and, rarely, in pink as well as blue, and has been developed by selection to include sky blue, red, lavender and maroon as well. The sandy land bluebonnet, *L. subcarnosus*, bears its royal blue flowers a little earlier in spring.

Lychnis CARYOPHYLLACEAE
The dusty miller or rose campion, *Lychnis coronaria* (z4–8), makes rosettes of white-felted leaves, topped by brilliant magenta flowers on gray 36in/90cm stems. There is a delightful white variant, the Alba group, while the Oculata group has white flowers with a pink eye. The flower of Jove, *L. flos-jovis* (z5–8), has wooly gray leaves and purple-red flowers on 18in/45cm stems; again, there is a white form, and a rose-pink, 'Hort's Variety.' The hybrid between the dusty miller and the flower of Jove, *L. × walkeri* 'Abbotswood Rose' (z4–8), is a splendid thing with silver leaves and vivid cerise flowers on 24in/60cm stems.

Marrubium LABIATAE
Marrubium cylleneum (z5–7) is wonderfully soft and silky in leaf, as the name 'Velvetissimum' (not a validated name) implies. It forms a 12in/30cm mound and bears small pink flowers of no particular consequence. The better-known, but scarcely widespread *M. incanum* (*M. candidissimum*) (z3–9) is a silvery-silky subshrub, larger in growth, with spikes of white flowers in wooly calyces. Both can be increased by division or cuttings.

Monarda LABIATAE
The wild bergamot, *Monarda fistulosa* (z3–8), is much more drought-tolerant than the bee balm, *M. didyma* (z4–8). The hooded flowers are lilac-purple or white, borne in whorls up the 4ft/1.2m stems; the foliage is fragrant. The wild bergamot can be increased by division.

Nepeta LABIATAE
The catmints are aromatic plants, easily grown in dry soils. The most popular with cats is the weedy catnip, *Nepeta cataria*, but the gardeners' favorite is *N. × faassenii* (z4–8), a grayish mound with a long succession of lavender-blue flowers on 18in/45cm stems. It is sometimes labeled *N. mussinii*, though the true plant, now called *N. racemosa* (z4–8), is of less value in the garden. The taller, spreading *N. sibirica* (z4–8) has bluer flowers and a similarly long season. The short, dense, blue spikes of *N. nervosa* (z4–8), are very different from the loose, cloudy effect of these catmints. They are all increased by cuttings or division.

Nipponanthemum COMPOSITAE
Nipponanthemum nipponicum (*Chrysanthemum nipponicum*) (z5–9) is a late-flowering, subshrubby perennial, with dark green foliage to set off its wide, pure white, lime-eyed flowers on 24in/60cm stems. It is increased by division. In cold regions, give it a warm sunny spot.

Oenothera ONAGRACEAE
The biennial evening primroses, valued for their night-time fragrance, are yellow-flowered, but there are some appealing small species with white or pink flowers as well as yellow. The day-awake species are known as suncups or sundrops. *Oenothera caespitosa* (z4–7), from the deserts of North America,

has narrow, toothed leaves and huge, fragrant white flowers on short stems. When happy, it spreads by underground runners. The tap-rooted *O. trichocalyx* (z7–10) is another desert native, with long, narrow, gray-green leaves and large white or pale pink flowers on short stems. The Mexican primrose, *O. speciosa* (*O. berlandieri*, *O. childsii*) (z8–11), is a spreading perennial with narrow, pointed leaves, and large white or pink cups on 6in/ 15cm stems. The dandelion-leaved *O. acaulis* (*O. taraxifolia*) (z5–8) has clusters of large, stemless white or soft yellow flowers. One of the easiest to grow in any well-drained garden soil is *O. missouriensis* (z5–8), the Missouri primrose or Ozark sundrops, its trailing stems set with narrow dark green leaves enlivened by pale midribs; it bears huge, clear yellow flowers in red calyces over a long summer season. More of a border plant, *O. fruticosa* ssp. *glauca* (z4–8), the common sundrops, has dark foliage and 18in/45cm stems bearing bright yellow cups opening from red-tinted buds; var. *fraseri* has mahogany-toned spring foliage. The smaller oenotheras are propagated by seed, but *O. fruticosa* can be divided.

Origanum 'Kent Beauty'

Omphalodes BORAGINACEAE
Omphalodes linifolia departs from the usual borage family tradition of blue flowers, displaying its skimmed-milk white blooms over glaucous-blue leaves. It is an annual, free-seeding in dry, well drained soils, growing to 12in/30cm or so.

Onopordum COMPOSITAE
Onopordum acanthium, the Scotch thistle, is an imposing biennial with silvery gray leaves, and large purple thistle heads on 7ft/2m stems. The leaf rosettes, in their first year, are wide and beautiful. Propagation is by seed.

Onosma BORAGINACEAE
The onosmas or golden drops all have nodding, tubular flowers, though not necessarily yellow. *Onosma alboroseum* (z7–8) has silvery hairy leaves and white flowers aging to pink, while *O. echioides* (z6–7) and the very similar *O. tauricum* (z6–7) have fragrant, soft yellow flowers. Both do well in a rocky crevice or dry wall.

Ophiopogon LILIACEAE/CONVALLARIACEAE
Ophiopogon japonicus (z7–9) is another lily turf similar to *Liriope*, with dark green, glossy, narrow leaves and small, white flowers on 12in/30cm stems. It is a spreader and can be divided for increase.

Origanum LABIATAE
The culinary herbs of the Mediterranean regions, *O. vulgare* (z4–8) and *O. majorana* (z5–8), which cooks call oregano or rigani (Greek wild marjoram), belong here, together with the dittanies, which are attractive, often gray-wooly plants for dry places, with their flowers held in hop-like bracts. *Origanum amanum* (z5–8) is a compact little bushlet with pale leaves and long-tubed lilac flowers in pink bracts, over a long season; it is a native of the Near East, as is *O. rotundifolium* (z4–8), which has round leaves clasping the short, woody stems, and pale pink flowers in whorls amid large, papery bracts. Its hybrid offspring, *O.* 'Kent Beauty,' is splendid with abundant pink flowers. The Greek *O. calcaratum* (*O. tournefortii*) (z7–9) grows to 12in/30cm, with leafy stems topped by lilac-pink flowers. *O. dictamnus* (z7–9), the dittany of Crete, is another delightful late-flowering plant, with round, white-felted leaves and nodding heads of pink flowers

with the same style of bracts. Another Cretan, *O. microphyllum* (z7–9), has pink flowers in rounded clusters at the tips of the 8in/20cm stems. The Levantine *O. × hybridum* (z7–9) has drooping pink flowers. Taller than these is *O. laevigatum* (z5–9), which has abundant, erect sprays of small, purple-pink, dark-bracted flowers, creating an open, airy effect very different from the dittanies.

Osteospermum COMPOSITAE

Another of the great tribe of South African daisies, the perennial osteospermums vary from trailing to upright bushes, all easily increased by cuttings. The annual species are grown from seed. *Osteospermum aurantiacum* (now correctly *Dimorphotheca sinuata*), the star of the veldt or Cape marigold, grows to 12in/30cm or more and bears bright orange daisy flowers with a dark brown disk. Seed strains offer different colors, including some charming pastel shades, as well as the short-growing 'Glistening White.' This name could apply to the perennial *O. ecklonis* (z9–10), a Cape species with pure white ray florets striped with mauve on the reverse, surrounding a dark metallic blue disk. The typical plant is upright; *O. e. prostratum* (*O. caulescens*) (z9–10), of similar coloring, spreads sideways. 'Weetwood' shows clear affinities to this. *O. fruticosum* (z9–10) is another sprawler, similar to *O. ecklonis*, forming wide mats up to 5ft/1.5m across in a single season. Plants with pink or lilac flowers are often attributed to *O. barberae* (*O. jucundum*) (z9–10), which is typically prostrate, with mauve-pink flowers, the petals bronzed on the reverse, among gray-green leaves. *O. b.* var. *compactum* (z9–10) is smaller and probably the most frost-resistant of all the osteospermums.

   Osteospermum hybrids and cultivars are many, varying greatly in flower color, habit and frost-hardiness. Among the more frost-resistant are three of spreading habit: 'Lady Leitrim' in white splashed with pink, around a yellow disk; 'Hopley's' in purplish-pink; and 'Langtrees,' similar to 'Lady Leitrim,' but with deeper pink-to-mauve flowers and a yellow and blue disk. Other spreaders, such as 'Tresco Purple' ('Nairobi,' 'African Queen,' 'Peggy') and the more upright, floriferous 'James Elliman,' with flowers like wine-purple corduroy around a dark purple disk, are frost-tender. Taller hybrids include pale lilac 'Bloemhoff Belle'; mauve-pink, blue-eyed 'Brickell's Hybrid'; pink-to-mauve 'La Mortola'; white 'Blue Streak,' so called for its blue disk and inky blue reverse; and soft yellow, bronze-backed 'Buttermilk.' Two curiosities with the petals pinched in at the center to show the blue reverse are white 'Whirligig' ('Tauranga') and 'Pink Whirls,' both of upright habit. Variegated leaves belong to 'Bodegas Pink,' and to white-flowered 'Silver Sparkler.'

Papaver PAPAVERACEAE

There is no mistaking the crumpled silk flowers of a poppy, whether it is the whopping oriental poppy or the diminutive *Papaver alpinum* of gardens (now attributed to *P. nudicaule*) (z4–7), which seeds itself about, forming little tufts of divided, pale leaves over which the solitary flowers hover, white, pink or yellow. Another miniature is *P. miyabeanum* (z4–7), very desirable with its gray-green, hairy, dissected leaves and large lemon poppies on 6in/15cm stems. Among annuals are the Shirley poppies, bred from *P. rhoeas* to a range of delicate colors by one of England's clergyman-gardeners; and the more substantial opium poppies (*P. somniferum*) (z4–10), with their soap-smooth, blue-gray leaves and large flowers, single or powder-puff double, in shades of white, pale to bright pink, and lilac. Even

Papaver rhoeas Double Shirley

the seed heads that follow are attractive, in the same blue-gray tones as the leaves; but beware, they shake their myriad tiny seeds out like pepper from a pot, and you can easily be overrun with seedlings. Would that *P. commutatum* were as generous. This is what a designer might have made of the red Flanders poppy: generous, scarlet flowers with a bold black spot at the base of each petal, over finely cut, soft green leaves. It is sometimes called, for obvious reasons, the ladybird poppy.

The typical perennial border poppy is *P. orientale* (z4–7), with hairy foliage that quickly dies down, and huge flowers, in the species bright vermilion-scarlet, black-blotched, with silky indigo-black stamens and velvety seed capsule; we used, as children, to turn the petals down, tie them about the stem with a blade of grass, and call the result a dancing lady – her scarlet dress contrasting with glossy black hair. Cultivars come in an increasing range of colors, from white – still with the enhancing black blotch – through pale pink, salmon and soft melon-orange, with or without contrasting picotee edge, to cherry red or deep crimson-maroon. There is a double orange-scarlet, and of the same style, but in miniature, is 'Fireball' ('Nanum Flore Pleno'), with running roots and absurd orange pompon flowers. Division and root cuttings are means of propagation.

Two smaller species are very much like each other: *P. atlanticum* (z8) from Morocco, and the more leafy *P. pilosum* (z5–8) from Asia Minor; both have delicate, silky flowers, soft orange in color, nodding on long stalks. *P. rupifragum* (z8), from Spain, has grayish foliage and soft tangerine flowers on 18in/45cm stems, while one of the most distinct, *P. spicatum* (*P. heldreichii*) (z4–7), has white-furred buds opening from the top of the 30in/75cm stems down, expanding to wide, tangerine-apricot flowers on short stalks, over blue-gray, hairy leaves. They can be increased from seed or by division.

Paronychia CARYOPHYLLACEAE

The whitlow worts are carpeting plants making good ground-cover among dry rocks. The Mediterranean *Paronychia capitata* (z5–7) is silver-leaved, and *P. kapela* (*P. serpyllifolia*) (z5–7) is very compact, with dark bluish-green leaves turning to rust-brown in the fall.

LEFT *Phlox subulata*

RIGHT *Pelargonium echinatum*

Pelargonium GERANIACEAE

The many species and countless cultivars of *Pelargonium* – a largely South African genus – have filled many a book on their own. This entry is merely to alert you to the ability of virtually all to survive periods of drought and neglect. This goes as much for the scented-leaf "geraniums" such as the rose-scented *Pelargonium graveolens* (z9–10), velvet-leaved, peppermint-smelling *P. tomentosum* (z9–10), lemony 'Citriodorum' and apple-scented *P. odoratissimum* (z9–10) as for the flowering hybrids. They are all easy to raise from cuttings, and seed strains have also been developed that make stout little plants, though only with single flowers. The ivy-leaved geranium, *P. peltatum* (z9–10), has given rise to several excellent trailing plants with semi-succulent leaves and bright flowers, often with narrow petals, such as the Balcon series in vivid pinks and reds.

Penstemon SCROPHULARIACEAE

From the gardener's point of view, penstemons fall into two groups: the border perennials, and the small, more or less shrubby species that look so pretty among rocks or in raised beds among other small plants. Of the border types, *Penstemon barbatus* (z3–8) bears a long succession of small, clear scarlet, tubular flowers with hairy throats on 36in/90cm stems, while the evergreen *P. campanulatus* (z8–9) has given rise to several more frost-resistant hybrids, of which two in particular are very popular in English gardens: 'Evelyn' (z6–8), with pink flowers on bushy 18in/45cm growth, and the deep wine-red 'Andenken an Friedrich Hahn' (z6–9), better known as 'Garnet.' Other hybrids range from the scarlet 'Schoenholzeri' ('Firebird' or 'Ruby'), 'Southgate Gem,' and others – which presumably derive their bright coloring from the vivid scarlet *P. hartwegii* (z8–9) – to the softer-toned 'Stapleford Gem' in opaline lavender or the tall 'Alice Hindley' (z4–8) in pale lilac. There are white, pale pink, and deep plum

('Blackbird,' 'Burgundy') penstemons, and at least one huge-flowered survivor from more expansive days that outdoes them all in triumphant vulgarity: 'Rubicundus,' its wide scarlet trumpets white-throated. Back with species, *P. glaber* (z4–7) is a small, front-of-border plant with opalescent pink and blue flowers over a long season on 10in/25cm stems, while the narrow-leaved *P. heterophyllus* (z7–8) has, in its best forms, purplish foliage as a foil to narrow tubes of purest azure blue. The lilac and cream *P. hirsutus* (z4) has a dwarf form, 'Pygmaeus,' of similar stature.

There are several small, woody-stemmed penstemons for rock gardens and raised beds, such as *P. davidsonii* (z6–7), at its best gray-green in leaf and bright carmine-pink in flower; the blooms are very large in proportion to the plant. *P. newberryi* (z7–8) has rose-pink flowers, and the almost prostrate *P. rupicola* (z6–7) has grayish foliage and rose-carmine flowers. *P. pinifolius* (z6–7) is of different character, making little bushes of very narrow green leaves set with slender tubes of bright orange-scarlet, or lemon-yellow in 'Mersea Yellow.' All penstemons except *P. barbatus*, which is best divided or seed-raised, can be increased by cuttings.

Perovskia LABIATAE

The Russian sage or Afghan sage, *Perovskia atriplicifolia* (z6–9), is a soft-wooded shrub with turpentine-aromatic, toothed, gray-green leaves, white beneath, and 4ft/1.2m open steeples of bright violet-blue flowers in summer. *P.* 'Blue Spire' (z6–9) is a hybrid of this and the feathery-leaved *P. abrotanoides* (z6–9); it has dissected leaves and branching spikes of violet-blue flowers. It is increased by cuttings or division.

Persicaria POLYGONACEAE

Persicaria capitata (*Polygonum capitatum*) (z9–10) is a fast-spreading, prostrate plant with rooting stems, also increasing by seed. In moist conditions it grows lush and green, but in dry soils it is more compact, and the pointed leaves, zoned with a dark chevron, take on pink and crimson tints as a pretty complement to the small spherical heads of candy pink flowers, appearing for most of the year.

Phlomis LABIATAE

The shrubby phlomis have already been described. From Syria comes the herbaceous *Phlomis russeliana* (z4–9), which has large, evergreen, leaves and 36in/90cm stems bearing whorls of soft yellow flowers.

Phlox POLEMONIACEAE

The border phloxes need rich living to do well, looking miserable in dry soils, but some of the small species commonly grown in rock gardens are tolerant of drought. *Phlox douglasii* (z5–7) is a perky little plant making little mounds of tufty foliage, with lavender, white, carmine-rose or pink flowers. The moss phloxes, *P. subulata* (z2–9), are offered in a wider range of cultivars still, though the basic color-range is the same. The prairie phlox, *P. pilosa* (z4–7), does well in hot, dry conditions, making 24in/60cm mounds of glossy foliage covered for weeks with pink, or sometimes lavender or white, flowers scented like jasmine.

Phormium AGAVACEAE/PHORMIACEAE

With their strong, evergreen sword foliage, erect or arching, phormiums have as much presence as many shrubs. *Phormium cookianum* (z9–10), the mountain flax, has somewhat lax, arching sword leaves and brownish flowers on 4ft/1.2m stems. 'Tricolor' has red and yellow stripes on the green leaves, while 'Cream Delight' has leaves broadly cream-margined, the green center with narrow cream stripes. The New Zealand flax, *P. tenax* (z9–10), is massive, with long, broadsword leaves held stiffly erect, and 10ft/3m spikes of blood-red flowers. The Purpureum Group have bloomy purple leaves, 'Variegatum' has yellow-margined leaves, and 'Radiance' is creamy yellow variegated. Cultivars deriving from crosses between the two species are many, including miniatures with grassy purple leaves such as 'Thumbelina,' and a range with arching or upright leaves colored in sunset shades of peach, orange and pink, scarlet and tan, such as the 'Maori' series, mainly compact enough for smaller gardens. The colored-leaf and variegated forms of both species are less hardy (z9).

Phuopsis RUBIACEAE
Phuopsis stylosa (z5–8) has tumbling stems set with narrow foliage and smothered in heads of tiny pink flowers over a long season; 'Purpurea' is brighter pink in flower. The whole plant smells powerfully of foxy garlic (though I have heard it described as "vanilla-scented"); it is propagated, if you can bear to get that near to it, by division.

Platystemon PAPAVERACEAE
Platystemon californicus, the cream cups, is a Californian annual of 12in/30cm or so, with gray-green, narrow, furred leaves, and creamy yellow flowers in summer. During hot, sticky weather, it takes a break, reviving as summer cools toward fall. It is increased by seed.

Plecostachys COMPOSITAE
Plecostachys serpyllifolia (z9–10) is a South African native with tiny, rounded, silver-felted leaves on stems that insinuate themselves sideways and upward through neighboring plants. In looks and behavior it evokes a miniature version of *Helichrysum petiolare*.

Polygonum POLYGONACEAE
Polygonum scoparium (*P. equisetiforme*) (z7–10) is very different from the herbaceous species now classed as *Persicaria*, for it resembles an *Ephedra* or a horsetail, with slender, leafless stems from which the tiny, white flowers burst late in the season.

Potentilla ROSACEAE
Several of the smaller species are worth trying in dry soils. One that is especially appealing is *Potentilla crantzii* (*P. villosa*) (z4–7), which has silvery furred evergreen foliage; the strawberry flowers are bright yellow with a deeper eye, on 12in/30cm stems.

Ptilostemon COMPOSITAE
The ivory thistle, *Ptilostemon afer* (*Cirsium diacanthum*) (z5–7), has wide, fiercely armed rosettes of narrow, white-spined leaves. The lilac thistle heads are valued chiefly as the source of seeds for the next generation of rosettes.

Ptilotrichum CRUCIFERAE
Ptilotrichum spinosum (*Alyssum spinosum*) (z7–9) is a spiky little shrublet of grayish cast, with white or pink flowers. 'Roseum,' the pink form, is prettier, a charming component of small-scale gray and silver plantings amid rocks with plants such as the small achilleas.

Pyrethropsis COMPOSITAE

Refugees from the genus *Chrysanthemum*, these are dwarf daisies for dry soils, increased by cuttings. *Pyrethropsis hosmariensis* (z9) has spreading, woody stems, silvery hairy leaves, and large, short-stemmed, pure white daisy heads with golden disks opening from silver and black buds, over a very long season. The Moroccan *P. gayana* (*Chrysanthemum mawii*) (z9) forms a 12in/30cm mound of finely cut bluish foliage, spangled with pink daisies enhanced by maroon disks.

Raoulia COMPOSITAE

Some raoulias are tricky customers, forming cushions, but the mat-forming species are easier. *Raoulia australis* (z7–8) makes the thinnest carpet of tiny silvery leaves and bears almost microscopic yellow flowers; *R. hookeri* (z7–8) is in effect a slightly larger version; and *R. tenuicaulis* (z7–8) is a very undemanding, gray-green spreader. All like gritty soil and are unhappy in cold, wet winters.

Ricinus EUPHORBIACEAE

Ricinus communis (z9), the castor oil plant, is a coarse plant, but useful for quick foliage effects, rapidly reaching 6ft/1.8m or more, with bold, palmate leaves. 'Impala' is an attractive strain with purple-flushed foliage. The seeds from which they are grown are very poisonous.

Salvia LABIATAE

The sages include shrubby plants and perennials, both hardy and frost-tender. Some of the woody species have already been described; it is now the turn of a mixed bag of perennials. *Salvia argentea* (z5–8) is an eastern

Salvia interrupta

Stachys byzantina and tall *Cynara cardunculus*

Mediterranean native, biennial or perennial (easy from seed), with gray-white, broad, basal leaves, textured as though composed of massed cob-webs. Candelabras of white flowers in gray calyces, on 36in/90cm stems, appear in summer. The southern European *S. aethiopis* (z6–8) is similar, with large, white-wooly leaves. The subshrubby *S. candelabrum* (z9–10), a Spanish native, has large gray leaves and branching 5ft/1.5m stems of small, purple flowers; *S. interrupta* (z9–10), from Morocco, is very similar. Both can be increased by cuttings or seed. The violet sage, *S. nemorosa* (z5–8), is a bushy plant with stems branching into erect spikes of violet flowers in purple bracts. 'Superba' grows to 36in/90cm, while 'Lubecca' reaches 18in/45cm and 'East Friesland' about 30in/75cm. *S. caespitosa* (z5–7) is a smaller plant for rocky places, with short, woody stems, very silvery, aromatic leaves, and lilac-pink, broad-lipped flowers in short clusters.

Saponaria CARYOPHYLLACEAE
Saponaria ocymoides (z2–7), the rose soapwort, is a good crevice, wall or dry bank plant, with tumbling leafy stems and many bright pink flowers. It self-sows freely, but named selections must be propagated by cuttings.

Scabiosa DIPSACACEAE
Scabiosa 'Butterfly Blue' (z3–9) is a charming recent hybrid with lavender-blue flowers over a long summer season on 18in/45cm stems.

Silene CARYOPHYLLACEAE
Silene uniflora (*S. maritima*, *S. vulgaris* ssp. *maritima*) (z5–7) is a plant of sea cliffs; in the garden, grow the double white form in a wall or rock garden, where its carnation-like flowers are very pretty amid the grayish foliage.

Sisyrinchium IRIDACEAE
Sisyrinchium angustifolium (*S. bermudiana*) (z3–9), the blue-eyed grass, has narrow, grassy leaves and blue, starry flowers on 6in/15cm stems in early

summer. It seeds itself freely and can be encouraged to settle in rocky
crevices or the gaps between paving stones. There are several other little
sisyrinchiums with blue flowers offered under a variety of names, at least
some of which are probably synonymous. *S. californicum* (z8–9) has yellow
flowers on 12in/30cm stems; in the Brachypus Group (*S. brachypus*) these
are reduced to 6in/15cm or less. It is a chirpy little plant, all too willing to
seed itself around. These little sisyrinchiums clump up fast and can also be
divided. *S. striatum* (z7–8) is a larger plant with evergreen, blue-gray, iris-
like leaves and primrose-yellow cups, faintly striped with purple on the
reverse, clustering along the 18in/45cm stems. Flowered fans die and
should be removed, but the plant increases freely both by forming new leaf
fans and by seed, so it is easy to maintain generous plantings.

Stachys LABIATAE

Stachys byzantina (*S. lanata*, *S. olympica*) (z4–8), the lamb's ears, is a favorite
old silver-leaved plant, as softly wooly as its pet name suggests, spreading to
form good ground-cover in dry places. The flower spikes are about 18in/
45cm tall, also gray-white, with tiny pink flowers lurking in the wool.
'Silver Carpet' is a non-flowering form, and 'Cotton Boll' dispenses with
the pink flowers, though not with the wooly, bobbly spikes that would
normally hold them. They are all evergreen, but susceptible to disfiguring
mildew; and can be increased by division.

Strelitzia STRELITZIACEAE

Strelitzia reginae (z9–11), the bird of paradise flower, has spiky blue and
white flowers crested with orange, like some exotic bird, and large, banana-
like leaves. It grows to 4ft/1.2m and can be propagated by rooting offsets.
The much larger *S. nicolaii* (z9–11) develops, with time, a palm-like trunk,
so that it may grow to as much as 25ft/7.5m, making it a noble foliage plant
with its broad blades. The flowers are whitish.

Stylomecon PAPAVERACEAE

Stylomecon heterophyllum, the wind poppy, flaming poppy or blood drop,
earns two of its names from its vivid flowers of coppery orange with crimson
center, scented like lily of the valley. The fleshy, gray-green leaves are
lobed. An annual from California and Baja California, the wind poppy is
increased from seed and thrives in the light shade of open-canopied trees.

Symphytum BORAGINACEAE

Symphytum ibericum (*S. grandiflorum*) (z4–8) is a compact, ground-covering
comfrey with nodding, tubular, cream flowers on 10in/25cm stems.
'Goldsmith' is a larger derivative of this, with primrose-variegated leaves
and bluish flowers. Both appreciate some shade, but are otherwise easy
spreaders increased by division.

Tanacetum COMPOSITAE

This genus is the present resting place of some former members of the genus
Chrysanthemum. These are small silvery plants for dry places: *Tanacetum
argenteum* (*Chrysanthemum argenteum*) (z8–9) is grown above all for its neat
silver carpets; pewter-gray *T. herderi* (*Hippolytia herderi*, *Achillea* 'Peter
Davis') (z8–9) smells rather unpleasantly of cold roast lamb when
handled; and two with leaves like silver feathers, *T. densum* ssp. *amani* and
T. haradjanii (z7–8), are wide mat-formers with impeccable manners and
attractive yellow flowers. All can be increased by division.

Strelitzia reginae

Teucrium LABIATAE

Teucrium scorodonia (z4–8) is a European weed, but it has a pretty variant in 'Crispum,' its fresh green leaves crimpled and ruffled at the edges; they are held on 12in/30cm stems. It is propagated by division.

Thymus LABIATAE

Many of the thymes are Mediterranean natives, well suited to growing in hot, rocky places. They have aromatic foliage and tiny but abundant flowers. The common thyme, *Thymus vulgaris* (z6–8), a wiry bushlet with gray-green leaves and purple flowers in summer, is often used in cooking. It is fun to collect thymes as much for their different aromas as for their looks. *T. herba-barona* (z4–7) is a carpeter; *T. serpyllum* (z4–7), with purple flowers has a distinct smell of caraway; the more bushy *T. × citriodorus* (z6–8) is, of course, lemon-scented; *T. camphoratus* (z7–8) is aromatic of camphor; and *T. mastichina* (z7–8) is turpentine-smelling. The shrubby *T. membranaceus* (z7–8) has pink flowers in showy white bracts, and *T. richardii* ssp. *nitidus* (z7–8) is another neat little shrubby thyme with grayish foliage and abundant lilac-pink flowers.

Trachystemon BORAGINACEAE

Trachystemon orientale (z5–9) is a big, rumbustious weed-smotherer, with huge, hairy leaves mounding up to 18in/45cm or so; the early flowers are blue. If you need to make more plants, simply divide the rootstock.

Tradescantia COMMELINACEAE

Tradescantia pallida 'Purpurea' (*T. p.* 'Purple Heart,' *Setcreasea purpurea*) (z9–11) is a Mexican native from arid regions, a low-growing plant with lance-shaped, purple foliage, enhanced by a faint metallic sheen, growing

Tradescantia pallida 'Purpurea'

to about 12in/30cm. Pink or pink-and-white flowers appear in summer. Though the top growth is killed by a few degrees of frost, the plant will spring again from below ground if the soil itself is not frozen.

Tulbaghia LILIACEAE/ALLIACEAE

A South African genus, the tulbaghias are easily increased by seed or division. Some, such as *Tulbaghia violacea* (z8–10), which has gray-green leaves to complement its heads of clear lilac-mauve flowers on 24in/60cm stems, have a distinct onion smell. *T. fragrans* (z8–10) has sweet-smelling, deep mauve bells in small agapanthus-like heads on 18in/45cm stems. The adorable *T. capensis* (z8–10) has 6in/15cm stems bearing nodding, cream and coppery orange flowers in early summer.

Verbascum SCROPHULARIACEAE

Several of the mulleins are imposing plants for dry places. *Verbascum bombyciferum* (*V.* 'Broussa') (z6–8) is a biennial, with large, white-wooly leaves forming a bold rosette during winter; the following summer narrow, self-supporting spikes, as white-wooly as the leaves, soar to 6ft/1.8m, studded with lemon-yellow saucers. Another noble mullein, *V. olympicum* (z6–8), has even taller stems of sulfur flowers and wide rosettes of silver-felted leaves. The leaf margins of *V. undulatum* (z6–8) are seductively wavy; the plant is no less silvery white. *V. chaixii* (z5–8) is a good perennial, nothing to shout about in leaf, but very pretty in flower, with its slim 36in/90cm spikes of soft yellow or white flowers, enhanced by the little tuft of mauve-pink stamens. *V.* 'Vernale' (z5–8) is a much more substantial plant, with handsome weed-suppressing basal leaves and huge plumes of bright yellow flowers on branching, 6ft/1.8m stems. The biennial verbascums are grown from seed; the perennials from seed or, to perpetuate particular clones, from root cuttings.

The small verbascums are also valuable plants for dry gardens. The Mediterranean *V. dumulosum* (z7–8) makes a hummocky 12in/30cm bush of stiff stems set with hairy, gray leaves and terminating in a short spike of yellow, purple-eyed flowers. *V.* 'Golden Wings' (× *Celsioverbascum* 'Golden Wings') (z8), the offspring of two Cretan parents, is a subshrubby bushlet of 10in/25cm or so, with dense spikes of pure yellow flowers over a long summer season.

Verbena VERBENACEAE

Bedding verbenas are often raised from seed, either as single-color strains or in mixtures. The best produce a sparkling mix of white, purple, scarlet and crimson. There are also many named varieties that are raised from cuttings; they tend to spread more widely than the seed strains, so you need fewer plants to fill a given space. Among them are 'Silver Anne' ('Pink Bouquet'), scarlet 'Huntsman' and cherry red 'Lawrence Johnston,' magenta 'Sissinghurst' and the scented, lavender-violet 'Loveliness.' They have a long flowering season and are drought-tolerant. *Verbena peruviana* (z7–10) is a small, mat-forming species looking very like a miniature equivalent of these bedding verbenas, spreading to 12in/30cm across or so, with brilliant vermilion flowers. There is also a pretty white form. In complete contrast, *V. bonariensis* (z7–9) is a tall perennial with sparsely leaved stems, so that it is worth growing at the front of a border where its small purple-violet flowers are at nose height. *V. rigida* (z8–10), used as a bedding plant in cooler zones, is a shorter plant, with tuberous roots, upright branching stems to 18in/45cm, and small violet flowers.

Bulbs

OPPOSITE ABOVE *Gladiolus callianthus* is one of the most elegant of late-flowering bulbs, with its arching stems topped by wide, white, crimson-hearted blooms endowed with a sweet fragrance.

OPPOSITE BELOW The brilliant flowers of *Anemone pavonina* color the hillsides and olive groves of the northern Mediterranean in spring, before the heat and drought of summer induce dormancy.

Bulbs are well adapted to providing color in dry gardens, for many are natives of areas where there is a long dry season. The *bled* or desert of Morocco, for example, is transformed in spring, while in Central Asia the bitter winter is followed by a hot, parched summer – and for a brief spell between the two the ground is carpeted with flowering bulbs. This is the home of many tulip species, as bright as jewels. The rather kinder climate of the northern Mediterranean is equally suited to bulbs; in spring the olive groves are lively with anemones and ranunculus. South Africa also offers a wonderful range of bulbs, including the fragrant belladonna lilies and freesias, gladioli, crimpled nerines and bright sparaxis.

The small bulbs can be tucked into odd corners among shrubs or beneath open-canopied trees, or in cooler climates should be given a position in full sun. Some taller bulbs make excellent border plants; alliums, the summer hyacinth (*Galtonia candicans*), crocosmias and crown imperials (*Fritillaria imperialis*) among them. Many can be grown in pots, brought near or into the house for flowering, and set out of sight to ripen during the summer.

Allium LILIACEAE/ALLIACEAE

The ornamental onions flower mainly in summer and vary from tinies suitable for a doll's house rockery to tall border plants. The following are just a selection from the dozens worth giving garden space in flower borders and among shrubs. One of the prettiest is *Allium cernuum* (z3–8), which bears nodding heads of amethyst-purple flowers on 12in/30cm, gracefully arching stems. *A. flavum* (z3–8) is a small charmer with shooting-star heads of lemon-yellow flowers on green or glaucous, 6in/15cm stems; *A. carinatum* ssp. *pulchellum* (z6–9) looks like a larger, rose-purple or white version. Naturally white-flowered species include *A. zebdanense* (z6–9), a slender creature safe enough to tuck into any border, and *A. neapolitanum* (z7–9), another attractive Mediterranean, but a bit of a spreader. Both grow to about 12in/30cm. One of the most striking of the larger ornamental onions is *A. christophii* (z4–9), stars of Persia, its 24in/60cm stems topped by large flower heads like skeletal footballs composed of metallic, pale mauve stars on spoke-like stems. The heads dry to crisp parchment, from which black seeds fall to increase the colony. *A. schubertii* (z4–9) somewhat resembles *A. christophii*, with smaller, pinker flowers on stems of varying length, so the large, spherical head is more haphazard than symmetrical. Another fine border onion is *A. rosenbachianum* (z4–10), which has solid spheres of violet-rose on 4ft/1.2m stems in early summer and palely glaucous leaf spears in spring; *A. giganteum* (z4–9), *A. macleanii* (*A. elatum*) (z4–10), *A. stipitatum* (z4–8), and the earlier-flowering *A. aflatunense* (z4–8) are similar, with rich or pale lilac flowers; some have white forms. The smelly but handsome *A.*

siculum (correctly *Nectaroscordum siculum*) (z4–9) grows to 4ft/1.2m, its bell-like flowers hanging on heads structured like a complex rocket – or like a fantasy castle in Bavaria as, after fertilization, they stand erect – but muted in their creamy green or tawny plum coloring.

Amaryllis LILIACEAE/AMARYLLIDACEAE

Amaryllis bella-donna (z8–10), the belladonna lily, bears its apricot-scented trumpets in autumn, prompted into growth by the rains. To make sure of a good display of flowers, it can be helpful to flood the bulbs with a liquid feed in late summer. The stout, dark stems push up amazingly quickly once the summer dormancy is broken; the dark, strap-like foliage follows in winter. The typical flower color is a soft pink shading to white in the throat; selected forms have deeper, richer-toned flowers and there is a beautiful hybrid with *Brunsvigia*, × *Amarygia parkeri* (z8–10), with rich pink flowers or, exquisitely, white in 'Alba.' All are best planted with their noses at the soil surface, except in cooler zones.

Anemone RANUNCULACEAE

The Mediterranean anemones color the fields in spring with their bright flowers of rose, pink, blue, white or scarlet. *Anemone blanda* (z4–8) has starry flowers, typically blue but also available in a brilliant white, pink, and a shocking magenta with white eye, 'Radar.' Flowering in spring on 4in/

Crocosmia 'Lucifer'

10cm stems, they spread readily into wide masses. *A. coronaria* (z6–9) has pink, mauve, red or white flowers on 12in/30cm stems. The florists' forms of the single De Caen and semi-double St. Brigid Groups (both z6–9) are easy to obtain; they flower in early spring in Mediterreanean climates and need light shade. Of similar style are *A. × fulgens* (z6–9), which has larger, broader-sepaled scarlet flowers, though selected strains such as St. Bavo have pink or soft mauve flowers, and 'Multipetala' has many narrow scarlet sepals; and *A. hortensis* (z6–9), usually some shade of purple. The poppy anemone, *A. pavonina* (z8–10), has vivid scarlet, pink or purple flowers, spectacular among the olive groves of the Mediterranean.

Chionodoxa LILIACEAE/HYACINTHACEAE

Chionodoxa luciliae (z4–9), glory of the snow, flowers in its native lands on stony hillsides, emerging as the snow melts. The blue flowers have a small, white eye. The brighter blue *C. sardensis* (z4–9) has more flowers on each stem; both are about 4in/10cm tall and spread freely by seed.

Crocosmia IRIDACEAE

Crocosmia × crocosmiiflora (z5–9), the montbretia, increases fast to form weed-excluding carpets of narrow, arching, fresh green sword leaves. In summer, branching 24in/60cm flower stems carry nodding, flared flowers of bright orange-scarlet, paler within to set off the tawny markings in the throat. Many selections have been named, including one named 'Citronella' (z6–9) – it is almost as vigorous and has clear yellow flowers. The bigger, bolder *C. paniculata* (*Curtonus paniculatus, Antholyza paniculata*) (z5–9) has broad, pleated, green sword leaves, and large sprays of small orange-vermilion trumpets on arching, 4ft/1.2m stems. 'Lucifer' (z6–9) is a tall and vigorous hybrid of *C. masonorum* and *C. paniculata*, with bold green broadsword leaves and arching heads of scarlet-orange flowers.

Cyclamen PRIMULACEAE

Cyclamen hederifolium (*C. neapolitanum*) (z5–9) will flower when its tubers are smaller than a fingernail and lives until they grow as large as dinner plates. They will grow even in the dry, rooty shade of trees. The small, dainty pink or white flowers appear in late summer into the fall on 3in/7.5cm stems. The leaves are variable in their marbled markings and in shape, vaguely recalling ivy in outline. *C. persicum* (z8–9) is the species from which florists' cyclamen have been developed. In its wild form it is a dainty creature with pink, scented, butterfly flowers on 6in/15cm stems. It is less frost-hardy than *C. hederifolium*, adapted to summer dormancy in the hot, dry season. Similar conditions suit *C. libanoticum* (z8–9), which is rare in its native habitat of dry, rocky hills in Lebanon. The thick-textured leaves are gleaming maroon beneath; the flowers are pink with crimson markings on the nose.

Freesia IRIDACEAE

Freesia refracta alba (z8–9) is a South African native with deliciously fragrant cream to warm yellow flowers, sometimes tinted with pale green, on 12in/30cm stems. *F. lactea* (z8–9) is similar, if not the same.

Fritillaria LILIACEAE

Fritillaria imperialis (z5–8), the crown imperial, produces stout 4ft/1.2m stems surmounted by a cluster of large, bell-shaped flowers hanging beneath a topknot of green leaves. Each bell-shaped flower, which may be

Galtonia candicans

Nerine bowdenii against a
background of *Santolina
chamaecyparissus*

tawny red or yellow, has a large drop of nectar at the base of each of the five petals; the legend is that the crown imperial once had white flowers held proudly erect, and that – alone of all the flowers – it refused to bow its head when Jesus entered the Garden of Gethsemane. Reproved by its Creator, it flushed red and bowed its head, hiding the tears of shame. The more slender *F. persica* (z7–8) has glaucous foliage beneath a 36in/90cm spire of smaller, nodding bells, of darkest maroon-purple in the selection 'Adiyaman,' bloomed with white on the exterior, opening in spring. Both species tend to be short-lived in the garden.

Galtonia LILIACEAE/HYACINTHACEAE

Galtonia candicans (z7–10), the summer hyacinth, is a South African bulb with 4ft/1.2m stems bearing large, white, nodding bells with a slight fragrance. Like so many of the larger bulbs, it is invaluable for adding color (for white is also a color) to the flowerbed in the minimum of ground space, interplanted with early-dormant perennials such as oriental poppies, or set among other flowers of summer.

Gladiolus IRIDACEAE

Although hybrid gladioli need a rich soil to feed their large, even gross blooms, many of the dainty species should succeed in dry conditions in improved soil. The European species known as corn flag, such as *G. communis* ssp. *byzantinus* (z7–10), are tough and hardy; this one has running roots and quickly makes a colony of 36in/90cm stems bearing magenta-crimson blooms marked with cream flashes on the lower segments. South African species include the spectacular *G. callianthus* (*Acidanthera murieliae*, *A. bicolor*) (z8–10), which bears its wide, gracefully arched, fragrant flowers on 4ft/1.2m stems in autumn. They are pure white marked with rich maroon blotches in the throat. The more demure *G. papilio* (Purpureoauratus Group) (z9–10) has 4ft/1.2m stems bearing small, hooded flowers of somber slate to mauve coloring, pale chartreuse within, over narrow, glaucous foliage. It, too, runs freely at the root.

Hermodactylus IRIDACEAE

Hermodactylus tuberosus (z6) blooms early in the year, on 12in/30cm stems, its iris-like flowers colored sober green with velvety black falls. They have a faint, slightly spicy perfume.

Hyacinthus LILIACEAE/HYACINTHACEAE

Hyacinthus orientalis (z3–7) is the wild precursor of the Roman hyacinth. It has pale blue bells in spring on 8in/20cm stems. Cultivated forms add white and pink to the color range; they are much daintier than the familiar, selected cultivars with club-like heads of close-packed blooms.

Iris IRIDACEAE

Iris histrio (z5–9) bears its pale blue flowers in early spring on 4in/10cm stems. The falls are marked with yellow and deep purple. The stouter *I. histrioïdes* (z5–9) has deeper blue flowers. 'Major' is a lusty form of this dwarf, early-flowering bulbous iris.

Ixia IRIDACEAE

These South African cormous plants have slender stems and stiff, grassy leaves. *Ixia viridiflora* (z8–10 with winter protection) has bowl-shaped flowers of metallic turquoise-green with a black-purple center. Other species have mauve, purple or pink, yellow, salmon or orange flowers. 'Venus' is rich magenta in bud, looking like a bright head of wheat, opening to show its white interior and yellow anthers.

Muscari LILIACEAE/HYACINTHACEAE

Most grape hyacinths are undemanding small bulbs with tiny, tight-lipped bells packed into a tapering spike. The usual color is blue, as in the fragrant *Muscari armeniacum* (z3–8); *M. botryoïdes album* (z2–8) is white. *M. azureum* (z3–8) is pale blue, *M. neglectum* (z3–8) dark indigo with white-rimmed bells. All grow to between 4in/10cm and 6in/15cm in height.

Narcissus LILIACEAE/AMARYLLIDACEAE

Narcissus tazetta (z6–10) is more drought-tolerant than most in a genus that often grows in the wild in moist meadows. It has several small, intensely fragrant flowers, white with a little yellow cup, to each 8in/20cm stem. The taller, yellow 'Soleil d'Or' belongs here. The paper white narcissus is *N. papyraceus* (z8–9), bearing several intensely sweet, small, white flowers on each 18in/45cm stem.

Nerine LILIACEAE/AMARYLLIDACEAE

The South African *Nerine bowdenii* (z7–10) bears its candy-pink flowers, starry with crimpled segments, in clusters at the top of strong 24in/60cm stems, late in the season; the rich green, strap-shaped leaves follow. Selections with richer or paler pink flowers have been named. *N. undulata* (z8–10) is, for garden purposes, a smaller version of *N. bowdenii*.

Muscari armeniacum

Tulipa clusiana var. *chrysantha*

Ornithogalum LILIACEAE/HYACINTHACEAE
Ornithogalum nutans (z6–9) is a plant that demands close inspection, for its hyacinth-like flowers are jade and ivory on the outside, silvery green within. They open in early summer on 18in/45cm stems. The "French asparagus," *O. pyrenaicum* (z6–9), opens its slim 24in/60cm spikes of ivory-green, starry flowers in early summer.

Pancratium LILIACEAE/AMARYLLIDACEAE
The pancratiums have stout stems supporting sweetly fragrant, white flowers, resembling a narcissus with long, narrow outer segments and a wide trumpet from which the long, white stamens protrude. *Pancratium illyricum* has smaller flowers than *P. maritimum* (z8–10).

Puschkinia LILIACEAE
Puschkinia scilloïdes (z4–9) is, as its name suggests, very like a scilla, with several ice-white flowers marked with azure to each 3in/7cm stem in early spring. There is a pure white form. Both have a curious, cheap-soap fragrance.

Ranunculus RANUCULACEAE
Ranunculus asiaticus (z7–10) is a native of the eastern Mediterranean, the Near East and North Africa, where it grows on dry, rocky hillsides, flowering in spring and dormant during the heat of summer. It varies in color from red to yellow, purple, pink or white. Florists' forms have double flowers like turbans.

Scilla LILIACEAE/HYACINTHACEAE
The squills are spring-flowering bulbs with blue flowers. *Scilla bifolia* (z4–8) has rich blue to violet flowers on 4in/10cm stems, while *S. siberica* (z2–8) is

Tulipa orphanidea

ultramarine blue. *S. messeniaca* (z4–8) has hazy blue flowers on 3in/7cm stems, and broad leaves; it is an enthusiastic spreader.

Sparaxis IRIDACEAE

South African bulbs resembling ixias, these are commonly offered as mixed hybrids in a range of bright, pretty colors. *Sparaxis grandiflora* and *S. tricolor* vary in color naturally from creamy buff and amber-yellow to salmon, orange, and vermilion, and *S. elegans* 'Coccinea' bears bright orange-scarlet flowers with black hearts on 12–18in/30–45cm stems (all z9–10).

Tulipa LILIACEAE

The highly bred garden tulips are unsuited to dry conditions, but many of the little wild species of Central Asia are adapted to cold winters and long, hot summers without rain (all z4–9). The choice is wide, ranging from the pale and starry *Tulipa turkestanica*, one of the first to bloom, to the brilliant scarlet *T. praestans*, or *T. greigii*, which adds maroon and green striated leaves to its charms. A still smaller vivid scarlet species is *T. linifolia*, with narrow, wavy-edged, glaucous leaves, while the Batalinii Group of this species have bluer leaves still, and amber or primrose-yellow flowers. *T. saxatilis* (z6–9) is a Cretan native with running roots and large, pale lilac-pink flowers. The lady tulip, *T. clusiana* (z6–9), is white marked with pink; var. *chrysantha* is yellow with coral. The eastern Mediterranean *T. orphanidea* (z5–9) has scarlet flowers.

Urginea LILIACEAE/HYACINTHACEAE

Urginea maritima (z8–10), the sea squill, is a Mediterranean and Near Eastern native, adapted to dry, rocky places and sandy soils. It flowers in late summer, the dark, 4ft/1.2m stems clad in their upper halves with many small, white flowers forming a slender spire.

Grasses & Bamboos

OPPOSITE ABOVE The tall
flowering stems of a variegated
form of *Miscanthus sinensis* are
topped by airy fan-plumes as
silky and neat as a fresh
permanent wave; they dry to
fluffy whiteness.

OPPOSITE BELOW The quiet
coloring and graceful arching
blades of grasses – here,
Pennisetum alopecuroïdes and
Miscanthus sinensis 'Strictus' –
contrast with the rigid
horizontals and verticals of a
painted fence.

Grasses are reticent plants. They do not advertise themselves in a blare of color, though they may announce themselves audibly in a range of subtle rustlings, and their proud grace is more enduring than the brilliance of many flowers. Some grasses make a speciality of their foliage, in color or bearing; others decorate themselves with whiskery, plumy, hazy or feathery flower spikes which may, if picked at the right moment, last for months in beauty when dried.

As a foil to the solid roundness of shrubs, rising from a carpet of lowly plants, or as components of a border planting, grasses fit into many designs. Though they look good by water, many are also ideally suited to dry or even desert gardens. Their muted coloring and vertical or arching outline look good in contrast with stone, rocks, or in a gravel mulch. Wherever you grow them, they are as a rule best planted as singletons. True, some grasses – and not just the kinds used in lawns – spread to form carpets, but most deserve to have their individuality respected. Massed, their outlines dissolve into a blur that does them no justice.

In mixed planting of contrasting shapes, color might be the unifying element. A grouping of plants with silver and glaucous-blue foliage, so well suited to dry gardens, could include *Helictotrichon sempervirens*, tufty little *Festuca glauca*, and the compact, stiffly poised *Elymus hispidus*, which reaches its apotheosis of blueness in a hot, dry place. Silver cotton lavender (*Santolina*) annually hard-pruned to neat mounds, lavender (*Lavandula*), the little platinum achilleas, and the wide gray-flannel rosettes of *Verbascum olympicum* or the blue, white-splashed *Argemone platyceras* with its thistly leaves and large white, golden-stamened poppies, would bring contrasting outlines to a subtly limited range of cool tones.

The effect created by the massive sugar-flower grass (*Miscanthus sacchariflorus*) is entirely different: not the pale brilliance of silver foliage, but a luxuriant fountain of green blades. Its one drawback is that it may become bedraggled at the base as summer advances. Plant a smaller companion, such as *Stipa calamagrostis* or *Pennisetum villosum*, at its feet, and the bare legs of the miscanthus will be concealed without masking its spraying foliage.

This and other large grasses have enough presence to stand as specimen plants, perhaps in an expanse of pebbles or contrasted with starkly modern concrete or decking. In the larger landscape, the miscanthus, *Stipa gigantea*, pampas grass (*Cortaderia selloana*), and even perhaps the aggressive lyme grass (*Leymus arenarius*) come into their own in wide plantings. Pampas grass especially – unlike many other grasses – can be grouped, though it would call for very large areas to evoke the native pampas of Argentina, where this social grass waves its feathery plumes of white, rose, blush and misty purple in massed clouds at head height or more.

Arundo GRAMINEAE

Arundo donax (z7–10), the giant reed, carrizo or cana brava of Mediterranean areas, is a massive grass growing to 10–15ft/3–4.5m, with spreading, rhizomatous roots, difficult to eradicate once it has taken hold, but valuable in controlling soil erosion. Although naturalized in ditches and damp areas, and recommended for moist soils, it will tolerate periods of drought. It is useful as a quick screen or windbreak, though being herbaceous it offers no protection in winter. It has also been used in mud and wattle construction buildings or for roofing adobe houses in Mexico.

Bambusa GRAMINEAE

Bambusa multiplex (*B. glaucescens*) (z7–11) is a tall, clump-forming bamboo of 13ft/3.5m or so. 'Alphonse Karr' has broad, olive-green leaves and variegated canes; 'Fernleaf' is a selection with angular stems and spraying, fern-like foliage.

Bouteloua GRAMINEAE

Bouteloua gracilis (z5–9), the mosquito grass, is a plant for detailed planting, not broad landscape effects. The curious horizontal, brownish-purple flower spikes appear in summer on 18in/45cm stems.

Briza GRAMINEAE

Briza media (z5–9), the quaking grass, has dainty flower heads composed of nodding, trembling green lockets, in summer, on 18in/45cm stems. The flowers dry well to pale parchment tones.

Calamagrostis GRAMINEAE

Calamagrostis × *acutiflora* 'Stricta' (z5–9), a sterile natural hybrid, has feathery brown flower heads on vertical 6ft/1.8m stems in late summer.

Cortaderia GRAMINEAE

Cortaderia selloana (z7–11), the pampas grass, is a luxuriant, leafy grass with razor-sharp blades and great plumes overtopping the clumps in summer or fall. It grows in most soils, and once established is drought-resistant, thriving in heat. Unfortunately it has become a noxious weed in Australia and New Zealand. Selections include 'Monstrosa,' with huge creamy, feathery, open plumes on outward-leaning stems up to 9ft/2.7m high; 'Pumila,' very compact at a mere 5ft/1.5m, with creamy white, dense, erect plumes; the pink pampas, 'Rendatleri,' which has arching, lilac-pink, one-sided plumes to 10ft/3m; and 'Sunningdale Silver,' growing to 7ft/2m, its very feathery, creamy white, open plumes clustered on erect stems.

Deschampsia GRAMINEAE

Deschampsia caespitosa (z4–9), the tufted hair grass, makes a clump of narrow, arching, dark green blades. The many erect 4ft/1.2m flowering stems bear large, elegant plumes of tiny, green or maroon flowers turning to parchment as they fade.

Elymus GRAMINEAE

Now that the wickedly invasive *Elymus arenarius* has been moved to *Leymus*, there remain some well-behaved, beautifully blue grasses in this genus. *E. hispidus* (z5–8) is a stiffly poised grass, intensely blue-silver when grown in a hot, dry place; and *E. magellanicus* (*Agropyron pubiflorum*) (z5–8) has vivid blue-gray blades bloomed with white, forming 30in/75cm clumps.

Hordeum jubatum

Festuca GRAMINEAE

Festuca glauca (z4–8) is a neat, small, tufted grass with steel-blue to glaucous, hair-fine blades, and blue-gray flower spikes in early summer; *F. amethystina* (z4–8) is twice the size at 18in/45cm, its blue-gray foliage with the hint of lilac suggested by its specific name.

Helictotrichon GRAMINEAE

Helictotrichon sempervirens (z4–9) is a clump-forming grass with rapier blades of bright blue-gray, up to 24in/60cm long, held erect and topped by slender flowering stems to 4ft/1.2m, adding to the blue-gray tones. It contrasts effectively with *Sedum telephium* ssp. *maximum* 'Atropurpureum.'

Holcus GRAMINEAE

Holcus mollis 'Albovariegatus' (z5–7) is a small, slowly creeping grass with soft, white-variegated blades, often almost wholly white.

Hordeum GRAMINEAE

Hordeum jubatum (z4–8), the squirrel tail barley, is a tufted grass bearing, in summer or early fall, flat, arching, feathery plumes with long, silky awns that shimmer gracefully in the breeze, on 24in/60cm stems. The seedheads vary in color from yellow-green to tawny bronze.

159

Miscanthus sinensis 'Strictus'

Pennisetum orientale

Leymus GRAMINEAE

Leymus arenarius (*Elymus arenarius*) (z4–9), the lyme grass, is a plant of sandy dunes, very well adapted to dry soils: too well, perhaps, for it is aggressively territorial, thrusting its way into neighboring plants. Its bright blue-gray blades grow to 24in/60cm and are overtopped by stiff spikes of flowers, like glaucous heads of wheat, in summer.

Miscanthus GRAMINEAE

Miscanthus sacchariflorus (z5–10), the sugar-flower grass or silver grass, is a giant, reaching 13ft/3.5m, with as much presence as a bamboo, though it dies down in winter. In summer it forms a shining fountain of arching blades, rustling in the breeze. It seldom flowers, at least in cool-summer areas, and may be confused with the similar *M. floridulus* (z5–10), which bears silvery mauve plumes. It, or they, are clump-formers, increasing at the root but not invasive. The maiden grass, *M. sinensis* (*Eulalia japonica*) (z5–10), a clump-forming Far Eastern species, is seldom seen in its wild form, but many different cultivars are offered, most growing to about 6ft/ 1.8m, their upright stems set with gracefully arching blades that fade attractively to pale parchment as winter sets in. Grow them as individual clumps, standing above neighboring plants; and cut them down in winter as they become weather-stained and torn. The flowering plumes last for years indoors as "drieds." One of the most elegant is 'Gracillimus,' its very slender leaf blades enhanced by the pale midribs common to the variants of this species. *M. sinensis* var. *purpurascens* has close-set stems flushed with purple, while 'Variegatus' has white striping the length of the leaf. 'Morning Light' has a gracefully arching habit and narrow, white-edged leaves. 'Cabaret' is strikingly variegated with well-defined stripes. The tiger or zebra grass, 'Zebrinus,' is unusually marked with horizontal yellow bands. 'Strictus' is similar, but holds itself more rigidly upright and develops brighter coloring; in both the cross-bands are most distinct after midsummer, and when the plants are grown in full sun. The flowers are borne late in the season, silky, fanning plumes of tawny pink evenly rippled with waves, fading and drying to near-white fluff. Finest of all for flower is 'Silberfeder' ('Silver Feather'), which is less reliant than the others on a summer baking to produce its fawn-pink sprays.

Pennisetum GRAMINEAE

These appealing grasses bear bottle-brush flowers in summer and fall. They form clumps and are not invasive. The rose fountain grass, *Pennisetum alopecuroides* (*P. japonicum*, *P. compressum*) (z5–10) grows to 36in/90cm, and flowers in the fall, its 5in/12cm indigo bottle-brushes each tipped with a white tuft. 'Woodside' is a form selected for its free-flowering qualities. *P. orientale* (z6–9) is a smaller plant, forming low tufts of narrow leaves topped by the 18in/45cm flowering stems. The flower spikes resemble a huge wooly caterpillar, the pinkish gray coloring enhanced by long mauve hairs. The fountain grass, *P. setaceum* (*P. ruppelii*) (z8–10), is another of the furry caterpillar types, forming clumps 24–48in/60–120cm high and wide, with narrow leaves, topped by bristly flower heads up to 6in/15cm long, white or tinged with pink or purple. The summer foliage is bright green, fading to straw color with winter frost. 'Cupreum' has deep fox-red foliage and coppery flower spikes, larger than the type; 'Atrosanguineum' is purple in leaf and flower, and 'Rubrum' has rosy foliage and flower spikes. The fountain grass and its cultivars cope cheerfully with drought and heat, surviving with as little as 6–12in/150–300mm annual rainfall. The dainty

Stipa calamagrostis

P. villosum (*P. longistylum*) (z8–10) makes grassy tufts, and the gracefully nodding, softly furry, white flower spikes are borne in the fall on arching 18in/45cm stems.

Phyllostachys GRAMINEAE
Phyllostachys aurea (z6–11) is a tall, graceful bamboo forming clumps of bright green, 8–13ft/2.4–3.5m canes, maturing to yellow and finally brown. The stake bamboo. *P. aureosulcata* (z6–11), grows strongly upright, with rough canes, yellow on the flat side, and dark green, almost translucent foliage.

Pleioblastus GRAMINEAE
Pleioblastus pygmaeus (*Arundinaria pygmaea*) (z5–11) is a dwarf bamboo forming carpets of slender canes up to 12in/30cm long, pale green at first, maturing to bright green.

Saccharum GRAMINEAE
Saccharum ravennae (*Erianthus ravennae*) (z9), the Ravenna grass or plume grass, makes bold clumps of gray leaves, and given enough summer heat will produce its great purplish flowering stems, up to 14ft/4m tall, topped by long spikes of gray-purple flowers in late summer.

Stipa GRAMINEAE
Stipa arundinacea (z5–10) is an evergreen grass forming dense clumps of arching, green leaves, becoming tinted with tawny orange as summer passes; in fall and winter they are entirely russet-orange. In summer the 36in/90cm flowering stems are a cloud of tiny, soft brown flowers. The large *S. calamagrostis* (z6–10) has silky green to brown, arching, loose plumes on 4ft/1.2m stems, turning to golden tan by summer's end. Unless the clump is lifted and reset every few years, the stems become lax and floppy. Another of the more modest stipas is *S. pennata* (z7–9), the feather grass, its long, white flower heads on 36in/90cm stems, over tufts of narrow leaves. Finally, *S. gigantea* (z6–9) is like a huge oat, with 6ft/1.8m flowering stems, the open heads of flowers tipped with a long awn, at first shining pink to purple, turning to corn-gold, and shivering in the slightest breeze.

Succulents & Xerophytes

OPPOSITE ABOVE *Aloe aristata* is one of the most frost-resistant of these African succulents, thriving outside even in some favored English gardens, where its spiny, symmetrical rosettes add a bizarre note.

OPPOSITE BELOW The blue-blade or dollar cactus, *Opuntia macrocentra*, adds an unusual note of color to desert plantings with its large, glaucous-blue and purple-flushed pads.

The days are gone when gardeners in desert regions could be prodigal with water and so create their own small oases. In areas where the natural rainfall is very low, succulents and xerophytes are the natural choice to join other desert plants in the type of conservation gardening known as xeriscaping – from the Greek *xeros*, dry; hence, also, xerophyte, a plant adapted to dry conditions.

Writing before the 1914–18 war, when neither industry nor agriculture had yet begun to deplete our dwindling water resources and gardens were full of flowery borders and lush lawns, that great English gardener E. A. Bowles spoke of his fascination with succulents, which the French call *plantes grasses*, and which Mr. Bowles described as "this thick-skinned race of plants . . . representatives in living vegetable tissue of the wine and water skins of the East." With their different ways of adapting to drought, succulents are as variable in appearance as any other group of plants. Within the cactus family alone, in the list that follows, there are the flat pads of prickly pears, the cylindrical barrel cactus, and the columnar saguaro, which may develop one or more arms with advancing years. Other succulents make thick, fleshy rosettes of blunt-ended or sharply armed leaves, or carpet the ground with trailing stems.

Plants with spiky or fat rosettes, and the spreaders, assort well with cacti and with other desert plants, but can spice up a more conventional planting of drought-tolerant trees, shrubs and perennials. In one of my gardens a curved path led suddenly to a long border, with a massive *Beschorneria yuccoides* as the opening component, backed by a gray stone wall. I set *Helichrysum petiolare* to swarm around its feet, and tucked in some bright bulbs to pop up in their season among all this gray and blue-white foliage. Elsewhere, on a hot, rocky slope, dudleyas and echeverias mingled with trailing osteospermums and succulent Hottentot figs (*Carpobrotus edulis*), curtaining the larger rock faces, with the silver wire of *Leucophyta brownii* adding another distinctive note. In many small town gardens in Amman, the Jordanian capital, plantings of two or three bold agaves in a sea of rounded pebbles are backed by walls decked with bougainvillea or perfumed white jasmine, in simple, bold statements that accord perfectly with the whitewashed desert houses.

Aeonium CRASSULACEAE

The Moroccan *Aeonium arboreum* (z9–11) has fleshy, rounded, bright green leaves in rosettes resembling a giant houseleek, on 36–72in/90-180cm stems. The flowers are yellow, in bold conical heads. It is easily propagated by offsets. 'Atropurpureum' is even more handsome, with burnished, metallic, purple-black leaves; 'Zwartkop,' though not apparently pure *A. arboreum*, looks like a particularly fine selection of this. *A. canariense* (z9–11)

162

Aeonium 'Zwartkop'

has bright green, thick-textured leaves, which are tinted with red, especially at the tips, in cold weather, and yellow flowers during high summer. The ground-hugging *A. tabuliforme* (z9) makes wide, very flat rosettes of soft green, closely overlapping leaves.

Agave AGAVACEAE

The agaves are among the most useful plants for hot desert areas, even thriving where the annual rainfall is as low as 3in/75mm, and some are hardy enough to grow in cooler, dry climates where they can help to create a desert atmosphere. Their rosette form guides every drop of rain that does fall to the roots; in consequence they are very sensitive to excessive wet combined with cold in winter.

One of the most familiar is *Agave americana* (z8–11), a Mexican native with broad, pointed, gray-blue leaves up to 5ft/1.5m long, forming bold rosettes. The toothed margins leave a shadowy impression on the reverse of the adjacent leaves. The pale yellow flowers are borne in flat, plate-like clusters on the short side branches of a stout, 20–33ft/6–10m stem, but only after many years' growth. In formal settings the variegated cultivars look right: 'Marginata' with creamy white leaf edges, 'Mediopicta' with a broad central splash of yellow, 'Striata' with yellow to white stripes, and cream and gray 'Variegata.' They all look good in large pots and make offsets which can be detached to grow into new plants. As the old leaves become messy, they can be cut off neatly as near the base as possible. The smooth-edged agave, *A. weberi* (z8–11), resembles *A. americana* except that the soft-textured, deeper blue green leaves up to 4ft/1.2m long are armed only at the tip, not at the margins. In hot climates it needs protection from fierce sun and more moisture, but it is more cold-resistant than *A. americana*. *A. atrovirens* (z8–11) is only slightly smaller than *A. americana*, though still with rosettes up to 6ft/1.8m tall and flowering stems of 20ft/6m. One of the most magnificent of the big agaves is *A. franzosinii* (z8–11), its huge, silvery gray or nearly white, curving leaves forming giant rosettes up to 10ft/3m high, topped by a flowering spike up to 36ft/11m.

Even without their massive flowering stems, these are big plants. In smaller spaces there are more manageable agaves to choose from. *A. parryi* (z7–11) is less than half the size of *A. americana*, and somewhat more frost resistant; its broad, spine-edged leaves are dark green. The still smaller *A. megalacantha* (z8–11), from Mexico, is said to be more trouble-free than *A. parryi*; it has small rosettes of broad, gray-green leaves with brown, hooked thorns. *A. utahensis* (z7–11) is rather variable, but typically forms a compact, gray-green rosette up to 16in/40cm wide, of stiff, tapering leaves with a sharp terminal spine and bears its yellow flowers on 8ft/2.4m stems. From Arizona comes *A. parviflora* (z8–11), which forms tiny rosettes, 4–6in/10–15cm high and 6–8in/15–20cm wide, of stiff, narrow, dark green leaves with white markings and white marginal threads, topped by a flowering spike reaching 36in/90cm. The very distinct *A. vilmoriniana* (z8–11), the octopus plant or midas agave, has blue-gray, twisting, slender, unarmed leaf blades to 32in/80cm, forming loose rosettes.

Aloe LILIACEAE/ALOEACEAE

The aloes are African succulents, many with showy, poker-like flowers, others with a branching inflorescence. They need free-draining soil. Like the agaves, they vary greatly in size. Among the larger species from eastern regions is *Aloe africana* (z9–11); it forms rosettes of long, spiny leaves, can grow to 7–14ft/2–4m, and bears deep orange, upward-curving flowers in late winter and early spring. The densely shrubby *A. arborescens* (z9–11) may grow even larger, 33ft/10m tall; it has glaucous leaf rosettes and spikes of bright scarlet flowers, often opening in midwinter in hot climates. One of the most familiar is *A. ferox* (z10–11), a tree-like aloe up to 16ft/5m tall, developing a trunk-like stem, with thick, sword-shaped leaves, spiny on both surfaces and edged with red-brown teeth. The spectacular branching inflorescence is formed of large, scarlet-orange, poker-like spikes. The similar *A. candelabrum* (z10–11) has scarlet, rose or orange flowers in erect racemes on candelabrum stems, in midwinter.

Smaller species from the eastern regions include *A. aristata* (z9–11), one of the hardiest. It has dense rosettes of dark green, pointed leaves, marked with white; the slender pokers on branching 24in/60cm stems are orange-red. Another, with a different style of inflorescence, is *A. saponaria* (z9–11), which makes clumps of pointed, succulent, medium green leaves tinged red with dull white spots, and margined with hard brown teeth, turning redder in extremes of cold, heat, sun or drought. The scarlet to yellowish flowers commonly appear two or three times a year in branching heads on stems to 30in/75cm. With its low growth, it is suitable for underplanting stem-forming plants such as palms or yuccas. It needs an open, rocky soil, in which it is reasonably hardy, for though damaged by a long, hard freeze it often recovers if already established. The pink or red flowers of *A. striata* (z10–11), a small plant with 18in/45cm rosettes, are held in flat-topped, branching panicles.

Agave americana 'Striata'

The western species are even more adapted to dry conditions. *A. variegata* (z10–11), the partridge-breasted aloe, is a miniature, forming rosettes of only 8in/20cm across, the leaves banded in green and white; the pink flowers open in late winter and early spring. From North Africa comes *A. vera* (*A. barbadensis*) (z10–11), the medicinal aloe or Barbados aloe, which was introduced by the Spanish to California and originally much planted in mission herb gardens for treating burns and skin complaints. The spiky, succulent rosettes are formed of upward-pointing leaves armed with sharp tips and white-to-reddish marginal teeth. The kniphofia-like spikes of yellowish or orange flowers are borne in spring on 36in/90cm stems. The Barbados aloe increases rapidly by offsets to 10ft/3m wide and is very drought resistant.

Aptenia AIZOACEAE
Aptenia cordifolia (z10–11) is related to the well-known "mesems" or Cape vygies (see *Carpobrotus*, *Lampranthus* and others), and makes good ground-cover for sunny, dry places, spreading to 24in/60cm or more in width. The tiny, red flowers are borne over a long season, but are scarcely showy.

Beschorneria AGAVACEAE
The beschornerias are semi-succulents with broad sword-blade leaves forming bold rosettes, and narrow, tubular bell flowers on stout stems. The most familiar in cultivation, *Beschorneria yuccoides* (z9–11), is a massive plant with gray-blue leaf blades up to 36in/90cm long, and very stout, leaning, rhubarb-red flowering stems up to 10ft/3m high, bearing slender jade bells hanging from pink and salmon bracts. Another species that is sometimes cultivated is *B. tubiflora* (z9–11), which has sword-shaped leaves up to 24in/60cm long, blue-green with a white bloom, and narrow flowers of green tinged with maroon dropping from purple bracts, on green or bronzed stems up to 4ft/1.2m in height.

Calandrinia PORTULACACEAE
Calandrinia umbellata (z9–11) is a compact, low-growing plant with gray-green leaves almost concealed by magenta cupped flowers all summer.

Carnegiea CACTACEAE
Carnegiea gigantea (*Cereus giganteus*) (z9–11), the saguaro, sahuaro, Arizona giant, or giant cactus, which is protected in the wild, is a columnar cactus which grows slowly to as much as 60ft/18m and may live for 250 years. At a comparatively youthful sixty to seventy-five years, it may develop one or more arms. Whether armless or branching, it makes a dramatic vertical silhouette, the very spirit of the Arizona desert. In late spring it bears white flowers at the branch tips, opening at night and lasting until the next afternoon. Red fruits follow in summer. Its water demands are minimal: irrigate only in periods of extended drought.

Carpobrotus AIZOACEAE
The Hottentot fig of South Africa, *Carpobrotus edulis* (z9–11), has succulent, three-angled, curving leaves on long, trailing branches and multirayed flowers in a range of colors from cream to yellow, apricot, lavender and magenta, in spring and summer. *C. acinaciformis* (z9–11) is distinguished by its two-angled stems and many-rayed, carmine-pink flowers. *C. chilensis* (z9–11), a native of the Americas from California to Chile, has purple flowers with a fruity fragrance.

Carnegiea gigantea towers over
Ferocactus cylindraceus, with
Fouqueria splendens in the
background.

Crassula CRASSULACEAE

Crassula sarcocaulis (z9–11) is a somewhat frost-hardy South African native
that grows like a tiny tree, with woody stems and small, pointed, narrow
leaves. The stems are tipped by crimson buds opening into pink flowers.
There are a large number of other species, most of them susceptible to frost,
all native to South Africa.

Dasylirion AGAVACEAE

The desert spoons are tolerant of drought (needing no irrigation except
when newly planted, provided the annual rainfall exceeds 12in/300mm)
and of alkaline soils, but detest damp. *Dasylirion glaucophyllum* (z8–11) has
rapier, blue-gray leaves with a prominent, off-center midrib, the margins
hook-spined, and white to alabaster-green flowers on 10–14ft/3–4m stems
in spring. The sotol, *D. wheeleri* (z8–11), also known as Wheeler's sotol or
spoon flower, gains the latter name from the shape of the trunk ends of the
leaves. A native of the southwestern United States and of northern Mexico,
it was used by the Indians for food, fiber, and, fermented, to make an
alcoholic drink. The narrow, toothed, gray-green blades radiate from the
crown; older plants develop several crowns and short trunks, giving overall
dimensions of up to 5ft/1.5m in height, with a greater spread. In late spring

to late summer the plants may bloom, bearing a plume of straw-colored flowers 5ft/1.5m above the leaves. Unlike the related agaves, flowering does not mean the death of the rosette. As a native of rocky desert soils, the sotol tolerates the fiercest desert sun and needs no watering once established unless in areas of rainfall below 10in/250mm annually.

Delosperma AIZOACEAE

The ice plant, *Delosperma nubigenum* (z8–9), tolerates severe drought and grows best in full sun. It is a rapid spreader with yellow-green leaves forming a close carpet and abundant bright yellow daisy-like flowers in early summer, followed by a sprinkling through until winter. The evergreen leaves redden with the onset of cold weather. The rosy ice plant, *D. cooperi* (z6–9), has potent magenta flowers and cylindrical leaves that turn purplish in winter; it is subshrubby, making a low mound.

Doryanthes LILIACEAE/AMARYLLIDACEAE

Doryanthes palmeri (z10–11) is an evergreen succulent which, in maturity, produces 10–16ft/3–5m stems topped by brilliant red summer flowers.

Dudleya CRASSULACEAE

Dudleya farinosa (z10–11) is a California coastal native, forming small, echeveria-like rosettes of fleshy, gray-green leaves covered with a dense white farina, which is easily damaged by rain or careless irrigation. The flowers are straw-yellow.

Dyckia BROMELIACEAE

There are many species of *Dyckia*, semi-succulents resembling *Fascicularia*, but rather less frost-tolerant. They are in other respects tough and hardy plants, ranging from miniatures of 4in/10cm to well over head height. *Dyckia fosteriana* (z10–11) is a very decorative small species, forming a spiral whorl of gray, narrow, spine-edged, metallic-sheened leaves mounding to 8in/20cm; the flowers are yellow, on an erect spike. The stiff, dark green rosettes of *D. brevifolia* (z10–11) are topped by orange flowers on tall stems, and *D. rariflora* (z10–11) makes compact flat rosettes up to 12in/30cm wide, of narrow, tapering, sharp-pointed, silvery green leaves; the flowers are orange-red, on 18in/45cm spikes.

Echeveria CRASSULACEAE

A large and variable genus, the echeverias form rosettes of fleshy leaves and have well-shaped, pinch-mouthed flowers. They are not desert plants, but natives of high mountain areas, most from the highlands of Mexico. They are propagated by offsets. Among the easiest to grow, and often used as summer bedding in areas too cold for it in winter, is *Echeveria secunda* var. *glauca* (z10–11), which is quick to form offsets, each rosette of pale blue-gray leaves edged red. The red flowers are tipped with yellow. *E. secunda* itself (z10–11) is very similar, but with light green leaves, red at the tips. *E. agavoides* (z10–11) forms fleshy rosettes of rigid, triangular, sharp-pointed leaves, varying in color from fresh apple green to gray, the margins occasionally red-tinged. The red, yellow-tipped flowers are borne on 18in/45cm stems. The branched, semi-trailing stems of *E. microcalyx* (z10–11) are set with rosettes of glaucous-blue, pink-tinged leaves. The bloom on the blue- or white-leaved echeveria is one of the most attractive features, as in *E. elegans* (z10–11), which has very thick-textured, white-mealy leaves edged with pale green, and pink flowers.

Euphorbia EUPHORBIACEAE

In addition to the shrubby and perennial euphorbias already described, the genus includes succulent species, some of which closely mimic cacti. *Euphorbia caput-medusae* (z9–11), from the Cape Peninsula of South Africa, has succulent stems with crowded, tubercular branches. The glands of the 'Medusa's head' are green with white fringes. The crown of thorns, *E. milii* (*E. splendens*) (z10–11), is a shrubby, spiny, leafy succulent that can grow to 5ft/1.5m, the brilliant red bracts surrounding the insignificant true flowers, in summer. It is extremely sensitive to cold.

Fascicularia BROMELIACEAE

The fascicularias make excellent evergreen ground-cover in poor, dry soils, forming colonies of close-packed rosettes. The narrow, pointed leaves are gray-green backed with white or fawn, margined with fierce, backward-pointed spines. Round clusters of stemless, pale blue flowers at the center of the rosettes are framed by the vivid scarlet of the leaf bases at flowering time; as the flowers fade, so does the bright leaf coloring. The larger species, *Fascicularia pitcairniifolia* (z9–11), forms rosettes up to 30in/75cm wide; *Fascicularia bicolor* (z10–11) has narrow leaves and is often more reliable in flowering. Both do well in coastal gardens.

Ferocactus CACTACEAE

The barrel cacti, compass cacti, or fishhook cacti (all z9–11) are natives of Mexico and the southwestern United States, and are protected in the wild. Typically, they are of cylindrical form up to 12in/30cm in diameter, forming sunward-leaning, fluted columns with a green, waxy skin and clusters of spines on the outer ridges, each composed of several straight spines and one curved like a fishhook. Slow-growing, at maturity they may be as much as 13ft/3.5m tall, but are more often seen at 24–48in/60–120cm. Different species bear yellow to orange or red, waxy flowers from spring to fall. A sandy or gravel soil with free drainage is the most suitable; there is seldom or never any need to water.

Fouquieria FOUQUIERIACEAE

Fouquieria splendens (z7–11), the ocotillo, coach whip, or vine cactus, another protected native of the southwestern United States and northern Mexico, grows slowly to 14–18ft/4–5.5m with, after several years, a spread of 10ft/3m, forming woody, thorny, usually unbranched canes. In spring, and after summer rain, the canes sprout green leaves which endure for several weeks before turning yellow and falling. Spiny clusters of red, tubular flowers form on the new growth at the cane tips each spring for a period of several weeks before the plant goes dormant with drought. As its natural habitat is dry desert, the ocotillo needs watering only while becoming established; thereafter it should be given no irrigation unless the annual rainfall is below 6in/150mm. Grown "hard" in this way, it is frost resistant to 10F/−12C.

Furcraea AGAVACEAE

The furcraeas are beschorneria-like semi-succulents, forming huge rosettes of broadsword, gray-blue leaves. After bearing flowers, the rosette dies, leaving a massive corpse to be grubbed out and disposed of. *Furcraea longaeva* (z10–11) grows to about 20ft/6m when in flower, the pendulous side branches decked with ivory-white, green-tinted bell flowers. As the flowers fade, bulbils form, drop to the ground and, in congenial conditions,

Echeveria elegans

take root to grow into new rosettes. Another sometimes cultivated is *F. bedinghausii* (z10–11), which has fragrant, waxy, pale green flowers in fountains on 25ft/7.5m stems.

Hesperaloe AGAVACEAE

Hesperaloe parviflora (*Yucca parviflora*) (z8–11) is a Texas native forming a clump of many very narrow sword leaves, bright green with whitish marginal threads. The slim flower panicles are aloe-like, their many nodding, coral-scarlet flowers marked with yellow inside.

Kalanchoe CRASSULACEAE

These succulents are popular house plants in cold areas and a standby for dry gardens where there is no frost. They can be propagated by cuttings, best left to dry off for a couple of days before rooting. The familiar *Kalanchoe blossfeldiana* (z10–11) is a small succulent plant grown above all for its pretty flowers. A compact bushlet, it has polished green leaves edged with red, toothed near the apex, and clusters of bright scarlet flowers. A great many hybrids have been raised, with flowers of differing colors including yellow, pink and white. Others, such as *K. marmorata* (z10–11) and *K. pumila* (z10–11), are of grayish cast. The first has stout, fleshy, erect stems, branching from the base, and gray-bloomed, pinkish to blue-green, brown-mottled leaves with scalloped margins; its flowers are white. *K. pumila* is a bushy plant at first growing erect, but becoming prostrate as it matures, with close-set, purplish-gray to red, white-bloomed leaves. The urn-shaped flowers are pink to lilac.

Lampranthus AIZOACEAE

The shrubby mesembryanthemums of South Africa are splendid plants for hot, dry places, with many-rayed, daisy-like flowers in a range of bright or soft colors (all z10–11). Under a fierce sun, the brilliant colors of orange-scarlet *Lampranthus aurantiacus*, orange-yellow *L. aureus*, coppery *L. brownii*, vivid scarlet *L. coccineus*, and bright crimson scarlet *L. spectabilis*, with its forms or hybrids ranging from apricot-orange to magenta, blend in Byzantine mixtures. The softer coloring of *L. glaucus*, which has especially pretty lemon-yellow flowers, can be trusted in any company, and in the pink range there is palest blush *L. blandus*, *L. multiradiatus* (*L. roseus*) with linear leaves and large, soft pink flowers, and *L. falcatus roseus*, which is low growing and bears pink flowers. *L. zeyheri*, which is of more prostrate growth than most, has magenta-pink flowers.

Nolina AGAVACEAE

These natives of Arizona, California and Baja California (all z9–10) resemble the dasylirions, with their radiating rapier leaves recalling fiber-optic ornaments. Some, such as *Nolina longifolia*, form a distinct trunk, in this case up to 10ft/3m, swollen at the base and branched at the top, the branches terminating in great tufts of narrow leaves. *N. parryi* has gray-green leaves finely toothed at the margins, and *N. wolfii* is similar with wider, green leaves. The shorter-growing *N. bigelowii* has very long, narrow, glaucous leaves. All these have spikes of flower topping the leaves by up to 10ft/3m. *N. microcarpa* has no evident trunk; its long, finely toothed leaves end in a tuft of fibers, and the flowers are plumy panicles held above the foliage. The Californian *N. interrata* has very narrow, glaucous leaves and 6ft/1.8m flower spikes. Nolinas need frost-free desert or semi-desert conditions and are increased by seed.

Lampranthus aureus

Ochagavia BROMELIACEAE

Ochagavia rosea (*O. lindleyana*) (z10–11) resembles the fascicularias in leaf, but the pink flowers are borne in domed clusters on a short stem at the center of the rosette.

Opuntia CACTACEAE

The opuntias – prickly pears and chollas – are instantly recognizable, with their characteristic pad-like, jointed segments, which may be set with large spines, or with barely visible but sharp bristles (known as glochyds) in polka-dot clusters on the waxy surface. They are the most widely distributed cacti, many native to the Americas, but planted worldwide wherever the climate permits. Few plants are more tolerant of desert conditions than the prickly pears; whole groves can develop in a few years from segments simply stuck in the ground and left to fend for themselves, and they have become noxious weeds in countries such as South Africa, Australia and New Zealand and may only be grown indoors in many places. Some of the cholla group, with their fierce thorns, make excellent living barriers, though they are harder to transplant successfully than the prickly pears, slower to get away after planting, and not so long lived.

In flower, opuntias can be very decorative, their waxy blooms opening in late spring and early summer, in a range of colors from yellow, orange and salmon to pink, red, and occasionally white. The fruit, which is like a berry or a pear, ripens from mid- to late summer, varying from green to shades of orange, red and purple, often changing color as they ripen.

The species range from tree-plants as much as 15–20ft/4.5–6m high, to spreading, prostrate forms under 24in/60cm in height. They vary in their resistance to cold; a few species are remarkably frost-hardy. Almost all will grow without irrigation where the rainfall exceeds 10in/250mm a year. Among the taller species is *Opuntia ficus-indica* (*O. megacantha, O. occidentalis*) (z10–11), the Barbary fig, Indian fig or spineless cactus, which grows tree-like to 13ft/3.5m, forming a woody trunk with several branches composed of smooth flat segments, each up to 18in/45cm long, with no thorns, but a few sharp glochyds in each polka dot. The yellow flowers are followed by edible fruit maturing from yellow to red. It roots incredibly easily; even fallen pieces take root, so that it can become invasive. The prickly pear, *O. microdasys* (z10–11), also called rabbit ears or goldplush, is a much smaller, ferociously prickly plant, reaching 36in/90cm in height, or sometimes spreading along the ground. The segments, up to 6in/15cm long, are rich to bright green or gray, set with velvety yellow, white or russet polka dots of very sharp glochyds. The flowers are yellow.

Englemann's prickly pear, *O. phaeacantha* (*O. engelmannii*) (z5), is a variable species native to a wide area from California to Texas and Mexico, some growing up to an altitude of 7,800ft/2,250m. Plants from different habitats vary in growth, size or pad, number and length of thorns, and flower color, though lemon-yellow is the most common. The fruits are green, ripening to red and finally purple. A particularly attractive species is the blue-blade or dollar cactus, *O. macrocentra* (*O. violacea santa-rita, O. santa-rita*) (z9–11), subtly colored in blue tinged with purple, or totally purple. The segments, which are up to 8in/20cm long, may be virtually spineless or bear long brownish to pink spines. The large yellow flowers are followed by red to purple fruits.

Among the hardier opuntias is the beaver-tail prickly pear, *O. basilaris* (z5), a striking plant with blue, red-purple or bronze pads, and large violet flowers. Easiest of all is *O. compressa* (z5), an Illinois native, growing low

Puya chilensis

and spreading to 5ft/1.5m, with rounded or oval, flat pads, and silky yellow flowers touched with red or orange. The Utah grizzly bear opuntia, *O. erinacea* var. *utahensis* (z5), makes a wide, prostrate mat with short upright branches to 18in/45cm, covered with white spines; the flowers are yellow or bright red. Plants of the same variety which become purple-flushed in full sun have been known as *O. rhodantha* (z6–11); their fruit is spiny. Toughest of all is *O. fragilis* (z4), which will even stand wet, but is drought-tolerant. It is a cholla type, easily broken – hence its name – and every little piece will root. High-altitude forms of *O. whipplei* (z7–11) are hardy, shrubby and low growing, with cylindrical pads and yellow flowers.

Portulaca PORTULACACEAE

Portulaca grandiflora (z9–11), the sun plant of South America, is a low, spreading plant with cup-shaped flowers in a wide range of colors from white, sulfur-yellow and vermilion-scarlet to rose and purple. A popular seed-raised ephemeral for sunny, dry places in cool temperate climates, it produces both single and double flowers.

Puya BROMELIACEAE

The puyas are viciously spiny plants, like *Fascicularia* in this way. If you are so misguided as to put your hand among the leaves of either, the backward-pointing spines will make sure you cannot withdraw it without leaving some flesh behind; one grower calls them the rottweilers of the plant kingdom. *Puya alpestris* (z8–11) forms rosettes of arching, prickly, gray-green leaves, from each of which, after some years, a 36in/90cm flower spike develops. The close-set, three-petaled flowers are bizarrely colored in metallic sea-green and turquoise, with orange anthers and bright green stigma, set in red bracts. *P. berteroniana* (z8–11) is similar, with taller, denser spikes of metallic blue-green flowers with orange anthers. The flowers of *P. caerulea* (z9–11), a smaller, clump-forming plant, are turquoise to sky blue, closely packed on a 4ft/1.2m spike over dense rosettes of narrow, spiny leaves. *P. mirabilis* is an Andean species with yellow flowers.

   P. chilensis (z9–11) is a very large plant, forming great rosettes of upward-pointing, narrow, prickly leaves, each up to 4ft/1.2m long, topped by flowering stems up to 10ft/3m high, the upper third forming an immense cone of chartreuse and orange flowers. It can clump up to form patches up to 25ft/7.5m across, bearing up to a hundred flowering spikes. But the giant of the tribe, in height at least, is *P. raimondii* (z9–11), which has unbranched flowering stems as much as 33ft/10m tall.

Rhodiola CRASSULACEAE

Rhodiola rosea (*Sedum rosea*) (z2–7), the rose root, is particularly decorative in spring when the young shoots, set with blue-gray, toothed leaves tinged red at the margins, are tipped by deep pink flower buds. These later open to yellow stars, giving the rose root a look akin to a small spurge.

Sedum CRASSULACEAE

There are many species of sedum, of which only a few resent drought, and some are at their best in poor, dry soils. Among them are traditional border plants, a variety of neat little species safe enough for rock gardens, and some rumbustious spreaders good for walls or rough places, but quite unsuited to manicured areas. What follows represents just a fraction of the species available; all are easy to propagate, every scrap willing to form roots.

   Sedum acre (z3–8), the wall pepper or goldmass stonecrop, is a hardy little plant, too invasive to admit to most gardens, though it has some pretty varieties such as *S. a.* var. *aureum*, in which the stems are tipped with yellow, silver-tipped *S. a.* var. *elegans*, and *S. a.* var. *majus*, which is larger than the species but, strangely, better behaved in the garden. Another European, *S. anglicum* (z4–8), makes close carpets of fleshy leaves, red-flushed if grown in poor, dry soil, and bearing starry pink flowers. Similar coloring belongs to *S. dasyphyllum* (z8–10), a Mediterranean species, its tufts of short, branching stems packed with tiny, pink-flushed leaves. The flowers are blush-white. *S. sieboldii* (*Hylotelephium sieboldii*) (z6–9) is a larger plant, big enough for the front of a dry border, its trailing stems set with rounded, blue-gray leaves in threes; the flowers are red-purple and open late in the season, and the leaves flush pink in winter. *S. cauticola* (*Hylotelephium cauticola*) (z5–9) is similar, with very blue leaves margined with purple, and pink flowers aging to carmine-rose, opening a few weeks earlier.

As small-scale ground-cover, the evergreen *S. spurium* (z3–8) is a competent weed-excluder with broad leaves and pink flowers, or, in the selection 'Schorbuser Blut' ('Dragon's Blood'), deep red; 'Green Mantle' is a non-flowering, green-leaved form. Several small species have yellow flowers, though in the case of *S. spathulifolium* (z6–7), the leaves are the thing. It makes generous evergreen mats of rounded, thick-textured leaves forming rosettes; named kinds include 'Cape Blanco,' which is heavily dusted with white farina, and the more robust 'Purpureum' with deep purple leaves. Another evergreen, *S. oreganum* (z6–8), has fat, paddle-shaped leaves turning deep mahogany-red in poor soil and flat heads of yellow flowers. *S. floriferum* (z5–8) 'Weihenstephaner Gold' has spreading, sprawling stems topped by heads of yellow flowers in late summer, popular with bees. *S. middendorffianum* (z4–8) makes tufts of upright stems set with narrow, russet-red leaves in contrast to the cheery yellow flowers.

S. sediforme (z7–9), a Mediterranean native, is a bigger plant, its stems as much as 12in/30cm in height, with rather narrow, close-set, spiraling leaves and greenish or pale yellow flowers. The favorite old border plant *S. spectabile* (*Hylotelephium spectabile*) (z4–9), the ice plant, is a fleshy, gray-green-leaved perennial with, in late summer, flat heads of muted pink flowers, dancing with butterflies wherever the use of agricultural chemicals has not banished these insects from our gardens. 'Herbstfreude' ('Autumn Joy') is a taller hybrid with flowers of richer, warmer pink, turning to russet as they age; in leaf it is just as decorative as the ice plant. Both bees and butterflies love it. The European orpine, *S. telephium* (*Hylotelephium telephium*) (z4–9), is represented in gardens by selections such as 'Munstead Dark Red,' which has dark green, purple-flushed leaves and flat heads of maroon-red on 18in/45cm stems, a striking contrast to silver foliage or blue grasses. The Allegheny stonecrop, *S. telephioïdes* (*Hylotelephium telephioïdes*) (z6–8), grows on dry cliffs and in rocky places in the Appalachian Mountains, making a dense 12in/30cm ground-cover, with blunt, light green leaves suffused red-purple, on reddish stems. The flowers are white tipped with red, giving a pinkish effect which deepens with age to red and, in the seeding stage, to dusky maroon.

Sempervivum CRASSULACEAE

The house leeks form mounds of rosettes, their succulent leaves varying in shape and coloring, and sometimes cobwebbed, as in *Sempervivum arachnoideum* (z3–8). Devotees select forms which differ only minutely from one another; most of us will be content to choose a few that we like, tucking them into odd dry corners, persuading them to settle on tiled roofs, or filling shallow pans with them, to stand out on a terrace or cosset in an alpine house. For edging dry borders and coping with difficult spots, the easiest is probably *S. tectorum* (z3–8), green or purple according to cultivar.

Yucca AGAVACEAE

The plant that symbolizes the desert, at least since the pop group U2 made an album named after it, is the Joshua tree, *Yucca brevifolia* (z7–11), found only in the Mojave Desert. Its long, twisted branches, their upper portions spiked with narrow, grayish, sharp-tipped leaves, may soar to 40ft/12m. The greenish-white flowers are borne at the end of each branch. *Y. brevifolia* var. *herbertii* (z7–11) grows to only 15ft/4.5m, so is more suitable for the average garden. Both tolerate long periods of drought.

Another species that can stand long periods of drought is the soap tree, *Y. elata* (z6–11), a native of high deserts of northern Mexico and of the southwestern United States. It grows erect to 13ft/3.5m, with very narrow, pale, white-edged leaves set with marginal curling threads. The flower spikes, in their late spring season, are dramatic, the stems topping the drying leaves by 6ft/1.8m, and bearing clusters of wide, fragrant, white flowers. The Spanish bayonet or dagger plant, *Y. aloïfolia*, (z9–11), grows slowly to 10ft/3m, the stiff, rather short, smooth-edged, green leaves set closely along the stem and tipped with a sharp point. 'Marginata' has leaves edged with yellow. Clusters of white, purple-flushed flowers are borne on 24in/60cm stems in summer. The Spanish bayonet tolerates long periods of drought, though the lower leaves wither and can be removed to show the stem. The common names of these plants may be confusingly similar: *Y. gloriosa* (z7–11) is known as the Spanish dagger, palm lily, or roman candle. It has stiff, leaden green, fiercely spike-tipped leaves up to 30in/75cm long and develops several trunks, to reach a height of 8ft/2.4m. If the old, withered leaves are removed, the effect is almost palm-like. The cream to pinkish bells open in late summer. To increase the Spanish dagger

Yucca brevifolia

and its type, remove the secondary trunks, leave them in a shady place for a week to form a callus, then plant them. *Y. recurvifolia* (z6–11), the pendulous yucca or curveleaf yucca, grows rapidly to 6ft/1.8m, forming a single stem or several branches, set with rosettes of dark gray-green, flexible, arching leaves. The flowering spikes, more handsome than those of *Y. gloriosa*, are borne earlier as white flowers in loose clusters. Though it will tolerate some drought when established, this yucca needs moderate irrigation in desert gardens when first planted. *Y.* 'Vittorio Emanuele II' is a hybrid of *Y. gloriosa*, especially magnificent in flower, with burgundy-tinted buds opening to ivory flowers, and good foliage; another excellent hybrid, selected for its fine flowers, is *Y.* 'Vomerensis.'

Not all species make trunks like the Spanish dagger. *Y. filamentosa* (z5–11) is one of the smaller species, with rosettes around 24–36in/60–90cm wide. The gray-green leaves have thread-like hairs along the margins. The flowering spikes reach 5ft/1.5m, with erect sideshoots forming a compact head of cream bells. 'Variegata' has leaves striped with yellow, and 'Bright Edge' is yellow-margined. *Y. flaccida* (z5–10) is similar to *Y. filamentosa*, but its leaves are more lax, arching at the tips, and the flower spike is more open and graceful, with side branches held almost horizontally. 'Ivory' is especially fine in flower, and 'Golden Sword' has yellow-edged leaves. The very fetching *Y. glauca* (z9) has hemispherical rosettes of many, very narrow, blue-gray, white-margined leaves and alabaster-white flowers in a narrow spike. The glory of the genus is *Y. whipplei* (*Hesperoyucca whipplei*) (z7–9), our Lord's candle, which makes dense, trunkless rosettes of stiletto-fine, gray-blue, sharply spiked leaves. The ivory-white, lily-like flowers, tinted with purple, appear in their hundreds in massive clusters at ends of 8–13ft/2.4–3.5m stems. The flowered rosettes die after the effort of producing these great displays. A native of California and Baja California, *Y. whipplei* tolerates long periods of drought. Amazingly for so magnificent a plant, it is easy from seed.

Yucca gloriosa

Dry Garden Maintenance

It must be clear from the account of plants' survival strategies in Chapter 1 that drought-tolerance is a quality belonging to a wide range of species from many different climates. The corollary is that the range of plants any of us can regard as reliably drought-resistant will differ according to where we garden, for both climate and soil will play a part. Beyond those macro-limitations, which can themselves be modified to some extent, there are many ways in which gardeners can help to maintain their plants' survival.

If you are designing a drought-proof garden from scratch, you will make your gardening easier if you choose plants that are likely to do well in your climate and soil. Of course, it is never as simple as that bland statement implies. Increasingly, gardeners are realizing that hardiness zones, a measure of the capacity to survive a given range of temperatures, are the roughest of guides, especially to people who garden outside North America. Much of Britain, for example, is approximately equivalent to Zone 8 in the United States; but British summers are commonly cooler and cloudier – even when they are droughty – than US Zone 8 summers, so woody plants miss the sun that ripens them for the winter, and even some non-woody plants pine for summer heat. And the Zone 9 coastal margins of the British Isles are very different from either the Mediterranean climate of California west of the Sierras, or the summer-humid subtropics of eastern Zone 9 across to Florida. However, this book has tried to take these differences into account and has adjusted some zone numbers accordingly.

So a given plant's ability to survive depends on much more than the range of winter minimum temperatures that the zones are based on. Even precipitation statistics are little help unless they provide a clear picture not only of the amount of rainfall, but also its season, frequency, and periodicity, and its relevance to the wider climatic picture of the region. In a green and lush land such as Britain, or that tiny portion of territory around Seattle that resembles an island climate, plants might be severely stressed after as little as three weeks without rain, whereas in the tropics a much longer period without rain might not cause a drought, because the vegetation there is well adapted to a different pattern of rainfall.

Drought can be induced or exacerbated by factors other than a simple deficit in precipitation. In very cold winters, plants under a blanket of snow are protected not just from cold, but, very possibly, from cold-induced drought; if the soil is frozen, the soil moisture is no longer accessible and snow that falls on unfrozen ground helps to insulate it against subsequent freezes. Extreme cold without snow-cover is something gardeners learn to dread; thick mulches can help, but they need to be applied before the soil freezes. Plants in containers are even more vulnerable, as the rootball may freeze even in quite minor frosty spells; wherever there is a risk of frost, they should be well wrapped if they cannot be brought under cover.

Wind can be damaging to plants suffering from lack of moisture at any season. Anyone who has hung out wet washing on a windy day knows how much faster it dries than in still weather, cold or hot; the effect on leaves is identical, and if the roots cannot make good the moisture loss because the soil is dry, the result is a flagging or wilting plant. Cold, biting winter winds damage evergreen leaves, and the tender, unfurling leaves of spring are even more vulnerable. In the heat of summer, plants use a great deal of water at the best of times; they lose still more through their leaves in blowy weather.

All this is not to discourage you, but to alert you to the need to use common sense when choosing plants for a dry garden. If your soil is free-draining and your garden sheltered from wind, you are likely to succeed with plants too frost-tender for your neighbor with his exposed garden and heavy soil that lies wet in winter. Large cities are commonly several degrees warmer than the surrounding countryside; and though the streets may be windy because of the tunnel effect of tall buildings, small yards are often sheltered by fences or hedges. Gardens part-way up a slope, from which cold air can drain freely, are a more congenial home for plants than frost-hollows, at least at lower elevations; there comes a point at which the drop in mean temperature resulting from increasing altitude is greater than the frost-saving effect of free air drainage. All these factors affect the variety of plants from which you can choose.

Starting with the soil
Some gardeners say that a plant grown "hard" is more likely to survive adversity than one that is mollycoddled. But the line between growing hard and a stressed plant liable to succumb to disease, pest infestation, or just one more climatic blip is very thin, and drought is a prime stress factor.

A planting design suitable for a dry climate makes a drought-proof landscape of spikes and hummocks, in which the broad, dark blades of a phormium are prominent.

Some mollycoddling is in order if you want to raise healthy plants with the best chance of survival.

Everything starts with the soil, and dry gardening is no exception. The more you are able to do to improve the soil in your garden, the better chance your plants will have of survival. Different soil types present different problems, though the solution, in part at least, is almost always to add generous quantities of organic matter. In sandy or gravelly, fast-draining soils, it helps to retain moisture; while in dense clay, which often lies wet in winter but sets concrete-hard and cracks open in summer drought, organic matter helps to open the soil, making it more friable, better drained in winter and more moisture-retentive in summer.

Soils in arid zones – whether dense, or fast-draining sand or gravel – are often very low in organic matter. Worse still, they may be excessively alkaline or saline, or both, or sodic, when soils becomes pasty and impervious to air and water. Sodic soils can be improved by adding gypsum. Add sulfur or sulfate of iron to high-calcium soils, including caliche. Caliche or coffee rock is the name given to the impenetrable hardpan, a layer of cement-hard calcium, as much as 6ft/2m thick, lying beneath a thin layer of topsoil in some calcareous soils. (Sandy, acid soils also sometimes have their own hardpan of accumulated salts.) The roots are unable to penetrate to search for moisture and nutrients, while irrigation water cannot drain away, leaving standing water around the roots and causing still further accumulation of salts. It is essential to break up the hardpan, or at the very least to excavate the largest planting holes you can manage, breaking up the caliche enough to make sure irrigation water does not lie stagnant. If this is not possible, you may have to limit yourself to plants that will tolerate caliche soils, such as mesquite or palo verde, or build raised beds above the natural soil level.

Another type of hardpan is sometimes found in soils that have been long cultivated to the same depth with a plow, causing an accumulation of salts on the unbroken subsoil, exacerbated perhaps by the subsoil becoming compacted. This can usually be cured without too much difficulty by deep cultivation with a ripper plow or, on a small scale, with a pickax. This will enable deep-rooting plants to search for moisture in the lower soil levels and help to improve the drainage. It may sound paradoxical to insist on good drainage for droughty gardens – but it is essential that water – whether falling as rain or from irrigation – can drain away freely, as plants that are waterlogged will fail.

Once the hardpan is broken up, it is time to add the organic matter, such as composted forest bark, garden compost, chopped bracken, mushroom compost, or well-rotted manure. The coarser the material, the longer it will take to decompose and the more it will bulk up and aerate the soil. The hotter the climate, the faster organic matter decomposes; very fine materials may hardly last a year. Whatever the material, there should be enough of it to alter the soil structure; a layer 3–4in/7–10cm thick, incorporated into the top 8–12in/20–30cm of soil, would be about right. After planting, regular topdressing with the same organic material will help to maintain the soil structure, as well as retaining moisture and insulating the soil against temperature fluctuations.

Planting

Once the soil is thoroughly prepared and enriched with ample quantities of organic matter, planting can start. Excavate generous holes for each of your plants, amply large enough to take the roots without cramping, and save the topsoil, but remove caliche or hardpan and rocks. If your soil is hard-packed or close-textured dense clay or caliche, check the drainage. Pour in enough water to fill the hole to a depth of 4in/10cm; it should drain away in no more than three or four hours. Meanwhile, mix the excavated topsoil with composted organic matter, two or three parts soil to one part organic matter, and if the soil is a heavy clay, add one part of grit or sharp sand as well. Dig some of this into the surrounding soil so there is a gradual transition from the improved soil to the original medium.

Both bare-root plants and those that are grown in containers need to be thoroughly watered at the time of planting. Make sure that bare roots have not dried out – soak them in a bucket of water if they look at all dry – and stand container-grown plants in water to make sure that the rootball is moist all through. Set the plant in the hole, spread bare roots carefully, and start to fill again with the prepared topsoil, taking care that the plant is at the same level as in the nursery bed or container. Remember that the soil will settle. In free-draining soils, it can be helpful to plant in a shallow basin so that when you do irrigate, the water is directed to the roots instead of

Prosopis species, known as mesquite, are among the few shrubs that will tolerate caliche soils, their taproots penetrating to 150ft/45m or more. A good example is the Argentine mesquite, *Prosopis alba*.

running off. In poorly drained soils, it is better to make a raised rim of soil around the plant, well away from the collar, to prevent irrigation water from running off.

After planting, water generously, so the soil is thoroughly and deeply moistened, and also to make sure that there are no air spaces around the roots. Finally, add a generous mulch of organic matter, which will help to keep the soil cool, retain moisture, suppress weeds that compete for moisture, and continue to improve the soil structure as it decomposes. Inorganic materials can also be used as a mulch; gravel, chipped granite, or limestone perform the first two functions, but not the third, so are less suitable for poor, low-humus soils, while a plastic mulch retains moisture, but does little to insulate the soil. Experiments with various unconventional mulching materials suggest that pieces of old carpet, though unattractive, are useful to keep down weeds, retain moisture, and help insulate the soil.

Windbreaks

Drying winds can seriously exacerbate the effects of drought, while in coastal regions they may carry both salt and sand, and in desert regions sand alone, causing abrasions of plant tissues as well as desiccation. It is worth giving space to a windbreak designed to filter the prevailing wind. In exposed coastal gardens, indeed, planting a screen of trees and shrubs tolerant of both wind and salt spray is the priority. The stronger the winds, the wider the shelter belt will need to be, and it should present a sloping face to the prevailing wind; the outer planting should consist of lower shrubs that will stay well furnished to the ground, both to filter the wind whistling between the bare trunks of taller trees, and to deflect the airflow upward more effectively than would a sheer, vertical wall of vegetation.

For coastal gardens in the south and west of the British Isles, among the best salt-tolerant shrubs and trees that will also stand dry conditions are the maritime pine (*Pinus pinaster*) and the Corsican pine (*P. nigra maritima*), tamarisks, *Euonymus japonicus*, the saltbushes (*Atriplex* spp.), *Baccharis halimifolia*, *Bupleurum fruticosum*, and several *Brachyglottis* species, especially

BELOW LEFT The silver-leaved sea buckthorn, *Hippophae rhamnoides*, tolerates severe cold and salt-laden winds as well as dry, sandy soils. Where male and female plants grow together, the females are laden with amber-orange berries in the fall. Too bitter to appeal to birds, the berries remain on the branches throughout winter.

BELOW RIGHT The Russian olive, *Elaeagnus angustifolia*, is another hardy "silver" suitable for dry, coastal gardens. The tiny cream flowers in spring are deliciously fragrant.

the low, spreading *B. monroi*. In colder coastal regions the Scots pine, Russian olive (*Elaeagnus angustifolia*), and sea buckthorn (*Hippophae rhamnoides*) are especially valuable, with white poplar (*Populus alba*) and the goat willow (*Salix caprea*) as taller shelter.

In desert regions the outer row of wind-tolerant plants (suitable for a wide range of climatic zones) could consist of Russian olive, then a row of tamarisk, then one of Arizona cypress, and if there is space, another of Lombardy poplar and an inner, leeward row of Aleppo pine. In smaller desert gardens, an outer or windward line of casuarina or tamarisk and an inner of Arizona cypress, would be both attractive and reasonably efficient at filtering the wind. In both desert and coastal gardens, the rows of shelter-belt trees and shrubs should be set about 15ft/4.5m apart.

While waiting for these living windbreaks to grow, fences and louvered baffles, or materials such as woven plastic, can be used as wind filters, helping to create a comparatively still atmosphere in which plants have a chance to establish themselves. Shade from the hottest sun can also help, especially in regions where the sun's rays are very fierce.

All these artificial windbreaks can also be useful for emergency shelter, for example, if the loss of a plant in the shelter belt creates a gap. In regions where sudden storms may blow from unexpected quarters, it can be useful to have a supply of hurdles or louvered baffles available to set on the windward side of treasured plants.

The more formal and permanent a planting, the more important it is that its components be appropriate to the climate: the loss of a single plant could destroy the symmetry of the group. Here an immaculate hedge of *Cupressus arizonica* var. *glabra* 'Glauca,' the blue Arizona cypress, is lifted from the commonplace by the dark sentinels of *C. sempervirens* 'Stricta.'

181

Though not so soft underfoot as a well-kept lawn, paving makes no demands on limited water resources and is easy to maintain. Here, a sunny terrace is framed by a white *Wisteria floribunda* and decorated with seasonal flowers in terracotta pots. The Mediterranean *Convolvulus cneorum* adds its silvery foliage and silken white funnels to the summer picture.

Lawns and lawn-substitutes

It is not possible to make a good grass lawn without ample water. In climates where the rains always come sooner or later, even if too little, gardeners are learning to live with brown and dusty lawns in summer, knowing that with the rains of autumn the grass will turn green again. They are also looking at alternatives to grass: paving, cobblestones, brick and modern hard surfaces for walking on; gravel and sand for the open spaces between plants; ground cover for restful sweeps of greenery.

In arid, semi-desert regions a year-round green lawn is a luxury achieved only with the profligate use of water. Some people compromise by opting for a lawn in one season only. A warm-season grass such as Bermuda grass goes dormant in winter, turning to straw-color; even then, it needs occasional watering to survive (a soaking once a month, unless there has been more than a sprinkling of rain), but so long as it does not become dust-dry, it will revive with rain or irrigation. Some people dye their winter-dormant lawns with a special green paint; if well done, this can look quite acceptable, and it is of course much less wasteful of water than overseeding with annual ryegrass in the fall, which may also delay the recovery of the Bermuda grass in spring. It takes much less water to achieve a winter-green, one-season lawn, by seeding with cool-season annual or perennial grasses each fall. Though the turf will die back with the summer heat, it will nonetheless help to reduce dust and erosion.

Although dichondra (*Dichondra micrantha*) or pony foot is a popular and attractive lawn substitute, it is not suitable for heavy foot traffic and needs ample moisture, so it is not an appropriate choice for the drought-proof garden. An alternative is lippia (*Phyla nodiflora*), which is more resistant to being walked on, is good for stabilizing soil with its deep-rooting runners, and is more drought-resistant once established. However, its flowers are very popular with bees, so it is not a good idea to walk barefoot over it. Its small leaves are bluish-green or gray-green.

Irrigation techniques

However scrupulous you may be in choosing drought-tolerant plants, it will from time to time be necessary to provide artificial irrigation, especially in the early years after planting. Many plants that are remarkably drought-resistant once established need moderate to ample water at first. In all climates, it is far more effective to water deeply and infrequently than little and often; allow the water to penetrate deep into the soil and then apply no more until absolutely necessary. This is especially important in arid soils, because of the high level of soil salts; long, slow waterings help to leach the salts from the root zone. Allowing the soil to become almost dry between waterings enables air to reach the roots. However, only established xerophytes will stand bone-dry soil; watch all other plants for signs of stress such as wilting, changes in leaf color to darker, grayer, or bluer than normal, curling or dropping leaves (remember, though, that in some desert plants shedding leaves is a natural adaptation to drought). Leaves that are dry and crisp at the margins or turning yellow usually indicate a severely drought-stressed plant.

There are various ways in which you can help to direct the water where it is needed, at the plants' roots. A favorite technique is to knock a hole in the bottom of a wine bottle, or to pierce holes in a large plastic one (one hole in the base and, if necessary, two or three halfway up the sides), and push the bottle into the soil near the plant. Wine bottles go in neck down, plastic bottles neck-up. Fill the bottle with water, which will seep through to the roots, leaving the soil surface dry. A more sophisticated version of this uses narrow-necked, unglazed clay pots sunk into the soil so that only the neck is visible. The pots are kept full of water, which slowly seeps through the porous clay. Both these techniques also help to keep the soil surface dry, which cuts down on weed growth.

Drip irrigation is another efficient method; the drip or seep tubing applies water very slowly to the soil, so it can operate on low water pressure, and the tubing can be laid so that the seepage is directed to the roots of individual plants. It is especially useful for plants in containers, or on slopes, where other types of irrigation are likely to result in water-loss through run-off, wind deflection, and evaporation. Another good method when establishing individual trees and shrubs involves the use of hollow stakes, made, for example, of rigid plastic tubing with an internal diameter of about 1in/2.5cm. With one end buried near the roots, the tube is filled with water once every week or ten days.

These techniques for efficient water use can be combined with general water management, such as re-using "gray" household water on the garden; here, the waste water from dishwashers, washing machines, and baths is routed to a rainbarrell; simple plumbing kits are now available for this. Others conscientiously wash dishes by hand in a bowl, chucking the water at the roots of the most thirsty-looking plants. People living in areas where drought is a daily reality, such as southern California, have achieved dramatic savings, through voluntary restraint in some regions and strict rationing in others. Their lawns may be brown and dying, but new techniques of xeriscaping have shown the way to make beautiful gardens with almost no water, and with the right choice of plants you can make a drought-proof garden almost anywhere.

Plants with Special Characteristics

Plants for Ground Cover

Even in dry gardens weeds grow, competing with ornamental plants for nutrients and moisture. It is better by far to cover the ground with a carpet of foliage in contrasting shades and textures. This will help both to exclude weed growth and to reduce soil-moisture loss through reducing evaporation. Most of the plants listed have creeping or mat-forming growth or form low mounds. Some climbers, grown horizontally on the ground, can also be used as ground cover; those listed are especially suitable. Among perennials, in addition to the ones in the list, many of the lesser plants described as mat-forming make good small-scale ground cover. Some clump-formers, even those with sword leaves such as *Libertia*, when growing luxuriantly are sufficiently dense to exclude weeds.

Shrubs:
Acacia redolens 'Prostrata'
A. subporosa 'Emerald Cascade'
Arctostaphylos nevadensis coloradensis
Artemisia 'Powis Castle'
Atriplex semibaccata
Baccharis pilularis
Brachyglottis compacta
B. monroi
B. 'Sunshine'
Carissa grandiflora, some cvs.
Ceanothus 'Blue Mound'
C. divergens
C. foliosus
C. f. Austromontanus Group
C. gloriosus
C. griseus
C. griseus var. *horizontalis* & cvs.
C. prostratus
C. purpureus
C. thyrsiflorus var. *repens*
Cistus × *dansereaui* 'Decumbens'
C. × *florentinus*
C. × *hybridus*
C. parviflorus
C. × *pulverulentus*
C. salviifolius 'Prostratus'
C. × *skanbergii*
Cytisus × *beanii*
C. decumbens
C. demissus
C. × *kewensis*
C. procumbens
Ephedra distachya var. *helvetica*
E. gerardiana
Euonymus fortunei
× *Fatshedera lizei*
Genista hispanica
G. pilosa
× *Halimiocistus* 'Ingwersenii'
× *H. sahucii*
Halimium lasianthum
Haplopappus coronipifolius
Helianthemum, many
Helichrysum splendidum
Iberis sempervirens
Lantana montevidensis
Lonicera pileata
Mahonia aquifolium
M. nervosa
M. repens
Myoporum parvifolium
Ozothamnus ledifolius
Pachysandra procumbens
P. terminalis
Phlomis chrysophylla
P. fruticosa
P. lanata
Potentilla fruticosa, many
Rosmarinus officinalis lavandulaceus
R. officinalis cvs., some
Rubus calycinoïdes
R. tricolor
Ruscus aculeatus
Salvia lavandulifolia
S. officinalis
Santolina, all
Sarcococca hookeriana
S. hookeriana var. *humilis*
Teucrium × *lucidrys*
Ulex europaeus
Vinca major
V. minor

Climbers
Hedera, many
Trachelospermum asiaticum

Conifers
Juniperus, many

Perennials
Anthemis punctata ssp. *cupaniana*
Bergenia
Cerastium tomentosum
Euphorbia amygdaloides var. *robbiae*
Geranium macrorrhizum
G. × *oxonianum* 'Claridge Druce'
Lathyrus grandiflorus
L. latifolius
Leptinella squalida

Liriope muscari
L. spicata
Ophiopogon japonicus
Osteospermum jucundum var. *compactum*
Phlomis russeliana
Stachys byzantina
Trachystemon orientale

Succulents
Aptenia cordifolia
Carpobrotus acinaciformis
C. edulis
Delosperma nubigenum
Fascicularia bicolor
F. pitcairniifolia
Sedum acre
S. anglicum
S. spurium

Wind-tolerant Trees, Shrubs, and Conifers

Wind is the thief of moisture, so creating a good shelter belt is an important part of dry gardening. Within the shelter of trees, shrubs, and conifers, a still atmosphere can be created in which moisture loss through transpiration is greatly reduced, enabling plants to survive drought which might prove fatal in exposed, windy areas. Salt-laden winds are a further hazard, burning the foliage of susceptible plants, so those that are tolerant of salt are marked [S].

Trees and shrubs
Acacia arabica [S]
Atriplex canescens [S]
Baccharis halimifolia [S]
B. patagonica [S]
Brachyglottis elaeagnifolia [S]
B. monroi [S]
B. rotundifolia [S]
B. 'Sunshine' [S]
Buddleja globosa [S]
Bupleurum fruticosum [S]
Casuarina
Ceanothus griseus var. *horizontalis* [S]
Cordyline australis [S]
Elaeagnus, many [S]
Eucalyptus, some
Euonymus japonicus [S]

Griselinia littoralis [S]
Hakea laurina [S]
Hippophae rhamnoïdes [S]
Lavatera arborea [S]
Myoporum laetum [S]
Pittosporum crassifolium [S]
Populus alba
Quercus ilex [S]
Salix caprea [S]
Spartium junceum [S]
Tamarix, many [S]

Conifers
Cupressus macrocarpa [S]
Pinus banksiana
P. nigra var. *maritima* [S]
P. pinaster [S]
P. sylvestris [S]

Plants with Bold or Lush Foliage

In a dry landscape, plants that look lush and leafy bring their own special note to contrast with the silvers and grays or the fleshy succulents. To these could be added some of the trees and shrubs with pinnate leaves such as *Robinia*, where each individual leaflet is small but the overall effect is leafy. The plants in the lists that follow are those with large or bold leaves, simple or compound. They vary greatly in texture from the hard, spiny leaves of *Mahonia* to the great velvety leaves of *Paulownia*.

Trees and shrubs
Ailanthus altissima
Aralia elata
Catalpa speciosa
Ensete ventricosum
Eriobotrya japonica
× *Fatshedera lizei*
Fatsia japonica
Griselinia lucida
Mahonia japonica
Melianthus major
Musa acuminata
M. × *paradisiaca*
Paulownia tomentosa
Philodendron bipinnatifidum

Rhus hirta
Sparmannia africana

Perennials
Acanthus mollis
A. spinosus
Bergenia
Crambe maritima
Cynara cardunculus
Kniphofia northiae
Phlomis russeliana
Ricinus communis
Strelitzia nicolaii
S. reginae

Plants with Sword-shaped Leaves

In contrast to the mat-forming and mounded ground covers, to the feathery silvers and the lush piles of acanthus and others with bold foliage, plants with sword- or rapier-shaped leaves have a special role to play in the design of the dry garden. Some of the most prominent are listed here. Each creates its own special effect, from the huge rosettes of agaves or the fiercely armed fascicularias and puyas to the fans of phormium blades.

Agave americana
A. franzosinii
Beschorneria yuccoides
Billbergia nutans
Cordyline australis
C. indivisa
Dasylirion glaucophyllum
D. wheeleri
Eryngium agavifolium
E. decaisneanum
E. proteiflorum

E. yuccifolium
Fascicularia bicolor
F. pitcairniifolia
Furcraea longaeva
Hesperaloe parviflora
Iris foetidissima
I. pallida ssp. *pallida*
Phormium, all
Puya, all
Yucca, all

Fragrant and Aromatic Plants

Many aromatic plants are doubly so in dry gardens, the essential oils that give them their characteristic perfume and flavor more concentrated than when they grow lush and soft. Some must be rubbed to release their aroma, others waft it to you on the air. Some flowers, too, are "fast of their scent" – you must bend the nose to them to enjoy it. Others are endowed with fragrance that is free-floating on the air, and often at its most eloquent at dusk. For these, especially, a sheltered garden is vital; wind will blow away fragrance, but in still air it is held captive.

Trees and shrubs
Acacia, some
Amorpha nana
Artemisia tridentata

Azadirachta indica
Brugmansia, most
Buddleja, many
Callistemon citrinus

Carissa grandiflora
Carpenteria californica
Caryopteris × *clandonensis*
Cassia artemisioides
Ceanothus arboreus
C. gloriosus
C. ramulosus fascicularis
C. rigidus
Chamaebatiaria millefolium
Choisya ternata
Cistus, some
Citrus, all
Comptonia peregrina
Conradina verticillata
Coronilla valentina
Cytisus battandieri
C. canariensis
C. × *praecox*
Elaeagnus, all
Eucalyptus, many
Gardenia thunbergiana
Genista cinerea
G. monosperma
Helichrysum italicum ssp. *serotinum*
Hymenosporum flavum
Hypericum 'Hidcote'
Hyssopus officinalis
Laurus nobilis
Lavandula, all
Lonicera fragrantissima
L. × *purpusii*
Lupinus arboreus
Magnolia grandiflora
Mahonia japonica
Melia azedarach
Michelia doltsopa
M. figo
Murraya paniculata
Myrica pensylvanica
Myrtus communis
Osmanthus fragrans
Ozothamnus ledifolius
Pithecellobium flexicaule
Pittosporum tobira
Plumeria, all
Poncirus trifoliata
Romneya coulteri
Rosa pimpinellifolia
R. rugosa
Rosmarinus officinalis
Ruta graveolens
Salvia greggii
S. officinalis
Santolina, all
Sarcococca hookeriana
Sophora secundiflora
Spartium junceum
Umbellularia californica
Viburnum suspensum

Climbers
Gelsemium sempervirens
Jasminum, most
Lonicera, many
Podranea ricasoliana
Rosa banksiae
Trachelospermum, all
Wisteria

Perennials and ephemerals
Abronia
Artemisia vallesiaca
Calamintha
Datura inoxia
Dianthus, many
Dictamnus albus
Erysimum capitatum
Foeniculum vulgare
Geranium macrorrhizum
Hedysarum
Hemerocallis, some
Hesperis matronalis
Iris germanica
I. graminea
I. pallida ssp. *pallida*
I. unguicularis
Lupinus luteus
Monarda fistulosa
Nepeta, most
Origanum majorana
O. vulgare
Pelargonium, some
Perovskia
Phlox pilosa
Phuopsis stylosa
Stylomecon heterophyllum
Thymus, many
Tulbaghia fragrans
Verbena

Bulbs
Amaryllis bella-donna
Cyclamen persicum
Freesia refracta var. *alba*
Gladiolus callianthus
Hermodactylus tuberosus
Hyacinthus orientalis
Muscari armeniacum
Narcissus papyraceus
N. tazetta
Pancratium

Succulents
Carpobrotus chilensis
Yucca, some

Further Reading

Australian Plant Study Group *Grow What Where* T. Nelson, Melbourne 1980

Chatto, Beth *The Dry Garden* J. M. Dent and Sons, London 1978

Duffield, Mary Rose and Jones, Warren D *Plants for Dry Climates* HP Books, Tuscon 1981

Latymer, Hugo *The Mediterranean Gardener* Frances Lincoln, London/Barrons, New York 1990

Menzies, Y M *Mediterranean Gardening, A Practical Handbook* John Murray, London 1991

Sheat, W G *The A-Z of Gardening in South Africa* Struik, Cape Town 1982

Smalls, R *California Gardening* New York 1983

Van Ollenbach, A W *Planting Guide to the Middle East* Architectural Press, London/Nicholls Publishing Co., New York 1978

Zone Ratings

The hardiness zone ratings given for each plant – indicated in the text by the letter z and the relevant number – suggest the appropriate minimum temperature a plant will tolerate in winter. However, this can only be a rough guide. The hardiness of a plant depends on a great many factors, including the depth of its roots, its water content at the onset of frost, the duration of cold weather, the force of the wind, and the length of, and the temperatures encountered during, the preceding summer. The zone ratings are based on those devised by the United States Department of Agriculture.

Approximate range of average annual minimum temperatures.

° FAHRENHEIT	ZONE	CELSIUS
below −50	1	below −45
−50 to −40	2	−45 to −40
−40 to −30	3	−40 to −34
−30 to −20	4	−34 to −29
−20 to −10	5	−29 to −23
−10 to 0	6	−23 to −18
0 to 10	7	−18 to −12
10 to 20	8	−12 to −7
20 to 30	9	−7 to −1
30 to 40	10	−1 to 4
above 40	11	above 4

Index

Page numbers in **bold** refer to main entries; those in *italic* to illustrations

Acknowledgments

Author's Acknowledgments

My double existence as a writer, essentially a solitary affair, and as an activist, which is the very reverse, occasionally induces a mild sense of split personality. Thanks to the support and encouragement of Sarah Mitchell, Erica Hunningher and all the staff at Frances Lincoln, I was able to keep on track, or rather on both tracks, and meet my deadlines in writing this book. I received invaluable help on the finer points of nomenclature from Tony Lord, and very useful advice on growing conditions in regions of the United States with which I am less familiar from John Elsley. Any inaccuracies or infelicities which remain are entirely my own.

Publishers' Acknowledgments

Thanks are due to: John Elsley for horticultural advice; John Laing for initial design work; Caroline Taylor for editorial help; Sally Cracknell for design assistance; Gareth Richards and Georgina Harris; and Heidi Gildemeister, whose work with drought tolerance in Mediterranean regions alerted them to the need for a book on drought-tolerant plants in zones 2–10.

Horticultural consultant Tony Lord
Editor Sarah Mitchell
Art Editor Niki Medlikova
Picture Editor Anne Fraser
Production Annemarieke Kroon
Editorial Director Erica Hunningher
Art Director Caroline Hillier
Production Director Nicky Bowden

Photographic Acknowledgments
t = top, b = bottom, l = left, r = right
Deni Bown 21,
John Fielding 11, 126b, 149b, 152t,
John Glover 80,
Niccolò Grassi © FLL: 6tr, 32, 50, 61, 69, 97t, 145
Jerry Harpur 5, 157,
Saxon Holt 14, 16, 17, 22, 23, 27, 33, 47, 48, 49, 57, 59, 63, 64, 76, 79, 86, 87b, 101t, 113t, 127, 128, 139, 140, 164, 165, 167, 170, 174, 177, 179,
Andrew Lawson 3, 6bl, 9 © FLL, 34 © FLL, 68, 71 © FLL, 73 © FLL, 78 © FLL, 82 © FLL, 84 © FLL, 92, 95, 107, 111 © FLL, 116 126t, 129, 132 © FLL, 133 © FLL, 135 © FLL, 136b © FLL, 137 © FLL, 146, 149t © FLL, 152b © FLL, 159, 160, 164,
Georges Lévêque 2, 6tl, br, 7, 12, 19, 25, 26, 30, 36, 39, 41, 43, 45, 46, 53, 62, 65, 72, 75, 81, 83, 87t, 89, 91b, 93, 97b, 99, 101b, 103, 104, 106, 109, 113b, 115, 122, 124, 125, 130, 134, 143, 144, 153, 154, 155, 175, 180, 181,
Marianne Majerus 182 © FLL
Smith Collection 1, 29, 55, 67, 70, 91t, 118, 119, 161, 169, 172
Jane Taylor 121
Steve Wooster © FLL: 136t, 150